W9-ACB-322

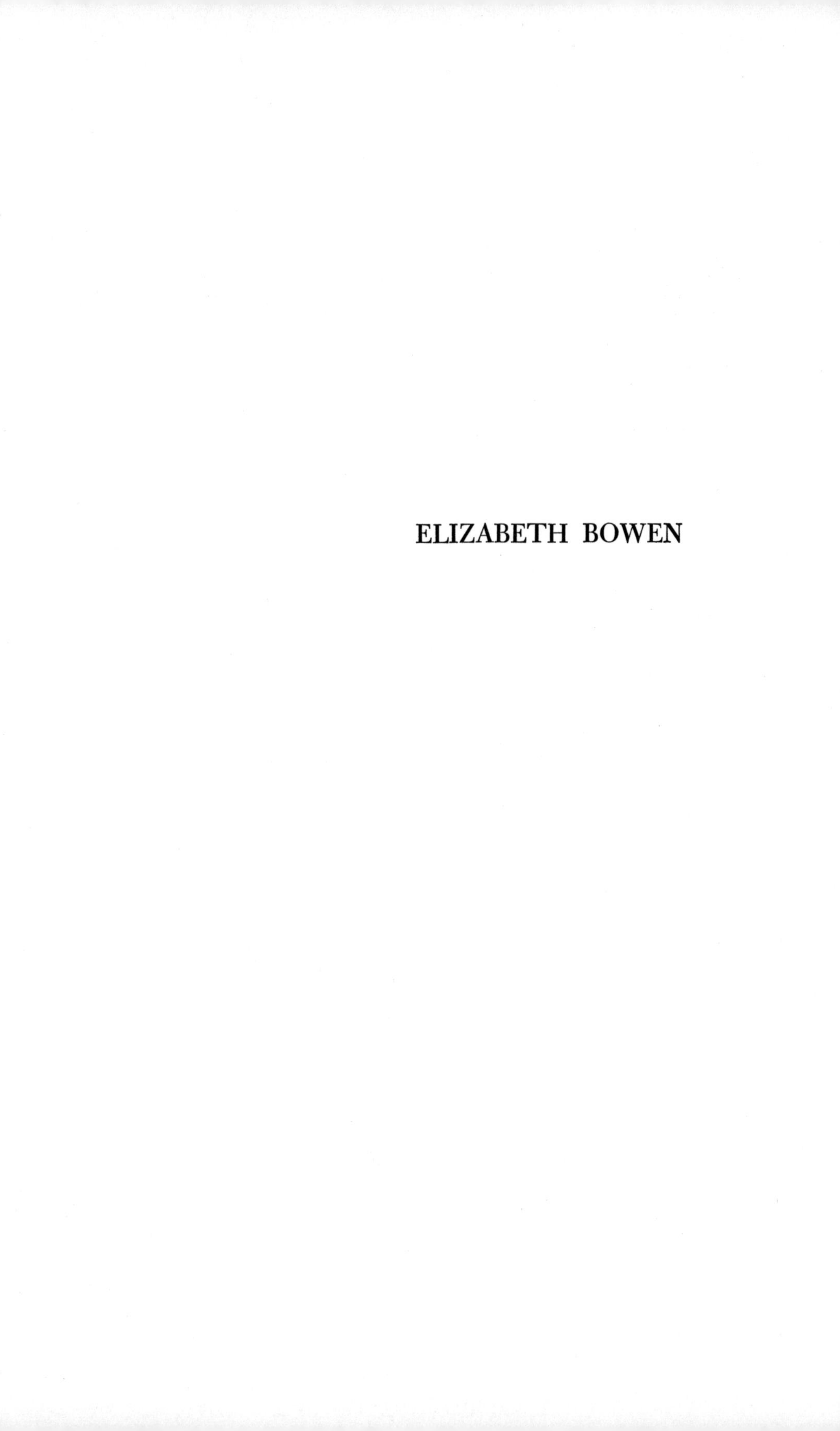

ELIZABETH BOWEN

WILLIAM
* HEATH

Elizabeth Bowen

An Introduction to Her Novels

THE UNIVERSITY OF WISCONSIN PRESS

Madison, 1961

Published by
THE UNIVERSITY OF WISCONSIN PRESS
430 Sterling Court, Madison 6, Wisconsin
*

Printed in the United States of America by
Vail-Ballou Press, Inc., Binghamton, New York
*
Library of Congress Catalog Number 61–10688

For my wife

* Preface

As Elizabeth Bowen says in her essay "Out of a Book," the adult reader of fiction, expelled from the Eden of innocent enjoyment, is doomed to have his brain "stand posted between his self and the story." This inevitable, perhaps unenviable, position should make the reading of any serious novel an act of literary criticism. To describe what happens, what is at stake, in the work of a novelist should be an attempt to define meaning, establish relevance, assess importance. And as long as the reading of that work continues, the act of literary criticism never ends. To say the book that follows is "finished" would be misleading. Other readers of Miss Bowen's fiction, ignorant of whatever claims for its importance I make here, may do more than I have done.

And the reading of the novels expressed by the chapters that follow is heavily dependent on readers who have preceded me. Any improvement that has been made in my understanding of the art of Elizabeth Bowen during the ten years since I first encountered *The Death of the Heart* obviously owes much to the essays and reviews listed in the bibliography. But other debts are more subtle and more important. Often, when they least expected it, my former teachers and present colleagues at Amherst College had their spoken words reclaimed, perhaps distorted, certainly used. My thanks to them must be tempered with apology.

For suggestions I have come by more directly, I owe a great deal to Professor Paul L. Wiley of the University of Wisconsin, whose extensive knowledge and scrupulous reading of modern English fiction contributed much to the thesis he directed and on which this book is based. Professor Frederick J. Hoffman, also formerly of the University of Wisconsin, has read the manuscript in more versions than he would care to remember and was substantially helpful in directing the process by which a thesis became a book. Professor Dean Doner of Purdue University, who read the first draft, was generous and helpful in his suggestions.

Without Miss Elizabeth Bowen's gracious encouragement, coöperation, and interest, this study would not have been possible in its present form. Like the others who have contributed, she is never responsible for my errors in taste, judgment, and fact.

Typing, proofreading, and indexing comprise the smallest part of the debt I owe my wife in making this book possible.

For assistance on particular points, I am indebted to Mr. John Perry of H. M. Tennant, Ltd., and to the libraries of Amherst College, the University of Wisconsin, and Yale University.

For permission to make extensive quotations from material in copyright, I am grateful to Miss Bowen and the following publishers: Alfred A. Knopf, Inc., the American publishers of *The Last September* (copyright 1952 by Elizabeth Bowen); *To the North* (copyright 1932, 1933 by Elizabeth D. C. Cameron); *The House in Paris* (copyright 1935 by Elizabeth D. C. Cameron); *The Death of the Heart* (copyright 1938 by Elizabeth Bowen); *The Heat of the Day* (copyright 1948 by Elizabeth Bowen); *A World of Love* (copyright 1954 by Elizabeth Bowen); *Early Stories* (copyright 1950 by Elizabeth Bowen); *Look at All Those Roses* (copyright 1941 by Elizabeth Bowen); *Ivy Gripped the Steps* (copyright 1941, 1946 by Elizabeth Bowen); *Stories by Elizabeth Bowen* (copyright 1941, 1946, 1959 by Elizabeth Bowen); *Bowen's Court* (copyright 1942 by Elizabeth Bowen); *Collected Impressions* (copyright 1950 by Elizabeth Bowen); and *Howards End* (copyright 1921 by E. M. Forster). The Dial Press, American publishers of *The Hotel* and *Friends and Relations.* Percival Marshall & Co., Ltd., publishers of *Why Do I Write?* (now out of print). The British Broadcasting Corporation, publishers of *The Listener;* The Statesman & Nation Publishing Co., Ltd., publishers of the *New Statesman.*

W. H.

October, 1960

*

Contents

ELIZABETH BOWEN

The final belief is to believe in a fiction, which you know to be a fiction, there being nothing else. The exquisite truth is to know that it is a fiction and that you believe in it willingly.

—Wallace Stevens, *Adagia*

But a man must live. Not for nothing do we invest so much of ourselves in other people's lives—or even in momentary pictures of people we do not know. It cuts both ways: the happy group inside the lighted window, the figure in long grass in the orchard seen from the train stay and support us in our dark hours. Illusions are art, for the feeling person, and it is by art that we live, if we do. It is the emotion to which we remain faithful, after all: we are taught to recover it in some other place.

—Elizabeth Bowen, *The Death of the Heart*

1 Introduction: Tradition and the Romantic Will

When Elizabeth Bowen enrolled at the London County Council School of Art in Southampton Row "as a sort of disguise" in the autumn of 1918, it was, she tells us, an essentially literary London that she entered, one defined for her by Dickens and Galsworthy, Compton Mackenzie and E. F. Benson, Conan Doyle and E. Nesbit. For the Anglo-Irish young woman leaving behind the isolation of her family's Big House in County Cork, London was filled not with people but books, and the invitations to the parties of Rose Macaulay and Naomi Royde-Smith, the readings by candlelight in the upstairs room of the Poetry Bookshop, were encounters with the "virtue" she hoped would proceed from the persons who wrote. Presumably the experience has been a common one, involving many more than the now successful few who look back at their arrival in the same London (as they do in John Lehmann's collection [1]) as a Beginning. Yet this young girl who saw other writers' books as the only reality, who thirty years later could still insist that her own books are her only relation to society, has succeeded eminently in that art in which a distinction between fantasy and reality is radical, has become, in fact, the most distinguished woman of letters now writing in English.

Miss Bowen has repeatedly insisted that the distinction between literary experience and experience in the world is tenuous for the reader, virtually absent for the writer. Yet in her definition of the novelist's activity she finds no fundamental distinction between art and lying, between tradition and debt. She assumes, without qualification, that the teller of stories is not a maker but one who returns, with willing "dishonesty and debt," to the mistaken but compelling childhood "age of magic" where "he once relied for life on being lied to."

The apparent choices of art are nothing but addictions, predispositions: where did these come from, how were they formed? The aesthetic is nothing but a return to images that will allow nothing to take their place; the aesthetic is nothing but an attempt to disguise and glorify the enforced return.[2]

The Platonic assumptions behind such a statement are at first surprising. Only in *The Republic* perhaps has such a negative definition of literature been put forth with such rhetorical force, and Plato, after all, had no need to reconcile his attitudes with his practice.

But within the statement lies its justification. The return is "enforced," lies are relied on for life, choices are predisposed, the vital images "will allow nothing to take their place." As she goes on to say in the same essay, "It could lead to madness to look back and back for the true primary impression or sensation . . . ." Although the statement implies that, from some point of view, a "truth" of experience exists, it is, even if attainable, an unbearable truth. Complete awareness for the writer, she implies, is madness and self-destruction. Only the disguise and consolation of fiction make bearable the inevitability of fact.

Although the essay is personal, its generalizations applied primarily to the writer's relation to experience, its implications apply to the reader of fiction as well. After all, he is solicited by the novelist to take part in this charade, to submit himself to the lies and the "new parade of the old mythology." In return for his lost integrity, he is, at one level, offered "synthetic experience" and "into that experience come relationships, involving valid emotion, between the child reader and book characters; a residuum of the book will be in all other emotions that are to follow." This, at any rate, is what fiction offers the child and "the great malleable bulk, the majority, the greater public," the uncritical reader. About the adult, critical reader, Miss Bowen has little to say, except that education inevitably, yet fortunately, casts him forth from this Eden:

. . . for evermore his brain is to stand posted between his self and the story. Appreciation of literature is the end of magic: in place of the virgin susceptibility to what is written he is given taste, something to be refined and trained. (*CI,* 264)

Presumably, though, this "virgin susceptibility" never entirely disappears, and the adult reader must always be a divided soul, passing critical judgment on what he willingly accepts; in Wallace Stevens' terms, he finds solace in knowing that the fiction he willingly believes *is* a fiction. Like Miss Bowen, who as a novelist can from some undefined area of truth see herself as a liar, the critical reader must from some similar point of self-awareness see himself as the child who enjoys being lied to. Art that allows, even encourages, such a complex position for its audience must be a great art.

In spite of the fact that an account of such power probably derives least from biography, the major events of Miss Bowen's career thus far should be identified. Although her comments on her early career emphasize that for her literature was power, a means for insisting on adult identity, the isolation her reading and writing compensated for was far too complex to be more than sketched in here. The image of stability and security implied by the name of the two-hundred-and-fifty-year-old Bowen's Court was partially undermined by both personal and public events. As Miss Bowen relates in the autobiography of her earliest years, *Seven Winters,* she was born in Dublin (on June 7, 1899) and spent the first seven winters of her life there, visiting Bowen's Court only in the summer. Then, while her barrister father, the sixth Henry Bowen, was undergoing treatment for "anemia of the brain," she and her mother (Florence Colley Bowen) spent the years from 1906 to 1908 in England, moving from Folkestone, to Hythe, to Lyminge on the Kentish coast. Although Henry Bowen was pronounced well in 1908, his family did not return permanently to Ireland until shortly before Mrs. Bowen's death in 1912.

Very soon thereafter Miss Bowen was sent to school in Kent (at Downe House), traveling to the continent with her father during the summer of 1913. In 1916, at the end of her formal schooling, she returned to Ireland to work in Dublin at a hospital for shellshocked war veterans. It was shortly after Henry Bowen remarried (Mary Gwynn, sister of Stephen Gwynn) in 1918 that Miss Bowen moved to London, living first in Earls Court and then with a great aunt in Queen Anne's Gate. The winter of 1921 she spent at Bordighera, presumably the setting for her first novel, *The Hotel* (1927).

Although Miss Bowen lived only occasionally at Bowen's Court, it is clear that its isolation and history, again in the form of literary images, served to shape her imagination. She speaks with both sympathy and amusement of the children who "grew up *farouches,* haughty, quite ignorant of the outside world" in such houses, which were even then before the Troubles, anachronistic reminders of the Anglo-Irish Protestant Ascendancy.[3] Thus to emigrate or return (neither word fits the member of a family living as semicolonials since Cromwell) to London was to achieve a geographic, if not yet an aesthetic, distance from a house where "lives . . . for generations, have been lived at high pitch, only muted down by weather, in psychological closeness to one another and under the strong rule of the family myth" (*BC,* 13). Apparently aesthetic distance from Ireland was to come later, for of the stories Miss

Bowen was writing during the years in London (later collected, in 1923, as *Encounters*) none is set explicitly in Ireland. In the year the collection was published she married Alan Charles Cameron and moved with him first to Northampton (1923–25), then to Old Headington where he was employed in the Oxford (city) school system. As a member of the University intellectual circle (including Lord David Cecil, C. M. Bowra, and Isaiah Berlin) and frequent visitor to the "multicellular" literary world of London, Miss Bowen wrote and published her first four novels —*The Hotel* (1927), *The Last September* (1929), *Friends and Relations* (1931), *To the North* (1932)—and two more collections of short stories: *Ann Lee's* (1926) and *Joining Charles* (1929).

After Henry Bowen, who had retired from the bar in 1928, died in 1930, Miss Bowen became the first female owner of Bowen's Court since its erection in 1776. However, she and her husband did not return to Ireland: in 1935 they acquired a house at Clarence Terrace in Regent's Park, London, which she still saw as "something out of (or in) a book." Here Alan Cameron worked on educational broadcasts for the B.B.C., later becoming educational adviser to the Gramaphone Company (Electric and Musical Industries, Ltd.); and Miss Bowen's literary acquaintanceship, begun during her early years in London, had by this time expanded considerably, to include Cyril Connolly and most of the Bloomsbury group, whom she met at the homes of Ethel Sands and Lady Ottoline Morrell. Her friendship with Virginia Woolf, begun in the early thirties, lasted until the latter's death: Elizabeth Bowen is mentioned as a house guest at Monks House in Mrs. Woolf's diary for February 1941.[4] Miss Bowen's novel of 1935, *The House in Paris,* only partially suggests the extent of her travels during this period. Though she traveled most often to France and Italy, she spent some time in virtually all the Western and Central European countries, either before or after the second world war.

The literary advantages gained from this cosmopolitanism are illustrated by her novels and stories of the late thirties. *The Death of the Heart* (1938) shows her close familiarity with the Regent's Park world of London; but at the same time, as a member of a virtually exiled class in Ireland, she has been able to see that country with the eye of an outsider (as she does in *The Cat Jumps*—1934). And since she was the first member of her branch of the Bowen family to live in England from childhood on, her detachment is no less pronounced when she regards English manners and morals. What she calls "the Anglo-Irish ambivalence to all things English, a blend of impotence and evasiveness, a reluctance to be pinned down to a relationship" certainly contributes to the tone of her collection *Look at all those Roses.*[5]

During the second world war Miss Bowen remained in London, working as an air-raid warden and writing for the Ministry of Information. Her short-story collection *The Demon Lover* (1945) is, as she says in a postscript, the "diary" she kept of her reactions to that period, although they are recollected as well in the comparative tranquility of 1949 in her war novel *The Heat of the Day*. In 1948 she was made a Commander of the British Empire and a year later was given an honorary Doctor of Letters degree from Trinity College, Dublin.

After the death of her husband in 1952 Miss Bowen gave up her house at Clarence Terrace to live at Bowen's Court, except for frequent trips to the United States as a lecturer and, earlier, as a member of a commission concerned with capital punishment. The setting of her eighth novel, *A World of Love* (1955), reflected her residence in southern Ireland. In 1960 Bowen's Court was sold, and Miss Bowen returned to Old Headington, Oxford.

Although Miss Bowen has written eight novels, over eighty short stories, one play (*Castle Anna*—1948), she has done a considerable amount of other writing as well. She has written a lengthy history of her family in Ireland (*Bowen's Court*—1942), a short impressionistic autobiography of her childhood winters in Dublin (*Seven Winters*—1942), a somewhat popularized history of the English novel (*English Novelists*—1946), a history of Dublin's Shelbourne Hotel (*The Shelbourne*—1951), and a book-length account of seven months in Rome (*A Time in Rome*—1960). In addition, she has contributed many book reviews to English and American periodicals, serving as permanent book reviewer for the *Tatler* for ten years (*ca.* 1940–1950). At present she is an associate editor for John Lehmann's *London Magazine* and regularly contributes essays on a variety of subjects to American and British magazines. Her *Collected Impressions* (1950) contains most of the essays and prefaces for which, she says, "I would wish survival."

As I hope an outline of her career demonstrates, Miss Bowen is quite frank in saying that her overtly significant experience, insofar as she wishes to discuss it, has been literary. To be sure, any critic of literature must assume that a writer's work is intimately related to his personal life, but in this case we have no choice but to see the relationship as an impossibly complex one, and any attempt to connect life and art would have to become factual biography rather than the heightening of perception toward which literary criticism is directed. As I suggested at the beginning of this chapter, one of Elizabeth Bowen's great accomplishments has been to see life *through* literature, to achieve a subtle position from which she can present life in literary terms—in the images, situations, and metaphors prevalent in prose fiction since its inception—at the same time that she can share with the reader their mutual awareness that this is an art. After all, to be able to see oneself looking at London as a literary experience, to be able to say "This romanticist's London I have never extirpated from my heart," [6] requires more than one self, more than a single perception. Beyond the Elizabeth Bowen that sees only literature is another that can see life steadily and whole by writing novels about it. This second self, this ironist's vision, can be located here and there, within the fiction, but it can probably never be defined, for it is genius. In her open letter to V. S. Pritchett Miss Bowen says,

> If I feel irked and uneasy when asked about the nature of my (as a writer) relation to society, this is because I am being asked about the nature of something that does not, as far as *I* know, exist. My writing, I am prepared to think, may be a substitute for something I have been born without—a so-called normal relation to society. My books *are* my relation to society. Why should people come and ask me what the nature of this relation is? It seems to me that it is the other people, the readers, who should know.[7]

If "society" is here taken to mean the world of Miss Bowen's ideal reader, his composite experience of life and art, present and past, then to define this relation should help to account for Miss Bowen's achievement. By selecting an image almost arbitrarily and watching it do its work, it may at least be possible to provide a pattern that suggests the whole.

In *The House in Paris,* Elizabeth Bowen's fifth novel and the one she herself most favors for its form, the willful Mme Fisher urges the child Leopold, the illegitimate product of an affair she has sponsored, to the life of the romantic:

> For you or me, Leopold, to have been born at all is an opportunity. For you or me, to think may be to be angry, but remember, we can surmount the anger we feel. To find oneself like a young tree inside a tomb is to discover the power to crack the tomb and grow up to any height.[8]

This image of a tension between apparently irreconcilable forces, which appears in similar forms throughout Miss Bowen's fiction, suggests one approach to her matter and manner as a novelist. The tree appeared earlier as the angel of *To the North,* reappears as the swans of *The Death of the Heart*—it symbolizes the romantic will, surging upward or serenely gliding forward, oblivious to external circumstance. Similarly the tomb, which appeared as automobiles and the mechanics of urban society in *To the North* and will appear again as the railway stations and subterranean cafés in the wartime London of *The Heat of the Day,* suggests cold indomitable fact, external circumstance, objective reality. "One is empowered to live fully: occasion does not offer" is the blunt, nonmetaphorical statement of the same opposition in the short story "The Disinherited" (*CJ,* 96–97).

The dilemma is conventional enough, the paradoxical situation from which novels have long been made. For Don Quixote, Simplicissimus, Joseph Andrews, Werther, Dorothea Brooke, Emma Bovary, even Leopold Bloom, life somehow fails to measure up to the protagonist's expectations. But of course the forms of this failure, and the resolutions, vary significantly. The picaresque naïf may achieve equilibrium at the cost of conformity, the romantic may preserve subjectivity at the cost of his life, the Victorian bourgeois may fall back to duty and domestic ritual. Two metaphors composed eighty-six years apart can suggest one such distinction. In his suicide letter to Lotte, Werther measures his love by a star and suggests a tree grown to such a height that it must fall of its own weight. But Silas Marner's domestic humanitarianism alone can destroy the walls of the tomb: "As the child's mind was growing into knowledge, his mind was growing into memory: as her life unfolded, his soul, long stupefied in a cold narrow prison, was unfolding too, and trembling gradually into consciousness." [9]

However, to simplify the paradox to a metaphor does as little justice to contemporary literature as it does to that of the nineteenth century. Modern novelists, with severe artistic self-consciousness and sophisticated social consciousness, have repeatedly questioned both the moral nature of the dilemma and the literary forms of its presentation. By choosing an uncommitted antihero as protagonist, they simultaneously expose the hypocrisy of absolute standards of behavior and the illusions they create by their own art. Though Byron's Don Juan was an almost personal exposure of Childe Harold, Mann's Felix Krull and Kingsley Amis' Lucky Jim have become prototypes of a literary fashion.

In its simplest form, this characteristic search for a position from which the narrator can honestly present the novel's events is manifested in a deliberate breaking of the novel's illusion, often by the imposition of an artificially "happy" ending. In the last few pages of Amis' *Lucky Jim* or *That Uncertain Feeling,* for example, the reader is the victim of a gentle joke: his expectations are being mocked at the same time they are being fulfilled. Or the novel may contain a narrator-character whose self-conscious struggle to put the world together is dramatized, his successes played off against his failures. Ratliff in *The Hamlet* can be seen as a portrait of the artist as travelling salesman, the novel itself as a serious comedy about jokes: stories of crooked horse traders, lusty monks, shotgun weddings, sold souls, sodomy, and salted gold mines.

The stories become *a* novel because storytelling becomes a subject when Ratliff sees more than he can say. The most elaborate dramatizations of the narrator's predicament occur in novels where the novelist and his narrator are not explicitly separated, or where the separation is almost too complex to define. Obviously there are degrees of complexity. John Dowell in Ford's *The Good Soldier* is, clearly enough, not Ford but a storyteller in a room before a fire, and the reader's reactions to this narrator's dishonesty are anticipated and relied upon. Nabokov's Humbert Humbert, however, is a writer who composes pages and who is given, by the fictitious narrator of the Foreword, a "life" beyond the chapters he has supposedly written. But the most confidential and complicated relation established between narrator and reader is probably that set up by Salinger's Buddy Glass in "Zooey" and "Seymour: An Introduction." The ideal reader of these stories is almost too explicit to exist: he must be a reader of Salinger's other works, he must be interested in Salinger's biography and rumors about it, and he must then accept the transformation of this information he has previously labeled "J. D. Salinger" into a fictitious form called Buddy Glass, whose problems as a composer he is asked to sympathize with: "I hate dramatic indentations with all my heart, but I suppose I do need a new paragraph for this matter." [10]

In all of these narratives, the most interesting adjustments the reader makes are not concerned with the events he is being told about, but with the manner of the teller. Whatever a "novel" is to the reader of Salinger and Nabokov (or, as I hope to show, of *A World of Love*), it is not a simple "imitation of life." This sort of complex relation between reader and novel is not, of course, an innovation—Fielding's interspersed chapters in *Tom Jones,* all of *Tristram Shandy, Moby Dick* would deny that—but the broken frame, what Robert M. Adams has called the effect of *trompe-l'oeil,* has become increasingly prominent in the work of intelligent and serious novelists of the mid-twentieth century.[11] What Northrop Frye says of contemporary poets is equally true of contemporary novelists: they are "deeply concerned with the problems and techniques of the age of sensibility." In various modes, they seek to reconcile "literature as process" with "literature as product." [12] The story the reader of such novels listens to is, in Frye's terms, both product and process, its teller both experienced man and self-conscious artist.

The novelist who would deal seriously with both moral values and a social reality to which they seem irrelevant must follow obscure paths through the maze of his world. The simple form, like the simple mind, cannot contain and order contradictions and chaos, especially when the language used in and for social and human realities—love, marriage, death—seems incomplete, unsatisfactory, inadequate to both the experienced reality and the ideals assumed for it. The novelist's desperation is a problem and function of form, not feeling. And it is this problem of form that the novelists I have referred to above have sought to dramatize. Though Elizabeth Bowen, reviewing a book of criticism by V. S. Pritchett in 1942, seems to talk of feeling and the age, the dilemma she defines is formal and timeless:

> These years rebuff the imagination as much by being fragmentary as by being violent. It is by dislocations, by recurrent checks to his desire for meaning, that the writer is most thrown out. The imagination cannot simply endure events; for it the passive role is impossible. When it cannot dominate, it is put out of action.[13]

Appropriately, what is here defined as the environment in which the artist must work is not substantially different from the enclosed air threatening the romantic consciousness of Miss Bowen's innocent young heroines. The problem of the romantic will is to arrive at a synthesis between the circumstance of external fact and the projection of an ideal world where feeling can be realized. As Miss Bowen has put it,

> Man matters—no dissolution of ideas around him, threats, pressures or changes in his condition can dislodge him from his individual fortress of importance. Man is the centre of the Universe—knowing he is not, he continues to feel he is. . . . As we now live, and see life, there would seem to be an increasing discrepancy between fact, or circumstance, and feeling, or the romantic will; and the novelist, in his search for a scale to work on, is increasingly worried by the discrepancy. But, looking back, is it not on that very discrepancy that tragedy for its force and comedy for its richness have relied? [14]

If the ethos of her own novels, wherein the problem is shaped by pattern if not resolved, can be stated as an abstract proposition, the process by which the romantic will arrives at a synthesis would be twofold. First the innocent must suffer a "death of the heart" and attempt to reënter the Garden of Eden by further consuming the fruit of the tree of knowledge, regaining the equilibrium of perfect innocence by approaching the ideal of absolute awareness. Losing innocence, as she portrays it, is dependent on the individual's ability to make connections between the various parts of his experience and, concomitantly, on his ability to make distinctions between good and evil according to an individual standard that is reconciled to the objective world of fact. And to make such distinctions, finally, is the power of language and literature. Synthesis is fiction, and the individual's definition of himself, like the narrator's literary position, is the "artificial" pattern of language he uses to compose and define his world. The alternative to such integration is destruction, the other form of the death of the heart. When a synthesis is impossible and the subjective vision finally bears no relation to the world outside it, madness or death, real or symbolic, are its consequences. Quiet perfidy and frank vulgarity are facts that the individual's art can transcend only if it acknowledges them, without submitting.

It is in treating the failure of the reconciliation of the tree to the tomb that Miss Bowen's indictments of society, especially middle-class banality, become most salient. The assumptions of her social criticism are particularly evident when she equates a perversion of the romantic will with twentieth-century violence in her epilogue to *Bowen's Court:*

> I have stressed as dominant in the Bowens factors we see dominant in the world now—for instance, subjection to fantasy and infatuation with the idea of power. . . . Fantasy is toxic: the private cruelty and the world war both have their start in the heated brain. . . . The outsize will is not necessarily an evil: it is a phenomenon. It must have its outsize outlet, its big task. If the right scope is not offered it, it must seize the wrong. . . . Not the will itself but its wastedness is the dangerous thing. (*BC,* 337–38)

Thus the romantic will to power, exemplified most simply in the novels by Mme Fisher, has its analogy in the second world war, the subject of *The Heat of the Day.* And in that novel, war is the disastrous situation in which there is no public language to control fantasy. To say that the second world war was the failure of art sounds absurd as a proposition, but *The Heat of the Day* makes such a proposition convincing. The contemporaneousness and relevance of Miss Bowen's fiction cannot be stated more directly than that.

The facility with which her comments on history and the role of the novelist in the modern world can be made statements about her own heroines is not surprising. In a very limited sense, each is a portrait of the artist, and the heroine's resolution is, in the more successful novels, the artist's way. The illimitable romantic will in conflict with external circumstance is a paradox that only metaphor, which is art, can resolve. And that resolution, as Miss Bowen points out in the letter to V. S. Pritchett quoted before, may be no more than pattern itself:

> Shapelessness, lack of meaning, and being without direction is most people's nightmare, once they begin to think. . . . Isn't the average thinker simply trying to trace out some pattern around himself? Or, to come on, detect, uncover a master-pattern in which he has his place? To the individual, the possibility that his life should be unmeaning, a series of in the main rather hurting fortuities, and that his death should be insignificant, is unbearable. . . . You and I, by writing a story, impose shape.[15]

Such an imposition of form or pattern on the events of "reality" is, most writers agree, the means by which literature, and particularly the novel, becomes a moral art. Though Arnold, speaking of Wordsworth, said that "whatever bears upon the question, 'how to live' " is moral, he added a condition for moral literature which would attain poetic greatness—that the application of ideas to life be noble, profound, and powerful. Arnold's convictions about form are hidden in his word "application," but Henry James, in his preface to *The Portrait of a Lady,* suggests a gloss. At the end of his familiar "house of fiction" statement he attempts to settle the "dull dispute" about morality in the subject of a novel by a metaphor. He has just said that "the 'moral' sense of a work of art [depends] on the amount of felt life concerned in producing it." Then,

> the spreading field, the human scene [before the house of fiction] is the "choice of subject"; the pierced aperture [of the house] . . . is the "literary form"; but they are, singly or together, as nothing without the posted presence of the watcher—without, in other words, the consciousness of the artist. Tell me what the artist is, and I will tell you of what he has *been* conscious. Thereby I shall express to you at once his boundless freedom and his "moral" reference.[16]

Lawrence, who changes the metaphor of building and architecture to that of a pair of scales, can be used to define the *concern* of the posted watcher with the "felt life" he confronts. For himself, Lawrence says, the value and beauty of the novel is that it can express, without nailing down, "the subtle, perfected relation between me and my whole circumambient universe."

> The novel is the highest example of subtle inter-relatedness that man has discovered. Everything is true in its own time, place, circumstance, and untrue outside of its own place, time, circumstance. If you try to nail anything down, in the novel, either it kills the novel, or the novel gets up and walks away with the nail.
>
> Morality in the novel is the trembling instability of the balance. When the novelist puts his thumb in the scale, to pull down the balance to his own predilection, that is immorality. . . .
>
> The novel is not, as a rule, immoral because the novelist has any dominant *idea,* or *purpose.* The immorality lies in the novelist's helpless, unconscious predilection.[17]

Though it has not always been her achievement to preserve this fluid, trembling balance, Elizabeth Bowen joins James and Lawrence in their plea for simultaneous concern and detachment, for honesty and openness in the powerful application of ideas to life. The moral nature of art, she says in writing of Ben Jonson, lies not in its legislation but in its "plumb-straightness of lines and trueness of angles." In literature, she says, "there must be . . . the mind's disengaged comment on enraged emotion—this *is* the work's morality" (*CI,* 116). To be sure, the consciousness of James's "posted watcher" is by no means equivalent to Lawrence's "me" or to Elizabeth Bowen's "mind," but it is clear that, replacing the eighteenth-century dualism of "delight" and "instruction" is a more subtle unity that cannot be successfully abstracted from the work itself, and that "form" is no less than the value of the literary consciousness by which the words are made active, by which art and life are related.

Thus far we have seen that form is a means of survival for Miss Bowen's protagonists. In one of the asides so frequent in *The Death of the Heart* the narrator says, "Illusions are art, for the feeling person, and it is by art that we live, if we do" (*DH,* 111). And we have seen that the literary form of any one novel is, for Miss Bowen and other modern novelists, the means of achieving a moral encounter with reality and the shape that that encounter assumes. But there is yet a further area in which form is essential to an understanding of Miss Bowen's role. As the individual defines his own identity by establishing his past, a writer can define the body of his work by establishing it within the larger continuity of a literary tradition. Since the well-read writer's experience is literary as well as "actual," he can hardly avoid seeing in the work of other writers ways of rendering his own consciousness, methods of achieving a literary identity, a role for his own relationship to the world and to history. So axiomatic has the idea of tradition become that Eliot's castigation of critics for using "tradition" pejoratively and most of the recommendations set forth with iconoclastic fervor in "Tradition and the Individual Talent" sound curiously dated forty years later. Obviously it is as compensation for a chaotic present that a writer accepts without question the reassuring position Eliot offers him, from which he can write "not merely with his own generation in his bones, but with a feeling that the whole of the literature of Europe from Homer and within it the whole of the literature of his own country has a simultaneous existence and composes a simultaneous order." And tradition in this sense offers power as well as security. When the writer's immediate social and cultural influence is minimal, he is given in its place the possibility of modifying the whole order of literature so that "the relations, proportions, values of each work of art toward the whole are readjusted." [18] Miss Bowen's acceptance of this role, her willingness to see her art as part of a permanent but impersonal continuity, is explicit:

> . . . the task of expression appears a vast one—the old simplicities of the world are gone. . . . We have to learn to live while we learn to write. And

> *to* write, we must draw on every resource; to express, we need a widened vocabulary—not only as to words, as to ideas. The apprentice stage, given modern necessities, cannot but be a long one: some of us there may be who will not outlive it. But at least we are keeping going a continuity; we may serve to link the past with the future masters.[19]

Since "literature . . . is a whole—a compost being added to continually,"[20] her own art gains continuity and expanded reference even though particular glory may have to be sacrificed to general achievement.

Although the concept of tradition, like critical axioms of other centuries, clearly reflects the cultural inadequacies of an age and compensates for them, it is difficult to define what being a traditional artist means as an activity. Eliot's essay posits two readers: the artist in search of a role and the critic in search of a method. What the critic can do who stands outside the literary "whole" has been excellently illustrated by F. R. Leavis in *The Great Tradition,* where the "line" of writers he forms is based on their balance of technical virtuosity and moral seriousness, the extent of their knowledge of English literature, their aliveness to environment, and "a vital capacity for experience, a kind of reverent openness before life, and a marked moral intensity."[21] The criteria thus reconcile "aesthetic" and "moral" standards, for the great novelist promotes an awareness of the possibilities of life by enlarging the possibilities of art, just as a new insight into the possibilities of life will require an enlarged art. But the line was drawn by Leavis, not by the novelists.

The ambiguity of "tradition" for a writer is evident, for example, in Elizabeth Bowen's later (1949) preface to the reissue of her earliest stories, *Encounters.* Although she expresses her indebtedness to E. M. Forster's *The Celestial Omnibus,* the reader can search in vain among the impressionistic sketches of *Encounters* for an echo of the involved plots and mythological fantasies of Forster's collection. The critic who depends on biography is left with an irrelevant fact. But the critic who, like Leavis, stands outside, is given considerably more:

> With regard to the short story, Katherine Mansfield was not only to be the innovator but to fly the flag; since *Bliss* the short story has never been quite ignored. I read *Bliss* when I had completed that first set of my stories which were to make *Encounters*—then, admiration and envy were shot through by a profound dismay. I thought, "If I ever am published, everybody will say I imitated her." I was right: this happened. (*E,* viii)

These stories clearly are in the tradition of Chekhov and Katherine Mansfield, and the critic interested in the body of literature as well as the individual writer is given a standard of evaluation. "Tradition," dependent on the awareness of the critic as well as his subject, can ideally be a concept that presents for the reader the nature of a writer's place in the literary world.

To call Elizabeth Bowen a traditional novelist entails a good deal of critical ambiguity. Although one can call attention to her comments on those writers who, seen externally, most resemble her, the most interesting evidence is found in her own literary practice, whether or not she could be aware of its precedents. *The Awkward Age,* for example, must be considered a precedent for *The Death of the Heart* even though Miss Bowen had not read it when she wrote that novel. To dispense with the ambiguity inherent in the term "tradition" would, in this case, narrow critical awareness.

Elizabeth Bowen's position in a tradition of the English novel, then, is a function of her moral concern and aesthetic practice as well as of her literary knowledge. Her essays and reviews make quite clear her knowledge of Jane Austen, James, and Forster, and the focus of her comments shows that her interest in their work is partly selfish. Like Miss Bowen, all three writers have concerned themselves with the romantic will as it is manifested in the sensibility of a young girl, and the drama of their most characteristic novels is similarly dependent on a readjustment of the heroine's moral vision. Emma, Isabel Archer, and Lucy Honeychurch have at least this in common. But there are other, more compelling reasons for arguing connections. In her novels, as D. W. Harding has pointed out, Jane Austen spoke repeatedly for moral autonomy by presenting "the separation of important private feelings from the routine of social behaviour" through heroines subject to the tension between personal affection and "moral fastidiousness." [22] The same terms could be applied to Miss Bowen, for the final decorum in the fiction of both writers is neither the autonomous rule of a society nor the private standard of an isolated saint—it is rather the metaphorical world created by the dynamically moral person who can find language, tone, and manner to reconcile both standards. Miss Bowen's summary (in *English Novelists*) of Jane Austen's achievement might be her answer to those critics who find her own concerns too limited:

> . . . what [Jane Austen] at once depicted and penetrated was not just *a* world, it was *the* world. She arrived at, and was able to fix for us, the denominators of desire, self-delusion and passion that are common to every kind of human experience. . . . It is true she has drawn no rebels: her people expect, and derive, pleasure from the straight-forward living of life. But they plan; they seek, with degrees of determination, ideal circumstances, ideal relationships inside that world they already know. They locate, and never far from themselves, possible darkness, chaos. . . . The world Jane Austen creates remains an absolute world because of its trueness to its own scale.
>
> (*EN,* 24–25)

Although removing novels and novelists from their historical contexts may seem to be ignoring all that literary historians have established about them, the reader of Elizabeth Bowen (and Miss Bowen herself) does read Jane Austen (or James or Forster) as extensions of his own culture. Precisely because Jane Austen's art is absolute and true to its own scale, it is timeless. The relationships defined within it are self-contained, and the art of their containment can be measured against Miss Bowen's.

But the boundaries of Jane Austen's world are obviously not congruent with those of Miss Bowen's. It is in the novels of Henry James that the romantic will is portrayed struggling to achieve realization in innocent, though active, moral integrity. Henrietta Stackpole, speaking to Isabel Archer, defines the struggle in terms that also characterize the prototype of Elizabeth Bowen's heroines:

> . . . you think you can lead a romantic life, that you can live by pleasing yourself and pleasing others. You'll find you're mistaken. Whatever life you lead you must put your soul in it—to make any sort of success of it; and from the moment you do that it ceases to be romance, I assure you: it becomes grim reality! And you can't always please yourself; you must sometimes please other people. That, I admit, you're very ready to do; but there's another thing that's still more important—you must often *dis*please others. You must always be ready for that—you must never shrink from it. That doesn't suit you at all—you're too fond of admiration, you like to be thought well of. You think we can escape disagreeable duties by taking romantic views—that's your great illusion, my dear. But we can't. You must be prepared on many occasions in life to please no one at all—not even yourself.[23]

If Miss Bowen's tone was anticipated by Jane Austen, analogues of her characters appear throughout James's novels. The helpless sensitive children confronted by moral (or metaphysical) evil who appear in *The Turn of the Screw, The Awkward Age,* and *What Maisie Knew* are reflected by Leopold of *The House in Paris* and Portia in *The Death of the Heart.* James, in fact, may have helped to give Miss Bowen's Portia her name, for in discussing the "frail vessels [in whom] is borne onward through the ages the treasure of human affection" (George Eliot's phrase), James goes back to Shakespeare to find a prototype—"even with Portia as the very type and model of the young person intelligent and presumptuous." [24] Certainly James, as a moral novelist, is like Jane Austen and Miss Bowen in seeing manners as the outward and visible signs of codified behavior that may not be moral. Decorum as an art of living, as a matter that "bears upon the question 'how to live,' " receives no fuller exploration by any novelist. His moral concern, of course, is in complete accord with Miss Bowen's emphasis on disengagement, for, James insisted in "The Art of Fiction," "with a relation *not* imaginative to his material, the story teller has nothing whatever to do."

When Elizabeth Bowen speaks of the morality inherent in James's novels, it is a comment on their range of implication, the intelligence of James's mind, not his didacticism:

His sense of beauty is matched by his sense of evil: his villains do worse than oppress or threaten—they subtly and immeasurably corrupt. His innocent characters move through danger zones; the spirit is in peril, seldom the flesh. (*EN*, 42)

There are pertinent differences between Miss Bowen's and James's convictions about the attitude the narrator may take toward his audience (she repeatedly allows the explicit recognition of the novel as illusion), but the similarities of both subject matter and ethos clearly place James in the tradition defined here. Miss Bowen chooses a fundamentally different art for expressing the preservation of illusion and order (she would hardly be distinctive if she didn't), but James probably would have agreed with the substance (perhaps not the desperate tone) of Elizabeth Bowen's "Man has to live how he can: overlooked and dwarfed, he makes himself his own theatre" (*CI,* 44).

"Overlooked" and "dwarfed" are certainly not terms that would have occurred to Jane Austen, for whom hostility is harbored in people rather than in the world. But E. M. Forster's "moral consumptives," like Miss Bowen's, are facts of history as well as personality. As he points out in his "Notes on the English Character," their villainy consists not of overt autonomous acts of evil but in a passive predilection for innocence. The dramatic conflict of his novels, as of Miss Bowen's, often occurs when the undeveloped, because incomplete, heart of the moral consumptive proves disastrously inadequate to the undeveloped, because immature, heart of the innocent. And the sick man is a counterpart of a sick society—Forster's terms for moral inadequacy and social injustice are usually organic, often medical. In betrothal and marriage especially the evil erupts. Lucy Honeychurch of *A Room with a View* barely escapes being crushed by Cecil Vyse as Sydney Warren in *The Hotel* barely evades the cage prepared for her by James Milton.

Forster differs from Miss Bowen in putting emphasis on the undeveloped male heart, but his ironic treatment of the encounter, his characteristic "double vision," is often echoed in her novels. There is no easy way to express what goes on in the mind of a man (or woman) who has become his own theater. Publicly viewed (and a novel's language must be largely public) his fantasy may be madness. Only irony allows a reader to read a statement from two separate points of view. In confronting such situations, a writer must take advantage of every resource available to him, so it is hardly surprising that both Forster and Miss Bowen have brought back to the novelist his prerogative to address the reader directly. Neither can afford to be afraid of tampering with the illusion of "real life" and empathy on which the novel of escape depends.

I have tried to indicate, partly by arbitrary choice, partly by allowing Miss Bowen's criticism to choose, the peaks of the tradition of the novel with which she seems to have allied herself, the forms of literature through which she has seen life. As Arnold said of the Romantics, she has been born in an age when she "could not know enough." Lacking an accessible intellectual milieu in the society she shares with her readers, Miss Bowen has turned to Arnold's alternative: "Even when [a 'society . . . permeated by fresh thought, intelligent and alive'] does not actually exist, books and reading may enable a man to construct a kind of semblance of it in his own mind, a world of knowledge and intelligence in which he may live and work." [25] The tradition I have tried to define in this chapter is at least an outline for the "world of knowledge and intelligence" Miss Bowen seems to be working from—not the one she has made, but the one her reader can construct.

Other readers, of course, might make other constructions. For instance, it is difficult to understand Miss Bowen's exclusion of Victorian novelists from her interests: her dismissal of Dickens and her apparent lack of sympathy with George Eliot. Though Mario Praz argues (in *The Hero in Eclipse in Victorian Fiction*) that a prevalence of bourgeois standards of taste and behavior made violent conflicts between circumstance and the romantic will rare, Dorothea Brooke of *Middlemarch* would seem to be as obvious a prototype for Miss Bowen's heroines as any in James or Forster. Even the metaphor by which Dorothea is introduced anticipates *The Death of the Heart:* "Here and there a cygnet is reared uneasily among the ducklings in the brown pond, and never finds the living stream in fellowship with its own oary-footed kind." Yet the impulse to excel, in Dorothea, is expressed as intellect, not feeling. What brings her grief is her inability to subordinate the forces of particular feeling to the abstractions of lofty spiritual purpose. In this way her dilemma is the converse of the one faced by the romantic will, and Dorothea belongs with a Jude or a Quentin Compson, rather than a Lois Farquar or a Karen Michaelis.[26]

When Miss Bowen sees her art within a historical sequence, whether or not the particular one I have defined here, she is partially self-deprecating. Since even the least distinguished novels can be placed in some kind of tradition, value obviously lies in the particular contribution of the individual talent. A heritage of illustrious predecessors can at best provide examples for comparison; it is Elizabeth Bowen's honesty in presenting and giving life to the world she sees, the successful art of *her* fiction, that must finally provide reasons for admiration, just as the limitations of her art must determine her position in such a hierarchy. Her conception of the novel's ideal form, for example, seems strangely ambivalent: the tone of most of the precepts she sets forth in her "Notes on Writing a Novel" is strictly Aristotelian, yet the assumptions underlying much of her criticism and practice seem narrowly romantic. In the "Notes" she speaks of Plot, Scene, Dialogue, not of organic form; yet her preference for the short story, her concern about sustaining mood for the necessary length of time, and the nature of *A World of Love,* all suggest that she feels the novelist must seek a metaphoric, spatial organization, that narrative bridges are "slimy tracts" disrupting unity and art.[27] Only some such conflict can account for the odd discrepancy between the manner of *The Heat of the Day* and that of *A World of Love* only six years later.

Indeed, it is Miss Bowen's own schematic approach to art that makes possible the approach of this study. Anyone who reads with intelligent enjoyment must recognize implicitly that a "reverent openness before life" is finally a more important quality in determining value than an abstractable thematic pattern, which can too easily lead the critic to value analysis at the expense of art. The bare skeleton of image, metaphor, or outline certainly is far more functional, far less destructive, when derived from the lyric rather than from the novel's discursive richness. But to talk about the novel as rather static and spatial, as I have done here, is merely to recognize that no other convenient critical language exists, and earnestly to hope that prolific quotation will suggest that the anatomy lesson is derived from and finally leads to a life that is something more, a vitality that lives beyond the scheme with full energy in the better novels, with flickering brilliance in the lesser ones. But Miss Bowen, who calls herself a "reviewer or, at most, an impressionistic critic," defines the literary critic's task as the presentation of a "reasoned analysis." [28] To provide one is the aim of the following chapters.

2 *Italy and Ireland*

The nameless hotel in the nameless Italian Riviera town in Miss Bowen's first novel, *The Hotel* (1927), is a curious structure. Its anonymity enhances its symbolic suggestiveness, for it is an outpost of British society in a primitive land, a fragile doll's house of suspended activity set slightly apart from a society that demands action, a sanctuary for relationships lost in the greater world. The motif of perilous existence amid danger is echoed literally and metaphorically throughout the book, and many scenes involve persons speaking from balconies, surveying from hilltops, huddled in self-protecting groups. Thus,

> The Pinkertons imposed themselves on the world by conviction. The damage at which they now stood aghast was not a personal affront, and they were ennobled by the absence of personal resentment. The poor old things had, after all, ventured out into the world along a kind of promontory.
>
> (*H*, 44)

Or Sydney, the heroine, speaking to the Reverend James Milton, says

> They all take for granted—down there—that there aren't any more Saracens, but for all we know they may only be in abeyance. The whole Past, for a matter of fact, may be one enormous abeyance. (*H*, 57)

Yet the melodrama inherent in these metaphorical situations is partly mocked by events. The "damage" that has shattered the composure of the Hon. Miss and Mrs. Pinkerton is the innocent use of their reserved bathroom by the newly arrived clergyman; the invasion of the Saracens turns out to be no more than the entirely honorable proposal of a young vitiated Englishman to a rather silly doctor's daughter. This complex interaction of tone and event in *The Hotel* requires some account of the novel's precedents in Miss Bowen's own short stories and in the novels of her older contemporaries.

The sophisticated ambition evident in *The Hotel* is somewhat less surprising if one remembers that it followed the publication of two volumes of short stories, *Encounters* (1923) and *Ann Lee's* (1926). Though most of these early stories are inferior to the early novels in technical competence and intellectual awareness, they serve to define the background of literary concerns from which the novels arise. As Miss Bowen points out in her 1949 preface to the reissued *Encounters,* she was not as yet aware of the difference between story and sketch, art and "accomplished reportage." With relatively few exceptions, they are the stories that would be expected of a young woman of literary bent, living in London, who "had already, at twenty, failed to be a poet, and was in the process of failing to be a painter." Her aim, she frankly admits, was publication (but for "affirmation" rather than "glory"), and she says that she hoped by writing to extend her sense of reality, which she had found thus far only in books. She herself has defined the paradoxical tone, the "social motive" that so often mars the stories: the desire "at once to approximate the grown-ups and to demolish them."

In publishing *Encounters* and *Ann Lee's* together, as *Early Stories,* Knopf did American readers a service, for the second collection less often demonstrates a literary talent in search of a role as compensation, more often replaces promise with achievement. The *Ann Lee's* stories were, she says in her preface to *Early Stories,* "half-way between the first bright stage of experimentation and the required next degree of command." The social satires are given the psychological turning points she found lacking in the earlier collection; a sense of place and atmosphere ("The hazy queerness places and persons had for me") give the actions tangible environments, and fantasy appears in a new and important role.

Both collections present in embryonic form the concerns defined in the last chapter; and although that definition is abstracted from all her fiction, Miss Bowen's first published works can help to separate indebtedness from originality in *The Hotel.* Even in the earliest collection, two parallel interests are evident. Laura, the "big fair girl" with "virginal starts and blushes" disconcerts the pretended naturalness of a sophisticated discussion in "Sunday Evening"; the young wife Esmée is possessed by Mrs. Windemere (in the story of the same name), who disintegrates her married life, invites herself to look over Esmée's husband and, having obtained a free lunch, leaves the Regent Street restaurant "firmly encircling Esmée's wrist with a thumb and forefinger." Possession and militant freedom, on which the conflict of *The*

Hotel depends, also appear in the Forster-like story of an encounter between a strait-laced young woman and a household of questionable morality in "The Parrot" (*Ann Lee's*). But unlike a Forster prude, who is typically rescued by the spirit of Pan, Eleanor rejects the release offered by her bohemian neighbors and returns, like the parrot, to the "cage" of respectability. Suggestive of seriousness as these stories are, however, they are often inconclusive, as if the material uncovered by the technique were too complex to handle. Miss Bowen emphasizes in her preface to *Early Stories* that many of them "are questions asked; many end with a shrug, a query, or, to the reader, a sort of over-to-you."

The Hotel—the product, Miss Bowen remarks, of a winter at Bordighera—is her first attempt to consider at length the world she saw, and it would seem to be a first novel more dependent on influence and precedent than tradition.[1] Twenty-four years earlier Forster had begun his first novel (though it was not published until 1908), *A Room with a View*.[2] In 1915, Virginia Woolf's first novel, *The Voyage Out,* appeared. *The Hotel* has a strikingly close resemblance to both its predecessors: all three novels have a similar protagonist, an upper-middle-class girl of sensitivity and intelligence moving from youth to maturity; the major setting of each is a predominantly English hotel in a foreign, "primitive" country; the crucial scenes of all three novels include a discovery of sexual passion during a pastoral excursion. Though the "transportation plot," as F. W. Dupee calls it in his biography of James, was inaugurated in *Daisy Miller,* Forster was apparently original in his use of a hotel as a microcosmic outpost of civilized society, and Forster's ironic tone makes *A Room with a View* considerably more complex than *Daisy Miller* or the novels of Mrs. Woolf and Miss Bowen.[3]

The appeal of a hotel as the locale for a first novel is easy enough to imagine. For the timid novelist who has read more than he has seen, it is a limited world separated from history and society, a definable unit of rendered characters surrounded by stereotypes labeled "foreigners." To a more ambitious novelist the narrowed field of vision can allow depth, as it does when the characters of *The Sun Also Rises* move to Pamplona. Or the limited field can be itself symbolic, so that the more elaborate relationships established within it are made to carry meaning that would be impossible if the world were not excluded, as they do in Iris Murdoch's *The Bell.* A distinction between limitation as technique and limitation as evasion seems to differentiate Forster's novel from those of Miss Bowen and Mrs. Woolf.

The relationships and moments focused on by the three novelists are astonishingly similar. In each a young girl becomes a woman—not biologically or psychologically as the usual novel of adolescence presents it, but morally and socially. Youthful romantic expectations are met by adult facts (only in Forster's novel are the facts "cultural" as well as social); and the "profession" anticipated in novels of adolescence is replaced by a vaguely threatening marriage. Especially in Miss Bowen's novel, where the suitor is actually a clergyman, the heroine's choice is almost religious: she must determine whether or not she has been called, whether the language imposed upon her as a wife will allow her freedom as well as possibility. For example, Sydney finds an attraction in the fact that as the wife of the Reverend J. D. L. Milton "death" would have a meaning in their vocabulary that it now lacks in her own. But the threat of marriage is both personal and institutional, for the will of society that sanctions marriage is allied with the will of the husband. Lucy Honeychurch's replacement of Cecil Vyse with George Emerson substitutes a living language for a dead one, a man who knows how to criticize his society for one who accepts it.

Naturally there are significant differences among the novels. The innocent primitivism and joyful socialism that Forster, with tongue in cheek, uses to free Lucy from the vise of Cecil, and offers her in the form of George, are far different from the macabre unnamed fever that prevents Rachel's loss of freedom in marriage to Terence Hewet by killing her. But in a common concern with adolescent heroines encountering death and love, the three novels are congruent. When Lucy, misled by the coachman's misunderstanding of her phrase "the good man," literally falls into the arms of George on a terraced hillside that is "the well-head, the primal source whence beauty gushed out to water the earth," the pattern is set for Mrs. Woolf's Rachel to pause at the summit of Monte Rosa just in time to see a young man and woman from the hotel embracing. Miss Bowen, presenting a very similar situation during the picnic expedition in *The Hotel,* alters only a few particulars when Sydney and James Milton separately witness the embrace of Veronica and Victor. For each pair of lovers, participating or watching, the experience opens up what Mrs. Woolf calls a "terrible possibility in life," at once exciting but threatening. And at this point each heroine, depending on her creator's skill, must enlarge her world (and the language that creates it) in order to include the unexpected event. In a quite literal sense, she must "come to terms" with an overwhelming experience.

Like love, death too can test a heroine's sense of the existence of minds other than her own. Death in Mrs. Woolf's novel, both destruction and solution for Rachel, is absolute and final, a conclusion rather than an event. But for Sydney descending the mountain and Lucy witnessing the murder in the Piazza Signoria, a death anticipated or seen also dramatizes the fact that there is something beyond and above "the world of rapid talk." The emotional awareness of the "fact" of death is presumably one of the most difficult situations any novelist can undertake to present, and perhaps for that reason is rarer in fiction than in life. When death in a novel explicitly causes changed relationships among connected persons, these changes can be dramatized: Stephen Dedalus' guilt, Gerald Crich's new dependence on Gudrun, the myth of Mrs. Ramsay. But the anticipation of one's own death or the witnessing of an irrelevant person's death is more often the subject for poetry ("When I Have Fears"). Forster is successful in this instance by using metaphor, the blood on the photographs Lucy was carrying; but Miss Bowen's Sydney can only say, in effect, "I'm alive" and "I'm different."

Yet death is only one aspect of the situation that Miss Bowen and Forster must find a language to realize. Since both novelists present the romantic will with sympathy and admiration, they must find a way to reconcile freedom to both violence and social restriction. Here Forster, by regulating his tone, strikes a balance of attitudes that Miss Bowen, following his direction, never quite achieves. As Lionel Trilling has pointed out, the attitude of sympathy with the romantic will that Forster urges is heavily qualified by irony.[4] In *A Room with a View,* where every autumn is reminiscent of spring, the "depths of strangeness" that give Miss Bartlett the strength to make sure that Lucy sees Mr. Emerson are equally evident in Cecil's good manners when he is rejected. Cecil and Charlotte, though medieval, can approach the Renaissance; Mr. Beebe's humanism, conflicting with his belief in celibacy, still bears the scars of its emergence from the dark ages. Just as there are "shadows because there are hills" on earth though not in heaven, so too do Forster's characters resist categorizing. The idealism according to which Forster applies his tests of moral realism exists simply in the proposition that "the Garden of Eden . . . which you place in the past, is really yet to come. We shall enter it when we no longer despise our bodies." [5]

The irony, the divided vision, implicit in such an attitude and essential to Forster's novel (and, as I hope to show, attempted in *The Hotel*), is significantly absent in *The Voyage Out,* where an ethos that presents extinction as an almost preferable alternative to marriage badly needs some sort of qualification. Rachel, it should be remembered, dies in a mythical South American city from an unnamed tropical disease. This translation of a social, emotional, and intellectual problem into a biological one seems too simple a solution of the novelist's dilemma. The futility of the romantic will, whose defeat is only suggested by Forster's irony, appears in a blatantly obvious manner in *The Voyage Out,* and death is a hastily dropped curtain rather than a light suddenly thrown on reality.

In one sense, Miss Bowen's novel is the least complex of the three, for the nameless hotel is explicitly a symbolic structure, a "little world of suspended activity where there was time for the finest of shades," where the adult social world of the lounge is connected by a symbolic lift to the bedrooms which are "the regions of intimacies," and when Sydney leaves the hotel at the end of the novel it is to rejoin a "real" world:

> I think we have been asleep here; you know in a dream how quickly and lightly shapes move, they have no weight, nothing offers them any resistance. They are governed by some funny law of convenience that seems to us perfectly rational, they clash together without any noise and come apart without injury. (*H,* 247)

And even the inhabitants of this dream world, as Sydney sees it, are puppets "surprised doing appropriate things in appropriate attitudes as though they had been put there to represent something and had never moved in their lives" (*H,* 108).

Although the narrative simplicity of *The Hotel* has been responsible for its misinterpretation as a social satire, the role of Sydney Warren makes such a reading impossible. Like the heroines of Forster and Mrs. Woolf, she is young, intelligent, and sensitive: she has "passed too many . . . examinations," is "curiously dammed up," has "the strangest possibilities of shining." And, as in the case of her two predecessors, intellectual preparation has not provided a sense of identity, which Sydney finds only in her devotion to the middle-aged, sophisticated widow, Mrs. Kerr: "If she did not exist for Mrs. Kerr as a tennis player, in this most ordinary, popular of her aspects, had she reason to feel she existed at all?" (*H,* 25). Although the attitude of guilt and secrecy with which Sydney surrounds and protects her relationship with Mrs. Kerr has led some readers to see in it a suggestion of homosexuality, Sydney's guilt has a more subtle basis: "Sydney professed herself (to friends of her own age) a Realist, and it was perhaps because of this that her imagination, which she dealt with austerely, was able to revenge itself obliquely upon her" (*H,* 25). Because Mrs. Kerr alone among the inhabitants of the Hotel is able to accept her own isolation and yet manage to live in the present, she becomes the center of admiration for the other inhabitants, who less successfully order their lives, and the object of Sydney's devotion.

James Milton and Ronald Kerr, who help to destroy the false, because unrealistic, equilibrium of the two women's friendship, are unlikely agents of the imagination's revenge. Milton, a broad-minded clergyman like Mr. Beebe in *A Room with a View,* asserts his independence from convention by aggressively taking over "a hospitable looking bathroom" the moment he arrives at the hotel, but his independence is ascribed to provincialism rather than sophistication. The kiss of Victor and Veronica reveals to him with disconcerting suddenness a realm of feeling outside the society of widows and spinsters who compose his parish and his security. When he and Sydney watch Veronica and Victor embrace beside the water tank, the effect on both is shock:

> Sydney's imagination had failed her, she found herself disappointed in her own society and was coming back slowly to rejoin the others. To her, looking down unawares, the couple gesticulating soundlessly below her in the sunshine appeared as in some perfect piece of cinema-acting, emotion represented without emotion. Then she wondered by what roads now unknown to her she might arrive at this: to be seen swinging back against a man's shoulder in that abandon of Veronica's. She wondered whether at such a moment she would be cut off from herself, as by her other emotions. (*H,* 68)

And Milton "had never seen a man and woman kiss before and was battering in a kind of despair against the glass wall that divided him from experience. He was thankful, with a tinge of regret, that Sydney had not been among them" (*H,* 69).

Though the situation here has been close to that in *The Voyage Out,* the tone with which it is anticipated is much closer to Forster's irony. The leader of the expedition, Mr. Lee-Mittison, an anemone-collector, has been their Moses, Milton their Aaron, and when they all reach the spot at which the kiss is to take place, "Veronica Lawrence, wildly exclaiming 'The Promised Land!' stumbled forward into the thyme and lay crucified" (*H,* 55). However serious the effect of the embrace of Veronica and Victor on Sydney Warren and James Milton, the love affair of the first pair functions throughout the rest of the book as an ironic subplot mocking what is to be the engagement of Sydney and Milton.

But the tone of amused irony is not consistently sustained. The reader is asked to take straightforwardly the threats to Sydney's apparently secure relationship with Mrs. Kerr that are presented by the arrival of her son Ronald and by Milton's proposal of marriage. Sydney's ideal, the imagery suggests, is a static relationship of object to object "in which emotions ceased their clashing together and friends appeared only as painted along the edge of one's quietness." But Milton's proposal and Ronald's impending visit force her to see that any human relationship is one of "being to being," not object to object. The metaphors used to present Milton's proposal imply the necessity for such a transition; and Italy in this novel is not Forster's land "in the eternal league with youth," but first a painted backdrop to the imperceptive, then a mysterious territory of the emotions to the one threatened by "being":

> Their conspicuous if isolated situation, the matter-of-fact sunshine and the sense that with all said and done they were English Visitors, he and she, sitting appropriately on a bench before a view designed for their admiration, had up to now kept her purely impersonal. So objective did she feel that she imagined a delighted Commune gazing down at the two of them: 'English Visitors.' In the expansion of the free air she had laughed and felt that neither of them were realler than the scenery. Now, at some tone in his voice she was surprised by a feeling that some new mood, not of her own, was coming down over them like a bell-glass. The bright reality of the view, the consciousness of their unimportant, safe little figures were shut away from her; they were always there but could no longer help. She felt the bell-glass finally descend as he, after a glance round at the other benches and over the edge of the plateau, said quickly, "The thing is, Sydney, aren't I ever to know you?" (*H,* 130)

As Sydney sees it, the conflict continues to be one between life and art. Interrupted in her reading of *Jude the Obscure,* she can urge Veronica to "go by yourself" in deciding whether or not to marry Victor, and sees that the simpler girl, even though (or because) the word "love" is not in her vocabulary, is able to take a "position midway between defiance and resignation" that will make her "very likely to achieve serenity."

Milton too is forced to consider past art's failure to order life when he and the cynical Ronald visit the deserted villa formerly occupied by Russian aristocrats. In the decay and ruin they see the inexorable victory of the permanent—raw nature, natural time, women's nature—over anything that man's intellect and conscious will is able to oppose to it. "It strikes me more and more as I live," says Milton, "that the world is no place for anyone with any real notion of anything, and that its expulsion of them must be almost automatic" (*H,* 164).

Thus both Sydney and Milton, forced to realize their dependence on chance and circumstance, on nature and society, over which they cannot will dominance, are vulnerable to almost any influence. In the process used throughout this novel, the abstract "sense" of something brought to a character's attention is almost immediately followed by a dramatization of that awareness. When Mrs. Kerr tells Sydney that she has expected too much of her, either by taking Mrs. Kerr too much for granted or by giving too much, Sydney is cast directly into the fatalistic world she has seen only in reading Hardy, and even then from the remove of her friendship with Mrs. Kerr. Whatever freedom she gains is ambiguous, a "terrible possibility": "The facility with which it would be possible for her to cover larger distances and her present complete inability to move from the kerbstone presented themselves simultaneously" (*H,* 182–83). The presence of Mrs. Lee-Mittison, the frustrated and self-sacrificing Martha of the picnic expedition, looking on with pity when Sydney agrees to marry Milton, suggests to the reader that Sydney's fate could easily be hers.

In accepting this kind of via media, the compromise of the romantic will in marriage, Sydney has presumably put herself on the same level as Veronica. Though Milton defends to Mrs. Kerr his right to accept Sydney's hand even if it has been extended only for protection, he must accept Mrs. Kerr's demonstration that his offer of protection, not "wrong," nevertheless eliminates the possibility of love: to offer protection he must acknowledge in Sydney a quality not "pretty or admirable." What might have been seen romantically as a love affair is reduced, by the analysis of Mrs. Kerr and the narrator, to a pact of alliance.

Just as Mrs. Kerr has made Milton aware of his own motives in wishing to marry Sydney, so too Ronald, encountering Sydney in the solitude of the valley near the hotel, faces her with her own adolescence. Ronald has been led to Sydney by a man who "also had shouted a word of encouragement, the same mystifying reference to some 'bellissima,' " and in having to explain to Ronald that the Italians "wouldn't be able to imagine why you should want to walk up a valley alone unless there were a woman at the end of it," she sees in him a naïveté she must lose and an honesty she must accept. To encounter adolescence in this way is to recognize a distance from it.

> While Ronald talked she often had a giddy sense of watching all she had ever said being wound off from a spool again backwards. Now and then came a truth that she had let slip away; she received this last one [love as a "misapprehension"] back again ice-cold. It went too deep and she wasn't grateful to Ronald. (*H,* 222)

Although Sydney and Milton, meeting later in the same valley, have become more clearly aware of the desperation that has driven them together and fear to meet "in this bare narrow place, the stage for a crisis, where no side-issue could offer itself to be grasped at," the conflict between and within them remains unresolved because Sydney continues to linger between contemplation and act. A discontinuous person, a "succession of moments," she admits that marrying Milton is "going back through the door," but attempts to subordinate her desire for individuality to the desire to escape from the silence that surrounds a life in which personal relationships deprive her of identity:

> She stood between Tessa and Mrs. Kerr as inanimate and objective as a young girl in a story told by a man, incapable of a thought or a feeling that

was not attributed to her, with no personality of her own outside their three projections upon her: Milton's fiancée, Tessa's young cousin, Mrs. Kerr's protégée, lately her friend. (*H,* 242)

For a moment, travelling down a mountainside in a car with the three who have "projected" her, Sydney sees death as the only pure, positive, and desirable alternative, but when the car almost crashes into a load of timber blocking the road, the closeness of the disaster Sydney has anticipated brings her a new sense of life and identity, much as the death sentence is a gift of freedom for Camus' Meursault. She is suddenly able to make distinctions between the lifeless art of her past, the defeat that marriage to Milton would have brought her, and death. For the first time she feels not a victim of time as a senseless succession of moments, but a person capable of extending time for herself:

This isolation above the regular approach of night connected itself in her mind with her present shocked sense of having been flung back on to living. The depths of shadow from which they were barred away would have been to her infinitely grateful. Above, in this unnatural, endless prolongation of the daylight she for the first time felt life sharply, life as keen as death to bite upon the consciousness, pressed inexorably upon her, held to her throat like a knife. Dazed by a realization of their import, she stared at her hands, at her body, at the hills round her. (*H,* 245) [6]

"It was the shock of being alive," she explains in breaking off her engagement, and Milton is able to feel that "at this moment of swinging apart he was one with her, and was able to say 'she is right.' " Somehow, Sydney has awakened from the dream the Hotel represents.

The emphasis put on Mrs. Kerr in the last two chapters of the novel is significant, for Miss Bowen defines the "new" Sydney by analogy. Mrs. Kerr's self-chosen isolation and independence (threatened more by kindness than death) is what we are asked to see Sydney attaining. Milton can return to the outside world exactly as he had left it, but Sydney, like Mrs. Kerr earlier, has become "a hard-sounding name with a cool-sounding echo" to the guests of the Hotel. Like her teacher, she has taken the lonely road that is freedom, acknowledging that it may lead "to an empty town at the top," but her future is no more explicit than that.

Having been brought face to face with chance and circumstance in a setting where time is suspended, Sydney has been shown to recognize that the process of integrating the personal will with these facts is neither easy nor simple. The intellectual preparation with which she arrived at the Hotel and the development of "feeling" that takes place while she is there are forces that pull in opposite directions, and any resolution must necessarily be an ambiguous compromise. She may "insulate" her feelings, but she is presumably able to rescue her will, and that cannot be said for the Lee-Mittisons, Veronica and Victor, or the spinsters.

The vagueness of the ending of *The Hotel,* and the haziness of Sydney's present and future, seem valid objections to the novel. The long conversation between Sydney and Ronald in the chapter called "The Valley" and the elaborate, apparently deliberate, symbolism suggested by the garden of the ruined villa demand a seriousness of attention from the reader that is not rewarded. Is Ronald's admiration of water—Milton calls his haunting of the tank "suspicious" and refers to his mother—intended as serious Freudianism? If so, the point is dropped before it is made.

Yet when indirection is used as a façade to civilize devastating social encounters, Miss Bowen's control of dialogue is remarkable. Milton's interview with Mrs. Kerr remains entirely restrained and polite even though she accuses him of attaching Sydney because it brings him power, of taking advantage of her wounded pride. The scene is a duel of innuendo in the manner of Henry James, with Mrs. Kerr obviously victorious when at the end "she looked round with relief as though rising again to the surface," at the same time "swimming back to the place she had come from, kind superficiality." Milton's defeat is metaphorical as well, though its causes are not: "He felt the light slanting down on him stupefyingly from the mirrors and ceiling a protection from feeling, a barrier, like an orchestra above which one could not, even if one had wanted to, make oneself heard" (*H,* 213). In Milton's case, the outpost is overwhelmed, the tree stifled by the tomb.

But few of the novel's most interesting scenes, including this one, involve Sydney. The cleverness that is alleged to be her distinction is never shown in action, nor are the values she gains from her friendship with Mrs. Kerr ever made explicit. Putatively the relationship with the older woman represents a kind of escape from the self, as does her temporary acceptance of Milton, but that self—with its intellectual cleverness—remains undefined except by metaphor.

These flaws can perhaps be traced to a single cause, evident as well in many of the short stories of the same period: Miss Bowen's unsureness as a narrator. Even in the reviews of this first novel, critics had begun to talk of Jane Austen and Henry James, and the two names do represent separate, often conflicting, narrative attitudes. The conversations based on innuendo, the intense moral seriousness of theme, echo James; but unlike Forster Miss Bowen was unable here to join moral seriousness and comedy in the manner of Jane Austen. The use of social comedy in *The Hotel* is bold—in the Veronica-Victor subplot, in the descriptions of the "flat" characters who inhabit the Hotel, in the ironic light cast on Sydney's romantic will by her cousin Tessa's completely subjective, hypochondriac romanticism. But the limits of lightness, or disapproval, are not always clear to the narrator, and metaphor often is allowed to become an easier substitute for action. When Milton, speaking to Sydney on the bench, destroys the static world she has controlled, the image for "life torn across" is just as static. The bell-glass falling is, presumably, Sydney's image, but to what is it appropriate? Certainly its relationship to the theatrical metaphors—"stage," "scenery," and (earlier) "perfect piece of cinema-acting"—is obscure. Miss Bowen, like Forster and Faulkner, presents frequent tableaux of frozen time, of moments in which life is arrested as art, but in *The Hotel* these moments fail to become dramatically relevant to the novel because she finds no way to move out of them.[7]

Whether or not Miss Bowen had read *A Room with a View* or *The Voyage Out* in 1927 is immaterial. Even if she had been completely ignorant of both novels, even if *The Hotel* was based more responsively than one would assume on her experience at Bordighera, her first novel would nevertheless appear derivative. Its brash comedy would still inevitably diminish the dimensions of the world into which Sydney's dilemma is born, and the reader still would lack the complex position from which he can simultaneously view two worlds—one simple and self-sufficient, the other seriously connected to the complex world of his own experience. All three novelists, to be sure, use a foreign background to circumscribe their characters, but Forster alone, by assembling the most important guests of the Pension Bertolini later at Summer Street and Windy Corner, shows the group reinstated among the complexities of the society from which it had been abstracted. In Miss Bowen's novel, the emphasis is placed on the Hotel as a vague metaphor for an abstract society, and less effectively on its position as an outpost of civilization in conflict with the manners and morals of another race. Her characters exist with few attachments to the world. No "Italians drive them" as in *A Room with a View:* they are "driven" by themselves, and these selves are often rather indistinct.

Much of the indecision in the narrative point of view in *The Hotel* disappears in Miss Bowen's second novel, *The Last September* (1929). When the scene is shifted from Italy to Ireland, the motif of the outpost is even more prominent, for the order and tradition of the Irish Big House are set amid a chaos as clearly defined as the outpost itself: southern Ireland in the time of the Troubles. By integrating political history with what she herself calls "transposed autobiography" Miss Bowen wrote one of her most complex novels, rich (in Empson's sense) in ambiguities left for the reader to explore. Not until twenty years later in *The Heat of the Day* was she to make so comprehensive an attempt to deal with factual and intellectual history in a novel, and only her eighth novel, *A World of Love,* explores the milieu of Ireland in a manner that can more fittingly be called metaphysical.

A reader's assumptions about any novel's genesis in what Miss Bowen has called the writer's "idea" must be speculative, but one feels that *The Hotel* began as a metaphor, and that the novel's world is deduced therefrom. The "idea" in this case seems to have been more limiting than germinal, and as creator of the limiting metaphor the narrator too perfectly and easily controls what it contains. In *The Last September,* however, Miss Bowen's relationship with her donnée appears to be more dynamic, and the novel's carelessness is perhaps the result of too much "life" for the narrator to handle. Its complexities may be unresolved and unordered, but they are more interesting than the neat (but unrelated) metaphors of *The Hotel.*

In his chapter on Elizabeth Bowen in *The Vanishing Hero* Sean O'Faolain, her native Irish champion (his *The Short Story* includes an analysis of "Her Table Spread" that is both admirable and admiring), perceptively points out the fated quality of her heroines and persuasively argues for the thematic importance of controlling fate in *The Last September.*[8] However, in his eagerness to generalize about all the novels, O'Faolain does not acknowledge the peculiar contributions of both place and period to this one novel. Certainly Miss Bowen is concerned with the conflict between fate and possibility, but, she insists with italics, it was "*here* she [Marda] was certainly fated," this particular house that "became a magnet to their dependence," the island status of Ireland itself that reinforces the sense of dependence. Though fate is often the substance of things hoped for in the later novels, here it exists in full strength as an external force. The moral and political correlatives of the fate, diminished possibilities, regrets, and failures that predominate are most clearly defined outside the novel's scope in her later (1942) history of the Bowen family in Ireland.

Since in *Bowen's Court* she undertakes in expository prose what she had earlier presented in fictional form in *The Last September,* a synthesis between the lives of individuals and the history of their environment, the later book can be read as a creative interpretation of the past in which she defines the relationship between the ten generations of the Bowen family and the events occurring in Ireland as a conflict, often unconscious, between family will and historical necessity.

> I have stressed as dominant in the Bowens factors we see dominant in the world now. . . . the idea of the power of the idea of power has governed my analysis of the Bowens and of the means *they* took—these being, in some

cases, emotional—to enforce themselves on their world. I have shown, if only in the family sphere, people's conflicting wishes for domination. That few Bowens looked beyond Bowen's Court makes the place a fair microcosm, a representative if miniature theatre. Sketching in the society of which the Bowens were part, and the operations behind that society, I have extended the conflict by one ring more: again, its isolation, what might be called its outlandishness, makes Anglo-Irish society microcosmic.

(*BC,* 337–38)

Only a few of her terms, such as "analysis," indicate that the book she describes is a history, not a novel, and some of its substance can certainly be seen as what was "transposed" to become *The Last September.* Although Miss Bowen's nationality is conveniently labeled "Anglo-Irish," *Bowen's Court* explains some of the ambiguities hidden behind this deceptively simple term. The Bowens made their home in Ireland after Colonel Henry Bowen, of Gowersland, Glamorganshire, Wales, was awarded land there in return for his services to Cromwell in the Revolution. Bowen's Court, the house built by the third Henry Bowen in County Cork in the late eighteenth century and inherited by Elizabeth Bowen in 1930, is the only surviving representation of the estates of the Bowens in Ireland—a property that had expanded with marriages and contracted in times of hardship. The Bowens as members of the Protestant Ascendancy, the largely English ruling class in Ireland and for many years the only class that could legitimately own land or vote, were cut off from the native Catholic Irish by nationality, religion, social and political position. Elizabeth Bowen herself, though the first of the Irish Bowens to live in England as a child, was so removed from the native Irish culture then being espoused by Yeats and Synge that she first heard of the Irish Revival when she was at school in England in 1916. The novel's Anglo-Irish heroine, Lois Farquar, shares this curious detached position from which she sees her country not emotionally but as "a way of living, abstract of several countrysides, or an oblique, frayed island moored at the north but with an air of being detached and drawn out west from the British coast" (*LS,* 50).

The world of the Big House of the Ascendancy, the oblique attacks on it by the Irish nationalists, and the futile defense of it by the Black and Tans, that form the violent background of *The Last September,* Miss Bowen relates to aberrations in the early nineteenth century. In ascribing the Earl of Kingston's madness to the fact that his tenants voted against his candidate in a bye-election, she sees a characteristic example of power relying on fantasy, romantic will pointlessly opposing political reality, and the replacement of society by "the dire period of Personal Life."

During the crucial years from 1907 to 1912 Miss Bowen (who was born in 1899) lived primarily in England with her mother and, after her mother died at Hythe in 1912, with an aunt at Harpenden. Since her visits to Ireland during this period that prepared the violence shown in *The Last September* were only fleeting, the first-hand impressions she records in *Bowen's Court* are necessarily limited and she does not attempt to deal with the complexities of the 1916 uprising or the Civil War (". . . the events and plans and passions of the years between 1914 and 1941 would make a book that should be as long again as the book that I have written by now"—*BC,* 324). But she does mention the intrusion of these conflicts in the society with which *The Last September* is concerned:

> Between the armed Irish and the British troops in the country, reprisals and counter-reprisals—tragic policy—raged. Fire followed shootings, then fires fires. In the same spring night in 1921, three Anglo-Irish houses in our immediate neighborhood . . . were burnt by the Irish. The British riposted by burning, still nearer Bowen's Court, the farms of putative Sinn Feiners—some of whom had been our family's friends.
>
> . . . .
>
> In 1921 came the Treaty, to be followed by the disintegration of Civil War—the dissentients to the Treaty, Republicans, in arms against the Free Staters who had accepted it. (*BC,* 326–27)

Although *The Last September* is actually concerned with events taking place before the Treaty—when the Anglo-Irish, the native Irish, and the Black and Tans still constituted three separate groups—the novel's narrator deliberately speaks from a point in time some eight years later, after "the Civil War gave place to at least a surface of peace—a surface beneath which, in the exhausted country, many people were not anxious to probe" (*BC,* 329). The novel was written at the time Henry Bowen retired from the bar to Bowen's Court and Elizabeth Bowen was married and living outside Oxford. She explains, in her preface to the American re-issue of the novel (in 1952), her reasons for looking backward and the advantages she gained by creating a narrator removed from both the scene and time of action. The reader's position must be complex enough so that he can see an immediate action within a historical context:

> "All this" [the events of the novel], I willed the reader to *know,* "is over." Yet I wished him to *feel:* "But see, our story begins!" From the start, the reader must look—and more, must be aware of looking—backward, down a perspective cut through years.[9]

In *The Last September,* then, both the political events in Ireland at the time of the Troubles and Miss Bowen's own memories of life in the Big House when it had become an isolated outpost are brought together. With an arrival at such a house, Danielstown, the novel opens, and with its burning it closes. In writing about such houses for *The Bell,* she defines what it meant to grow up struggling in isolation, "queered" by pride, indignant at decline, divorced from countryside. Clearly the determination of Sir Richard and Lady Naylor, the owners of Danielstown, is thus "obsessed" and "exalted"; and in *Bowen's Court* the psychological atmosphere that pervades such houses is described even more vividly. For *The Last September* (and later *A World of Love*) the peculiarity of such life is essential to the novel.

> Each of these family homes, with its stables and farm and gardens deep in trees at the end of long avenues, is an island—and, like an island, a world. . . . Each member of each of these isolated households is bound up not only in the sensation and business of living but in the exact sensation of living *here.* . . . Each of these houses, with its intense, centripetal life, is isolated by something very much more lasting than the physical fact of space: the isolation is innate; it is an affair of origin. It is possible that Anglo-Irish people, like only children, do not know how much they miss. Their existences, like those of only children, are singular, independent and secretive. (*BC,* 13–14)

All of these characteristics—the struggle, the isolation, the timelessness—form the body of circumstance, the fate, against which Lois, orphaned niece of the Naylors, weakly attempts to exert her will. Lois, within the prototype more vaguely defined by Sydney Warren of *The Hotel,* serves to set the pattern for all Miss Bowen's heroines. Though she can live well enough in the future she projects in her daydreams (when she is not forced by circumstance to adopt a role), she nevertheless sees the present and its boundaries, the immediate past and the imminent future, as occasions of ignorance and terror. Action already taken can be reinterpreted, altered by memory; events yet to come can be anticipated in terms of infinite possibility; only what must be done here at Danielstown in the particular autumn of the novel is commitment. Life surprised "at a significant angle" is her romantic dream, and her fate is to realize that "life, seen whole for a moment, was one act of apprehension, the apprehension of death."

It is the present that forces Lois to act in some predetermined but uncongenial way. Her attitude toward social convention is ambivalent, for although she insists on preserving her independence and acting "naturally," she realizes that her life exists in the talk of the drawingroom, that in her society the violation of convention is next to insanity, that "inconvenient" and "wrong" are synonymous descriptions of behavior. Her attitude toward Gerald Lesworth, the subaltern stationed nearby with the Black and Tans, has the same sort of ambivalence. Though she admires the vitality of a soldier's life ("Soldiers did not talk about food, they ate it") and Gerald pleases her with his "eagerness and constancy," Lois recognizes that Gerald's literal-mindedness does not allow him to know what she is like, and that she can only understand him when she imagines him as an object rather than a person. Like Sydney who prefers people as "painted images," Lois can look directly at Gerald only when "she saw him as though he were dead." The change of vocabulary, though, is significant. An overt contrast between art object and man is clear enough, but must remain an explicit simile. If, however, the distinction is made between a living man and a dead one, static simile gives way to metaphor. "Death" can be both stasis *and* dramatic event.

Other comparisons between this novel and the first one reveal similar attempts at greater subtlety. Veronica and Victor in *The Hotel* ironically suggest a simplicity Sydney cannot accept, but there are several love affairs in *The Last September* in which whole apprehension can take place because the apprehenders, in different ways, are more limited than Lois. Lois's school friend Viola in England is able to accept the conventions of her society without rebellion, and Viola's Anglo-Irish counterpart in Ireland, Livvy (the Viola-Olivia similarity is apparently deliberate), flouts convention in her naïve pursuit of soldiers. These simple alternatives of passive acceptance or spontaneous rebellion are both closed to Lois because her imagination forces her to see their futility.

The imaginative perception of futility is evident in the cool, distant, resigned tone of the narrator and reflected even in the titles of the three sections into which the novel is divided: "The Arrival of Mr. and Mrs. Montmorency," "The Visit of Miss Norton," "The Departure of Gerald." These events, the reader is constantly reminded, are in the past, involved characters who now can be known. Indeed, the narrator finds few mysteries in the permanent inhabitants of Danielstown: Sir Richard Naylor, Lois's uncle, is the completely social man "who did not like his friends to be distracted from him by lorries any more than by introspection or headaches or the observation of nature." His wife Myra, like Lady Bracknell in *The Importance of Being Earnest,* relies entirely on her own code of convention, finds truth she doesn't like "gossip," and rejects Gerald as a suitor for Lois partly because his having relatives "scattered about" in Surrey seems "exceedingly restless." Lois's cousin Lawrence, like Ronald of *The Hotel,* is a cynically precocious adolescent who is determined to see love and marriage as surrender, and is condemned by the others because he is not happy.

In spite of the narrator's tone, the "Arrivals" do contain some mystery, and the unfulfilled destinies of the Montmorencies enlarge the scope of the novel. Hugo, who almost married Lois's mother Laura, is repeatedly referred to as the man who did not go to Canada, the practical man *manqué* who loses chances to play tennis and fails to arrive soon enough to save Lois from her experience in the mill. He consummates his desire for a love affair with the Naylor's guest Marda in a fantasy he enacts for himself after she has gone, in a dream world he controls.

> Hugo was pleased with the place; here he seemed to have stepped through into some kind of non-existence. And here, divorced equally from fact and from probability, he set up a stage for himself: the hall's half-light. Marda's hand is on the wide scrolled curve of the baluster-rail: he touches her hand, electric and quiet, with the deliberation of certainty, all his senses running into the touch. She stares recognition fixedly, darkly back. . . . For though in actuality she had had only one mood for him—cool and equivocal—he, frantic with this power disconnected from life, could now command her whole range imaginatively: her features became his actors. And if this were not love . . . (*LS,* 242–43)

As the tone of Hugo merges with that of the narrator—"if this were not love" can hardly originate in the same place that "he, frantic with this power" does—the coolness becomes ironic understatement.

But while her husband seeks continuity in love affairs bred of fantasy, the invalid Francie tries to find it vicariously, watching the young lovers: "For the fact was, life attenuated to the snapping point; in Gerald's continuity, in Lois's, she must invest her own" (*LS,* 233). The protean narrator here, of course, is straightforward and engaged. By such literary resources, lacking in *The Hotel,* Miss Bowen is able to create a fuller, more interesting world for the events of *The Last September.*

It is the story of Lois, of course, that unifies these characters and tones, and gives them an organic relation to the novel. Although the dramatic events directly involving Lois, with one exception, are overtly prosaic (a tennis party is held at Danielstown, Gerald comes to lunch, Lois and Marda meet a revolutionary in an abandoned mill, the British officers give a dance in their huts), in the territory around the house events are more violent: patrols are ambushed, houses are burned, and Gerald is killed shortly after Lois has agreed to marry him. The separation of the prosaic and dramatic, adolescent love and civil war, is central to the meaning of the novel and is the reason I have emphasized the descriptions of Bowen's Court. The romantic and geographic isolation of the inhabitants of Danielstown is reflected in their political position: Lady Naylor rejects the English as vulgar and opportunistically loyal, but the native Irish, many of them friends of the Naylors, represent an active threat to their existence. When Marda asks Hugo about the war, he summarizes the Anglo-Irish position as "... our side—which is no side—rather scared, rather isolated, not expressing anything except tenacity to something that isn't there—that never was there" (*LS,* 115).

Though Lois's dependent position would seem to make her more susceptible than the others to this isolation, she, being young and innocent, is potentially able to mature and outlast the present. But first, presumably, some kind of awakening must bring about within her consciousness a unification of the worlds of love and war, prose and passion, innocence and experience, life and death. If the change is to amount to more than this rhetorical chain of antitheses, a dramatic scene defining the change (like Sydney's discovery as she descended the mountain) must require all Miss Bowen's art. The deserted mill that Lois and Marda encounter, exploring the grounds with Hugo, becomes more than itself:

> Banal enough in life to have closed this valley to the imagination, the dead mill now entered the democracy of ghostliness, equalled broken palaces in futility and sadness; was transfigured by some response of the spirit, showing not the decline of its meanness, simply decline; took on all of a past to which it had given nothing. (*LS,* 171)

And for these "meanings" to be more than a narrator's metaphors, the mill must be related to a quality in Lois's consciousness. Her anxiety in entering it is ambivalent, "a fear she didn't want to get over, a kind of deliciousness"; and the cause of the ambivalence is sexual:

> Marda put an arm round her waist, and in an ecstasy at this compulsion Lois entered the mill. Fear heightened her gratification; she welcomed its inrush, letting her look climb the scabby and livid walls to the frightful stare of the sky. Cracks ran down; she expected, with detachment, to see them widen, to see the walls peel back from a cleft—like the House of Usher. (*LS,* 171–72)

When the sleeping man the girls find in a further room wakes up and threatens them with a pistol, again they are frightened virgins, "embarrassed at this curious confrontation."

However, the fact that the details are given meanings extending to the past, to the consciousness of Lois, to the nature of sex and death, does not mean that the event is undramatic. "Meaning" emerges as well in the changed relations between the characters involved, and in the connections between this event and others in the novel. When Hugo finds them after hearing a shot, Marda has been grazed on the knuckle by a bullet accidently discharged, and in spite of the melodramatic nature of their adventure, the three agree that it would be best to tell those in the house that she has scraped her hand on a stone. Lois, thinking "how the very suggestion of death brought this awful unprivacy," perceives suddenly the potential illicit relationship between Marda and Hugo. Yet when Marda asks her if she is sorry they went into the mill, Lois answers positively "No" because she has had a "revelation." As the conversation and imagery repeatedly suggest, the revelation has involved both sexuality and death: life and death have both been surprised at a significant angle. (Marda even says "inconsequent," "I hope I shall have some children; I should hate to be barren"; and Lois can only wish that she too had been shot.) Though Lois herself has participated only indirectly in this loss of virginity, she is now part of a conspiracy of adulthood and adultery, knowing something of the thinness of the wall separating life and death, Marda and Hugo.

Yet all this action is accounted for by earlier events, for Lois had passed a trench-coated figure skulking in the shrubbery and there has been much talk of guns buried at Danielstown. Even Lois's discovery about Hugo and Marda could be explained by their behavior when he joined them. But in her selection of details, her metaphors, her deliberately equivocal vocabulary, Miss Bowen insists that more is involved, without resorting to a crude symbolism in which one object stands for a thing. From a more complex position than she ever attains in *The Hotel,* Miss Bowen defines far more satisfactorily the way in which the world changes for an adolescent who suddenly apprehends sex and death.

But finding a way to go on is as much a problem for the narrator as it is for Lois. Lois's perception of Gerald is even now not radically different from what it was when she could focus on him only if she saw him as an object. As she hoped, there has been "some change, some movement, . . . some incalculable shifting of perspectives," but it has not brought him, for Lois, "wholly into focus, mind and spirit" (*LS,* 75). What has changed, apparently, is Lois's definition of herself, so that she begins to see Gerald as an escape, their kiss as a loss of her own identity. But the voice of Lois is little changed from what it was before. As Milton in *The Hotel* offers Sydney kindness it would be destruction to accept, Gerald offers Lois protection; but it would be for Lois a future already fixed, therefore over and past, and Gerald would become "the instrument of some large imposture." Though Lois still seeks a direction, one imposed from without is a form of death. "You don't know what it's like for a snail, being walked on," she tells Gerald. When she learns that Gerald has been killed, again "life seen whole for a moment, was one act of apprehension, the apprehension of death." Her freedom, thus won, is the desultory action she and Marda had planned: tours.

Though a summary of the plot might suggest that the novel is a "tragedy of young love" in which a romantic feminist almost loses her independence, Miss Bowen emphasizes in her preface that this was far from her intention. Time and place are given precedence.

> ... the ambience of death and danger, often of violence, seemed as elementally natural to this girl as dance music, the sweet pea in the garden, rain, or the rising moon or the setting sun. Lois's tragedy was not that Gerald should die (what, indeed, was she to do with his life and hers?) but that he should die knowing she could not love him. Her tragedy was *not* Danielstown burning—which did, indeed, though violently, serve to free her.[10]

Moreover, any sentimentality that might attach itself to the story of Gerald's sudden death is banished by the manner in which it is announced. The vulgarity of the British officers' wives has been the target of the narrator's satire, and it is through such unsympathetic characters that the ambush in which Gerald has been killed is announced. Mrs. Fogarty "pressed her hands up under her vast and useless bosom" as she thinks of Gerald's mother, and the Vermonts agree with Denise Rolfe that Gerald's companion won't die (he does) because he's a sergeant. Even the title of the final section of the novel refers to the death as merely a "departure."

However, the success of the irony and satire in the closing pages of the novel is qualified, for it becomes too explicit a defense against the loss of control. The cool, distant narrator gives way, briefly, to an almost vindictive one, and the new narrator's targets—vulgarity and lack of feeling—seem to distract the reader's attention from Lois (and Ireland) to other matters entirely. It is as if Miss Bowen, fearful of asking for tears, insisted on cynical laughter.

The brief account of the later burning of the house at a time when "it seemed that an extra day, unreckoned, had come to abortive birth that these things might happen" reminds the reader that this is not intended as a novel about people or love in the usual sense at all, but a statement (or question) about death. The process by which Lois's identity is brought to birth through experiencing death has been echoed in atmosphere as well as in the burning of Danielstown. Autumn is the season not only of mists and mellow fruitfulness but also of decay, as the many descriptions of nature emphasize:

> In yesterday's dusk, the square with its flitter of leaves had been all autumnal: smoke was blue in the air and, later, the dark where they kissed had a sharp intimation of autumn. She [Lois] loved in autumn a stronger, more shadowy keen spring, sweet shocks of goodbye, transition. (*LS,* 228)

The elaborately metaphorical method on which a full reading of the novel depends accounts for both its distinctions and its weaknesses.

Conversations here count for considerably less than they did in *The Hotel,* and the voice of the narrator is correspondingly more important. The political and historical analyses of disturbed Ireland in *Bowen's Court* are translated into sensuous images—the sound of a lorry "crawling with menace" piercing a tranquil evening, branches brushing a trench coat, and a "resolute profile powerful as a thought." Every attempt is made to blur artificial distinctions between thoughts and emotions, people and places, ideas and things, As in the mill scene above, virtually every object exists in its emotional significance, every personal action as part of the suggested political scene.

The narrator, implicitly reminding us that this is being seen "down a perspective cut through the years," can make of formless action a patterned whole, yet, as Miss Bowen reminds us, we are simultaneously to feel that this is here and now. Lois, who may be said to represent the narrator without the perspective of time, seeks significant form, for to her the isolated action, thought, or state of being is terror and chaos. As she tells Marda, "I like to be in a pattern. . . . I like to be related; to have to be what I am. Just to *be* is so intransitive, so lonely." But the ultimate state of relatedness is death.

This concept of the saving pattern, defined first in *The Last September,* is to be a central one for Miss Bowen's later novels. Here the pattern is already an ambivalent duality: the Big House tradition is moribund, the dying animal to which Lois's soul is chained, a malignant restraint on her race. Fate, which in Miss Bowen's vocabulary is largely a synonym for circumstance and a specific human condition, acts through the agency of the Troubles to destroy the possibility of action determined entirely by the self. Yet the self *can* invest its security in the pattern it is able to apply to circumstance seen retrospectively. (A reader can imagine the immense significance the novel, as transposed autobiography, would have for its author.) The Ireland of Danielstown is a vanished civilization, and it is Miss Bowen's achievement as a novelist (and autobiographer) to be able to shape the personal and historical past into meaning without indulging in sentimental nostalgia.

But Miss Bowen's discoveries are not extended to her heroine. The writer of an autobiography, she said much later, sees that ". . . gradually one's years in the world add up into something which takes on size and shape and in which meaning may at least be sought for." [11] It is perhaps an indication of Miss Bowen's development as a writer that Lois can see the necessity for pattern but that the novel ends before she must use pattern to seek for meaning. Lois's interest in pattern is not very different from Miss Bowen's own (as George Orwell has remarked, the characteristic hero of a modern novel is a novelist), but in the later novels the fiction-making of the heroine will be far more explicit, perhaps as Miss Bowen herself begins to realize consciously as well as intuitively the dramatic possibilities of her own convictions.

Nevertheless, the development of Miss Bowen as a novelist during the two years separating *The Hotel* and *The Last September* was considerable. The reader's impression that the first novel is based on a factitious situation, the second on a "real" one, can best be accounted for on the grounds of style. The rather simple decision that Sydney faces is given no material by which its range of implications can be extended. The society that the Hotel represents is a deliberately exaggerated one, the countryside into which the characters wander is rather vague. The problem of the romantic will and its resolution does not extend beyond Sydney—its effect even on Milton is negligible.

However, in *The Last September* Lois's dilemma, though indefinitely resolved, is extended beyond her. Her fantasies reflect those of Anglo-Irish society, and their pervasiveness is seen even in the decaying landscape of autumn and the final destruction of the house. The author's attitude and tone too are far more consistent in the second novel, perhaps because all the events and characters are treated at the remove of time.

With the exception of *A World of Love, The Last September* is Elizabeth Bowen's only novel set entirely in Ireland, and though she is not really a regional novelist, much of what she has called Irishness is present in this novel. She does not specifically mention *The Last September* in outlining "The Writer's Peculiar World," but her remarks on the intuitive novelist (one who uses "memories, images, impressions" as opposed to a "framework of ideas") have an application to this novel that she herself would probably not agree with.

> Psychologically if not actually he [the intuitive novelist] is a regionalist, in his work relying not only for subject but for atmosphere, texture, color and flavor upon the particular enclave which has given him birth—and whose myths and taboos, ideas and sentiments, whether or not he knows it, have been absorbed by him. In return for the inspiration he gets from the natal landscape he owes pieties: his ancestor worship, however much this may be diluted by irony, is fundamental. His sensibility in his first working years, because of its sheltering, makes rapid esthetic growth. He has not yet touched the limits or felt the remoteness of his peculiar world.[12]

The great limitation of *The Hotel* is that it lacked a peculiar world, that of *The Last September* that a peculiar world, located, leads to a "rapid esthetic growth" at the expense of an exploration of limits. Miss Bowen's heavy reliance on imagery in the second novel, for instance, often leads to decorative elaboration, and too many sentences echo this kind of pointless verbal excess:

Chinks of sunlight darted up her like mice, and hesitated away like butterflies. She had been looking down at the party deployed in all its promise with greed and eagerness, as at a box of chocolates; eyes like a thumb and finger hovering to selection. (*LS,* 58)

Moreover, the heavy emphasis on mood tends to obliterate characters, especially the men, who are distinguished by little more than practicality (or its absence), cynicism, or lack of sensitivity. Not until the cads and bounders of *To the North* and *The House in Paris* (a type vaguely anticipated here by the unimportant and silly Mr. Daventry) do Miss Bowen's heroines encounter men as liberally endowed with alternatives for action and potentiality for change as they are.

But the "peculiar world" of *The Last September* is less "regional" than Miss Bowen implies. She depends for its construction far more on a "framework of ideas" than, say, Frank O'Connor, Eudora Welty, or other obviously regional writers, and has surprisingly little resemblance to the "intuitive novelist" she defines. The family, region, and myth of *The Last September* are *used,* not assumed and absorbed, and the "pieties" are observed from a considerable distance. In an essay written for the *Saturday Review* in 1928, when she must have been writing *The Last September,* Miss Bowen is far less insistent on the contribution of region to one aspect of her art. Exploring the effect of light on imagination, she found acute response to be the result of childhood ideas of light as mystery and the sharpening of this perceptive ability by writers (especially Flaubert, Conrad, Poe, Proust, and Emily Brontë).[13] Indeed, this reliance on intellectual preparation, particularly on her careful reading of her contemporaries and predecessors, makes possible a distinction between her novels of the twenties, *The Hotel* and *The Last September,* and those of the thirties: *Friends and Relations, To the North, The House in Paris,* and *The Death of the Heart.* Insofar as she does work from a "framework of ideas," the literary and intellectual history of the two decades offers the most interesting explanations of the directions her fiction took during them.

Brief historical statements about English fiction during such a twenty-year period have to be crude, but it is clear that most novelists' interest in their immediate society became decidedly more self-conscious in the thirties. Titles alone justify the historian's confidence that serious writers rather abruptly began to consider the society they opposed as capable of reform, even renovation. As late as 1929, major novelists seem to be pointing almost anywhere except at the world they inhabit. Though the first world war had been over for ten years, it was more in vogue than ever in 1929: Ford's tetralogy had been completed just a year before, and in 1929 appeared Aldington's *Death of a Hero,* Manning's *Her Privates We,* and an English translation of *All Quiet on the Western Front.* Hemingway's *A Farewell to Arms* (published in England and America in 1929) was frequently compared to them, and the one successful dramatic attempt to deal with the war, Sheriff's *Journey's End,* was also produced in 1929. Sean O'Casey, in *The Silver Tassie,* like Miss Bowen in *The Last September,* looked back to the Ireland of the war-time period.

To draw a firm line at the end of this decade and assert that a "new" literature of the thirties replaced that of the twenties requires selection, but the selection is so easily made, the exceptions so easily overlooked, that the generalization seems valid. Almost any year between 1931 and 1938 can be made to yield significant differences from 1929 and earlier. In 1932 John Lehmann, having persuaded Leonard and Virginia Woolf to publish *New Signatures* and ("after some hesitation" on their part) Isherwood's *The Memorial,* left the Hogarth Press partly because of "their sober check on all this youthful foisoning of ideas" and "currents that ran too deeply under the surface of the time for me to be entirely aware of them, currents that were affecting in greater or lesser degree all our friends and all our world." [14] Lehmann's metaphor is rather dramatic, but the directions of literature as well as the signatures of its writers did tend to be demonstrably "new" in the thirties. Huxley, who had been one of the first to survey the postwar world seriously, now looked ahead to *Brave New World* (1932), and self-conscious historical references became monotonously popular as titles for self-consciously modern books: *New Bearings in English Poetry* (1932), *New Country* (1933), *New Verse* (1933), *Art Now* (1930), *New Literary Values* (1936). "Of course," says George Orwell in his convincing essay toward this distinction, "a novelist is not obliged to write directly about contemporary history, but a novelist who simply disregards the major public events of the moment is generally either a footler or a plain idiot." [15] Miss Bowen, of course, is neither, and her third and fourth novels are exploratory attempts to find a theme, a voice, a world nearer her own. In both *Friends and Relations* and *To the North* she turns to societies more contemporary; they represent, in Orwell's phrase, Miss Bowen's relinquishment of the telescope.

As Mark Schorer pointed out in reviewing the reissued *The Last September* in 1952, Miss Bowen's early dependence on other writers is hardly surprising:

> The smaller units, the phrases and the sentences, tell us, of course, whom Miss Bowen had read with respect, but what bright young woman would not

have been reading Virginia Woolf with respect in 1927 and 1928, and what bright novelist today, young or old, would not still discover in E. M. Forster a kind of force of phrase and incident that is enviable? [16]

But to "read with respect" is a largely passive activity, part of a necessary but restraining apprenticeship. The quality of originality that distinguishes derivative craft from traditional art appears fleetingly in *The Hotel,* is too often submerged by a concern for "the smaller units" in the much finer *The Last September.* Having apparently exhausted that part of her past available to literature, and influenced by the literary concerns of a new decade (and her geographic distance from Ireland), Miss Bowen in the thirties turned to more "immediate" subjects —to England, and the present time.

Caught between a decadent tradition and external chaos, the heroine of *The Last September* discovers that to live is finally to die, though the artist succeeds in recapturing the past through the pattern of art. The novel's epigraph, appropriately, was from *Le Temps Retrouvé:* "Ils ont les chagrins qu'ont les vierges et les paresseux." *Friends and Relations* is Miss Bowen's first attempt to deal with a more immediate present and a marriage that, though as large an "imposture" as the ones Sydney and Lois escape, is nonetheless a *fait accompli.*

3 *Manners and Morals*

For what novelists, wonders Francis Wyndham, would the literary critic of 1931 have predicted a future? He concludes that the critic would have seen Lawrence, Forster, Joyce, Wyndham Lewis, Virginia Woolf as established, probably would have recognized the "brilliance" of Waugh's *Decline and Fall* and *Vile Bodies,* "might have mentioned" Rosamond Lehmann for *Dusty Answer* and *A Note in Music.* "Would he have spotted Elizabeth Bowen, who had published three novels and three volumes of short stories but whose name was not yet widely known?" [1] Wyndham is probably right in implying a negative answer to this question. O'Faolain's inclusion of Elizabeth Bowen in *The Vanishing Hero* as a "novelist of the twenties" is misleading. Like Waugh, Graham Greene, Faulkner—unlike Hemingway, Huxley, and Virginia Woolf—she was to achieve prominence in the following decade. Not until 1935 did she begin writing regular book reviews for the *New Statesman and Nation,* her stories began to appear regularly in *The Listener* in the early thirties, her first major essay for the *Spectator* appeared in 1936, the same year she edited the Faber collection of short stories and contributed the essay on Jane Austen to Verschoyle's *The English Novelists.* It is to her work of the early thirties then that one must look to account for her rather sudden achievement of fame and influence.

Although, with *The Hotel* and *The Last September,* she established for herself a characteristic theme amenable to her novelist's sensibility, neither novel represented a point from which she could go on. *The Hotel,* based on a single experience, derivative in approach, was followed by the particular retrospection of her "transposed autobiography." The worlds of both novels were limited by time, and neither world, for a writer in 1930, could be seen as contemporary. Miss Bowen's third and fourth novels, *Friends and Relations* and *To the North,* appearing in rapid succession (1931, 1932), represent a new search both for matter and for mode, but their tentative nature leaves them among the least successful of the eight.

As the short stories of the early thirties (especially those collected in 1934 as *The Cat Jumps*) indicate, her concerns were increasingly social, even sociological. The qualities she praises in her 1936 preface to *The Faber Book of Modern Short Stories*—attack on convention, revulsion against "inflated feeling," political bias—repeatedly appear in her own work. *The Cat Jumps* contains one of the most significant of these stories—one that Miss Bowen herself has found among her most satisfactory. In "The Disinherited," she illustrates quite clearly the advantages she found (in 1936) peculiar to the short story as a genre: the subject matter is sociological, the "drama" hovers between the "heroic" and the "pathological," the "outward acts" are presented in their "inner magnitude," and the manner in which the story is written puts the action on a level just short of poetry's "altitude line" (*CI,* 38–46).[2]

Like *The Last September,* "The Disinherited" takes place in a Keatsian setting where "this first phase of autumn was lovely; decay first made itself felt as an extreme sweetness; with just such a touch of delicious morbidity a lover might contemplate the idea of death." But this extravagance of language is deliberate. Davina Archworth, living with and at the expense of a wealthy aunt in the village overlooking a university city (Miss Bowen was living outside Oxford when the story was written) is revolted by the rawness "at once hygienic and intellectual" of the nearby housing development inhabited by her friend Marianne Harvey; but Davina is, in every sense, decadent: an attractive girl with "a touch of the sombre romantic," she is "a woman born to make herself felt." Lacking "sphere," surrounded by a class that is impotent, she borrows money from her aunt's chauffeur and repays him by sleeping with him.

The story is presented in two different, but equally macabre, forms: the letters that Prothero, the chauffeur, writes to a former mistress he has murdered and the description of a Walpurgisnacht held by Davina's friends at the uninhabited estate of "Lord Thingummy" where one of the friends, Oliver, is supposedly cataloguing the library. The two parts of the story are closely related. Prothero, as he indicates in the interior monologue of the letters, has escaped punishment for the first murder by killing a derelict in Marseilles and assuming his identity, and the respectable husband of his mistress, unaware of her infidelity until her corpse is discovered, has assisted Prothero by refusing to acknowledge the infidelity. The question of identity suggested by the stolen passport is essential to Prothero's story: he has murdered Anita to gain freedom from her demands, sexual and psychological (he writes: "I act my own way now, only I act that way because it is my way"), and only regrets that "... it makes me mad to see you don't see that I don't see you or want you." However, the letters reflect Prothero's wish rather than his conviction, as his despairing postscript to them indicates. By murdering his mistress and trying to extinguish his identity by becoming agent for another, Prothero has been psychologically disinherited. Complete freedom has for him merely brought deeper enslavement.

Conversely, the guests at Oliver's party are materially disinherited. Like Markie of *To the North,* another product of dislocation, they find satisfaction only in being "where we've no call to be!"

> Oliver despised the rich and disliked the poor and drank to the bloody extinction of the middle classes. He wished to call no man brother, and disbelieved with ferocity in himself. The old order left him stranded, the new offered him no place. He lived as he could, and thought well of Davina for settling herself on her aunt. (*CJ,* 69)

One of his guests is a White Russian, another a girl who has been forced to open a tea shop, a third "a dentist who had won five thousand pounds in an Irish sweep and shut up his surgery till this should all be spent: he regretted nothing." As the narrator's tone suggests, cool detachment is finding an object more appropriate than images from Ireland's past or the grown-ups an adolescent wishes to demolish. And the narrator controls the implied criticism by simultaneously imitating the character's voice—"wished to call no man brother"—and stepping back to comment on him—"disbelieved with ferocity in himself."

Achieving this position, the narrator can conclude the story by comment as well as by dramatized event. To Oliver, illegitimate host and irresponsible librarian, Marianne Harvey "had seemed ... as disconnected from fact as an angel or goddess," and when Marianne returns next morning to her husband after being seduced by Oliver, "she was disoriented: she did not know." Davina the same morning returns to ask Prothero for money, but is denied because, he says, "I'm buying not selling these days" and because he claims to be his "own man." Although Davina learns from her aunt that she will inherit the house, she sees that material inheritance is only of value in an established society, useless in a new order. In her recognition is Miss Bowen's bluntest statement of fate curbing the romantic will:

> She saw that events led nowhere, crisis was an illusion, and that passions of momentary violent reality were struck off like sparks from the spirit, only to die. One could precipitate nothing. One is empowered to live fully: occasion does not offer. (*CJ,* 96–97)

To Oliver, who has corrupted an angel, to Prothero who has murdered, to the innocent Marianne who has become an adulteress, the only fact is change: the story ends as "two men came uphill her [Davina's] way, stopped and debated: they were surveyors coming to peg out a new road."

But new roads in the thirties, according to Miss Bowen, too often led to morally empty destinations. "The Man of the Family," though markedly inferior to "The Disinherited," can be read as an allegory about the social evils against which Miss Bowen's writing of the thirties became increasingly directed. The very proper William objects to Chummy as a suitor for his cousin Patsey because he has already seduced another cousin; but Rachel, Chummy's victim, refuses to join William in condemning him because "morals are like clothes and I'd scrapped one lot and hadn't found others to suit me." Yet she does object to Chummy's manners because "I honestly do believe that manners (or people not having them) undermine happiness far quicker than morals." Though William goes to Patsey's mother to expose Chummy while "repeating that values were relative," he is nevertheless astounded when she assures him that she already knows the story and considers Rachel the transgressor. William, replaced by the new "man of the family," can console himself only by telling himself that "it really doesn't much matter. . . . They're all fools" (*CJ,* 147–64).

According to the stories, a change in moral order, like the displacement of governments, brings in a new set of standards in the midst of which the members of the previous order are stranded on islands of morality (like William) or become decadent romantics (like Davina). Those excluded have the choice of continuing to legislate impotently from their isolation, in which case they are "mad," or of accepting passively the standards of the new order and surrendering their ideals. The historical and social change with which Miss Bowen is here concerned is the substitution of manners for morals and she forces the reader to see the distinction by macabre comedy, as Waugh did in *A Handful of Dust,* published in the same year as *The Cat Jumps* (though most of Miss Bowen's stories, of course, had had previous periodical publication).

But the macabre in Miss Bowen's fiction is not the opportunity for cathartic laughter that O'Faolain finds it to be in Waugh. It is, rather, the presentation of the apparently indefinable, of the moment when "emotion crystallizes without going icy, from which a fairly wide view is at command." Only when the contrast between manners and morals is defined for the protagonist can his choice be an intelligent one. Jane Austen asked no more of Edmund Bertram, no less of Fanny Price.

However, Miss Bowen, for the most part, accepts the fact that "occasion does not offer"; not circumstance, but the attitude taken toward it, is the variable giving one an option. His is the opportunity, if he dares, to connect "outward acts" with their "inner magnitude."

But even though Miss Bowen's fiction of the early thirties reflects the social conscience of its decade and is frequently marred (not necessarily as a consequence) by its author's insecurity of direction, her second two novels also further establish her position as a traditional novelist. The central situation of the first, *Friends and Relations,* is the juncture, through marriage, between an accomplished adultery and a potentially adulterous situation in a younger generation; the characters belong to the lesser nobility and gentry without land; the scene is predominantly rural; and the narrator's tone, when consistent, an amused moderated irony. In *To the North,* a rural environment gives way to an urban one, outright seduction replaces potential adultery, and qualified irony too often yields to unreserved melodrama. In spite of these more contemporary subjects and scenes (the London of *To the North* is particularly explicit), the literary heritage of *Friends and Relations* can be traced back to Jane Austen and that of *To the North,* according to Miss Bowen herself, to Elizabethan tragedy. In both novels the cat's jump is not the less arbitrary because its direction is socially and culturally (as well as psychologically) determined, and once again the reader is faced with heroines who, like Janet Studdart, are vainly convinced that "there must be some kind of strength in growing, like a plant has, that pushes things, even paving-stones, out of the way and grows past them" (*F&R,* 152).

The world of *Friends and Relations* is perhaps more prosaic than that of any of the other novels: no deaths take place, and weddings are the only social events of significance. The ironic tone used to describe the first wedding (in which Laurel Studdart, the daughter of a retired Army officer and his wife living outside Cheltenham, is married to Edward Tilney, son of the divorced Lady Elfrida and a man who "had at any time more address than an occasion required") prepares the reader for the later failure of the marriage: Laurel's sister Janet "[paces] here and there, a heavy-lidded and rather sombre Diana, supervising the Wolf Cubs," and tries to prevent a "stoppage" when "the Tilney connection (here to shower on Edward for his marriage as well as his mother a loving depreciation) bright woof to a sober warp, [shuttle] their way to and fro through the Studdart connection" (*F&R,* 17–18). And the sly narrator never fully admits the destructiveness of the metaphors. Sentences follow one another as if no joke had been recognized.

The most relevant fact connected with the wedding is presented from the same distance, through the mind of the novel's least attractive character, the precocious, homely, adolescent Theodora Thirdman who, eavesdropping on Lady Elfrida, "inferred that Janet loved Edward, that his mother preferred Janet; that for Janet this was a day of chagrin, possibly of despair" (*F&R,* 21). When Laurel's marriage to Edward is complemented by Janet's to Rodney Meggatt of Batts Abbey in "—shire" (the pair have been brought together by a sick borzoi), the discovery that Rodney's uncle Considine had been the co-respondent in Lady Elfrida's divorce from Edward's father merely compounds the absurdity of the alliances. Although Janet and Edward, separated but linked by scandal, manifest their love in the anger provoked by Edward's strict propriety, the innocent Studdarts hope that "the growing up together of Meggatt and Tilney children might well heal the ugliness of that adultery, cheerfully re-linking the two names" (*F&R,* 28). On the outside looking in, as their name implies, are the Thirdmans, Theodora and her parents, who extol the lower-middle-class ideals of "air, milk, honesty, education, arrangement of scenery," and measure distances by department stores.

Thus, in the first section of the novel, a situation burdened with potential disaster is defined as a moral stasis: the naïve country piety of the Studdarts represents one pole, the amorality of the post-Edwardian lesser nobility (Lady Elfrida and Considine) the other. Between the extremes fluctuate the Thirdmans, who substitute material standards for both piety and tradition, and the undefined young married couples. In the second part of the novel, which takes place ten years later when both the young Tilneys and Meggatts have children, Rodney becomes more relevant. Both he and Batts represent an anachronistic world of tradition and noblesse oblige where work on the land and relaxation in the house are the realities and time is cyclical rather than linear:

> With the duress and vigour of country life as his point of departure he took indoors his relaxations and was accustomed to view his fine trees, the dip of his grounds and the rise of his land from the library window. The seasons only turned him from hearth to window, window to hearth. (*F&R,* 81)

And although the visits of the Studdarts and the Tilney children to Batts little threaten its illusory peace, the visits of Theodora Thirdman (now a masculine young woman with "passions for women . . . a tax on behaviour, like nausea at meals") and Lady Elfrida bring chaos. When Janet, encouraged by her own "unnatural sense of the natural" and Rodney's innocent, indifferent acquiescence, invites Lady Elfrida to Batts as a companion for Considine at the same time that the Tilney children are visiting, all order is relinquished and the fantasy is exposed:

Today proved to be one of those weekdays, vacant, utterly without character, when some moral fort of a lifetime is abandoned calmly, almost idly, without the slightest assault from circumstance. So religions are changed, celibacy relinquished, marriages broken up or there occurs a first large breach with personal honour. Rodney and Janet suddenly saw no reason why Elfrida should not visit at Batts with Considine. (*F&R,* 99–100)

But the crisis primarily affects Edward. The children he rescues from Elfrida and Considine have had their hair cut and have been filled with ices. Simon's hair reeking with violet oil and Anna's satiated stomach are clearly, for Edward, symptomatic of the corruption they have undergone, and the protective Edward's confrontation of the permissive Janet is strikingly reminiscent of the scene in *Mansfield Park* in which Mary Crawford defends her brother's abduction of Maria Rushworth as folly, while Edmund condemns it as evil. As the advocate of feeling and moral freedom, Janet argues that the memory of seeing Elfrida and Considine happy will be a pleasant one to store up against the time when they hear the scandal.

"Otherwise, I don't see how you can bear them to grow up."
"I suppose I hardly can," said Edward involuntarily.
"Oh Edward, don't be ridiculous! Then why were they ever born?"
"But their world—"
"But after all, there only *is* one world; and that's naturally awkward sometimes, like sharing a room." (*F&R,* 129)

Like Mary Crawford, Janet, seeing the predominant and necessary as the good, refuses to recognize separate, and different, worlds of morality, so that Edward, unable to retain a strictly moral and rational attitude, loses control though he wins his point.

Yet when Janet, in London for a night, meets Edward in her hotel room, the consummation of their adultery is prevented by her concentrated effort of will, and it is the will in harmony with necessity which alone is able to conquer the influence of Lady Elfrida, whose "nerve was the heart." Janet's return to Batts is a surrender to obligations (a tea for the Mothers Union) and Edward, returning to Laurel, surrenders his romantic will to the stronger power of feminine, almost maternal, forgiveness.

The reassertion of the power of the family and society over the romantic will, or at least romantic values, is echoed by the narrative summary of the yearly visits of the daughters to the home of their parents that concludes the novel. Against the romantic will and fantasy of Janet and Edward, against the forces working toward social disorganization, the family is presented as a force that has a permanent, dull strength of its own apart from that of its members:

Leaves falling danced their less than moment on the gold sunshine; spring itself could not have been gayer. A touch of chill on the air made the day brighter. Along a kerb, the polished cars were drawn up between white lines, diagonally: everyone was in Cheltenham. Here came the wind and a fine touch of spray: before the colonnades of the Imperial the long willow branches, the fountain blew one way, to meet the Studdarts. (*F&R,* 224)

As in the case of Miss Bowen's other less successful novels a plot summary suggests more than a skeleton of the whole: informing, at times replacing, the action, is a theme, pronounced by Elfrida to Janet after Edward has removed his children from Batts:

"*This* is a fiasco."

Elfrida's "this," though moulded by her long ring-laden fingers into a very small kernel of, as it were, intensive action, or pain, remained so comprehensive that Janet could not tell how far she ought to look back. With impassive docility she lent herself to the retrospect. She looked back to her very first sight of Edward, to what had been a false dawn for her, then at his wedding half in the rain. She looked beyond him steadily at the old branching sin that like the fatal apple tree in a stained glass window had in its shadow, at each side, the man and woman, Considine and Elfrida, related only in balance for the design. And in her confused thought this one painted tree associated itself, changed to another, the tree of Jesse; that springing—not, you would think, without pain somewhere—from a human side, went on up florescent with faces perplexed similar faces, to some bright crest or climax or final flowering to which they all looked up, which was out of Janet's view. If you felled the tree, or made even a vital incision, as Elfrida impatient of all this burden now seemed to desire (for if her heart were the root, it had contracted, if hers were the side, it ached), down they all came from the branches and scattered, still green at the core like July apples, having no more part in each other at all: strangers. (*F&R,* 148)

Metaphorically the organizing motif of the novel is the imposition of the apple tree on the tree of Jesse. The family tree is the means by which both sin and salvation are carried on or, as Forster has expressed it more abstractly, the characters are afflicted with a knowledge of the inseparability of good and evil. Janet is the passive victim of the danger implied by this imposition; Lady Elfrida, since the bonds that family represents have no meaning for her, is the agent by which the perilous situation can become an actively disastrous one. Love, to Lady Elfrida, is only the means by which order is destroyed, "a very high kind of overruling disaster," rather than the cohesive force preserving the structure of the family.

Yet it is the self-reliant Laurel who, though she achieves domestic success by repressing the romantic will and accepting her husband, remains the greatest problem to her parents:

They had married her well, properly, formally, with a marquee; but they had not, somehow, married her *off*. She remained. But then, she was Edward's affair. In talk, Mrs. Studdart again and again felt it proper to pick up Laurel's life, like a piece of unfinished sewing, and hand it back to her. Had she mislaid the pattern? Their house, on these visits, seemed to be littered with snipped muslins. (*F&R,* 221)

Thus the dilemma presented by the romantic will is not easily solved. Suppression of subjective will leads to dependence, dullness, retreat; expression of it to chaos. And always in the background of the novel are those who would replace civilization with codified vulgarity, the Thirdmans, who demand the patronage of Studdarts, Tilneys, and Meggatts but exist as a denial of the social order they represent. But unfortunately the characters are passive, the forces potential, life a piece of sewing, the tree painted, resulting in a scheme rather than a novel, an elaborate metaphor rather than a story.

In attempting to define the traditional quality they sense in all of Elizabeth Bowen's novels, critics have insisted on her similarity to Jane Austen. Christopher Morley, reviewing *The Hotel* in 1928, notes that "this is a book that two readers particularly would have been excited by—Jane Austen, Henry James." And twenty-seven years later, Carlos Baker finds *A World of Love* a novel with the matter of Jane Austen and the manner of Henry James.[3] In *Friends and Relations,* especially, both subject and manner inevitably bring Jane Austen to mind, though the correspondence is one that must be defined in static terms. When Laurel is married to Edward, for instance, we are told, in the understatement characteristic of the earlier part of the novel, that

The wedding went off delightfully. No one, even the bride, remained for more than a second clearly in view; there was some rather poignant gaiety, some confusion. The Cheltenham caterer justified his reputation. The little bridesmaids dived shrieking in and out of the marquee, tripping over the tent-cords. Laurel, very much elated, not nervous, cut a slice from the cake and traced another; Edward said surely that was enough; Janet took her place. Lewis Gibson, the best man, feared Janet might find this too much. Healths were proposed. The bride and bridegroom, the best man and the bridesmaids were photographed. The sun descended, the wet garden was staged in light; guests ventured out on duckboards to see the tulips. . . . The little girls were given champagne, champagne was taken away from the little girls. . . . Someone felt faint in the marquee. Someone showed some disposition to weep. Word came that the bride and bridegroom were going away. (*F&R,* 22–23)

The passage, as a tour de force of aesthetic distance gained through sentence structure, echoes closely the briefer description of the wedding of Mr. Rushworth to Maria Bertram in *Mansfield Park:*

It was a very proper wedding. The bride was elegantly dressed—the two bridesmaids were duly inferior—her father gave her away—her mother stood with salts in her hand, expecting to be agitated—her aunt tried to cry—and the service was impressively read by Dr. Grant. Nothing could be objected to when it came under the discussion of the neighbourhood, except that the carriage which conveyed the bride and bridegroom and Julia from the church door to Sotherton, was the same chaise which Mr. Rushworth had used for a twelve-month before. In every thing else the etiquette of the day might stand the strictest investigation.

It was done, and they were gone.[4]

To both narrators the wedding is a distant rather dull series of unimpassioned actions. For both novelists, the public event is an inadequate accounting of the human passions that are only dimly glimpsed behind the social ritual.

In every one of Jane Austen's novels the situation of the romantic will opposing social circumstance (broadly defined) forms the basic opposition. Like Miss Bowen's heroines, Jane Austen's meet experience assuming they are free agents, evaluating people and events according to subjective standards of their own. Awareness finally comes to them, too, as the product of social suffering: the encroachment of an experience—be it love, betrayal, death, or merely embarrassment—on a private world unable to cope without reference to a code external to the individual heart. Yet conventional decorum too often is inadequate, and Jane Austen's solutions, like those of Miss Bowen, rarely bring victory unalloyed.

Especially in *Mansfield Park* (and this is its important relation to *Friends and Relations*), failure in social vision is the outward and visible sign of a more basic failure to recognize a general underlying evil. The view that sees appearance and manners as negotiable counters for morality must be distinguished from that which sees an active metaphorical relation between them. The cruelty of the Crawfords is the necessary consequence of their moral indifference. Their high spirits, like those of Elfrida, produce a desperate, destructive, almost hysterical excitement. To be sensible, to be both civilized and independent, is to understand the nature of commitment, ordination, active principle. If such an achievement means sharing the dullness of Edmund, the priggishness of Fanny (or the complacency of the Studdarts), this is merely the author's recognition that the excitements of games and the theater are destructive cruelty when translated too simply into life.

While *Friends and Relations* is by no means as masterful and confident a statement in favor of preserving the autonomy of the family moral code as *Mansfield Park,* the tree of Jesse does eventually bring the penitent Janet to minor-keyed contentment while the tree of knowledge merely increases the discontent of the sinless Laurel. The paradoxical attitude informing the tone of the novel is like that of *Mansfield*

Park, where the most "attractive" characters are the least moral. Not only do Janet and Lady Elfrida here echo Mary Crawford in their arguments, but they imputedly share her attractiveness as well. In the case of Elfrida, in fact, this combination of attractiveness and immorality becomes the basis for a rather elaborate pun. She is usually described in terms of blinding light—in settings of sunshine, color, brightness—and is at the same time a morally "light" woman: ". . . she [Elfrida] had persistently sought the light man in him [Considine], match for her light woman" (*F&R,* 98–99).

As advocates of Virtue, Laurel, Rodney, and the Studdarts are as colorless as Fanny Price; and Edward, in his puritanical attitude toward his mother, is as strait-laced as Edmund Bertram. In both novels attractive appearance is rigidly separated from moral seriousness, and what Trilling has called "our modern impulse to resist the condemnation of sexuality and sexual liberty" is one of the assumptions both novels, in their complex irony, attempt to expose.[5] When this basic irony permeates *Friends and Relations,* when banality of language and tone is allowed to indicate the banality of daily life through which significant action can barely rise, the reader is conscious at least of his position, and "action" occurs in the interplay of attitudes. Miss Bowen's failure occurs when the distancing and detachment of tone are relinquished, and the reader sees only the sterile passive metaphors (since human actions, in this novel, do not count for much). For Edward's supposedly catastrophic interview with Janet at Batts, for the futile encounter in Janet's hotel room, no such tonal quadrants are supplied, and although the flowing fountain at the end of the novel may be as intentionally ridiculous as the guests' wandering out on duckboards during the wedding, the description of Mrs. Studdart's imaginary companion is the only suggestion in the later chapters of the novel that any position other than that of straightforward acceptance is possible for the reader. Fanny Price can acquire active principle, but Janet and Laurel, in spite of the irony of their creator, can only seem to submit when that irony is relaxed.

To be sure, the correspondence between *Friends and Relations* and *Manfield Park* finally becomes a matter of pieces and patches of style and attitude. The traditional materials Miss Bowen had absorbed were only partially assimilated therein, and, as in *The Hotel,* a literary precedent only fleetingly elevates her original material. Undominated by a static image, Jane Austen was able to work out her novel in freedom and discursiveness, while Miss Bowen, however successfully her comic moments approach Jane Austen's, has been constrained by her "idea" to force a conclusion, to solve her equation. The forced quality appears most noticeably in those scenes in which issues are brought explicitly into the open, in the conversations between Janet and Edward. With a polite social language appropriate to any occasion, Jane Austen could, at moments of crisis, suggest the frenzy behind its pattern. Miss Bowen, however, makes the aesthetic mistake of relinquishing patterned discourse (and its irony) to allow Janet and Edward to try to speak forthrightly to one another. The novel's failure is that they succeed too well. Five years later, in her 1936 preface to *The Faber Book of Modern Short Stories,* she defined the tendency that weakens both *Friends and Relations* and *To the North.* In arguing for the advantages of the short story over the novel, she notes that "the art of the short story permits a break at what in the novel would be the crux of the plot: the short story, free from the *longueurs* of the novel is also exempt from the novel's conclusiveness—too often forced and false: it may thus more nearly than the novel approach aesthetic and moral truth" (*CI,* 43). Miss Bowen had no reason to be so distrustful of the novel, for, as *The Death of the Heart* shows, she was later able to make a virtue of *longueurs* and to avoid forced conclusiveness. What she had not yet learned from Jane Austen were the immense resources of the narrator's position, the full potentialities of an ironic vision.

Almost as a deliberate act of conscious rejection, Miss Bowen abandoned what she has called the "muted Elizabethan world" of Jane Austen in favor of the violent actions in the melodramatic Jacobean terror of *To the North.* When the restraints in tone and the limitations on relevant action are removed, the effect is a boundless world in which the reader must ever more desperately seek his own position. In effect, *Friends and Relations* involved the working out of a relatively abstract problem, the paradox arising when the family tree simultaneously embodies the orderly salvation of the tree of Jesse and the destructive chaos of the tree of good and evil. By this rather calculated means, the family love of relations conflicts with the romantic affinity of friends, and the conscious ironic tone of the novel is even reflected in the title, for few here are "friends," and "relations" are more often the potential concerns of divorce suits than the participants in family reunions.

To the North, however, had an appropriately less rational genesis. Miss Bowen has said that she first conceived the "idea" of the novel when, driving outside London with her husband, she suddenly saw a road sign reading "To the North" outlined against the sky. And the novel that takes its form from this image is equally (and deliberately) nonrational in statement: in the midst of a realistic, modern London an innocent girl, Emmeline, is seduced by a Satanic villain, Markie, and brings about his death and hers when no alternative action is possible, the fire of their passion somehow creating the ice of their destruction. The author states this inevitability, from the point of view of Markie, in language as extravagant as the events it describes:

> She [Emmeline] had, as he saw, stepped in Paris clear of the every-day, of conduct with its guarantees and necessities, into the region of the immoderate, where we are more than ourselves. Here are no guarantees. Tragedy is the precedent: Tragedy confounding life with its masterful disproportion. Here figures cast unknown shadows; passion knows no crime, only its own movement; steel and the cord go with the kiss. Innocence walks with violence; violence is innocent, cold as fate; between the mistress's kiss and the blade's is a hair's-breadth only, and no disparity; every door leads to death.... The curtain comes down, the book closes—but who is to say that this is not so? (*TTN,* 248)

In this novel, however, the action does not take place in the relative isolation of an Italian hotel, an Anglo-Irish Big House, or an English Abbey, for Emmeline, an orphan, lives in a carefully described house in St. John's Wood with her widowed sister-in-law, Cecilia Summers, and manages a travel bureau in Bloomsbury. Her immersion in the midst of the everyday is contradicted by her attitude toward her environment. Her nearsightedness is repeatedly emphasized, and this physical defect is symptomatic of a similar psychological one, for "... she was short-sighted in every sense. Watching slip past her a blurred, repetitive pattern she took to be life, she adored fact—the exact departure of trains—and had taught herself to respect feeling" (*TTN,* 40). Emmeline's dedication to the travel bureau, then, is her attempt to join vicariously in the experience of others, compensating for the psychological retreat she herself has made and for the passivity of her acquaintances. In spite of her adoration of fact and action, her spiritual home is the country estate, appropriately named Farraways, of her cousin Lady Waters where "grief was a language she did not know" and she can feel that "free will was a mistake but did not know what this meant."

> Here Emmeline, stepchild of her uneasy century, thought she would like to live. Here—as though waking in a house over an estuary to a presence, a dazzling reflection: the tide full in—she had woken happy. But already a vague expectation of Monday and Tuesday filled her; looking out from the shade of the lime already she saw the house with its white window-frames like some image of childhood, unaccountably dear but remote. (*TTN,* 89)

Though Emmeline as the "stepchild of her uneasy century" can see life steadily and whole only in a retreat from London to childhood, Markie is decidedly the natural son of a dislocated age who is most at home in the flat he occupies in his sister's house in Lower Sloane Street where he and his sister "made a point of not meeting, cut each other's friends at the door, had separate telephone numbers and asked no questions" and where his only communication with the rest of the house is the speaking tube through which he whistles to the cook for meals. Visiting a country house for him is an experience not of peace but of hell:

> No birds sang: it had been worse than that day in Keats. Leaves, rotting and rusty, deadened his steps; the afternoon had been sodden and quite toneless; it began to be dark early. Down there, between the dreary trunks of the beeches, houses lay like a sediment in the cup of the misty valley: great gabled carcases, villas aping the manor, belfried garages where you could feel the cars get cold. (*TTN,* 80)

The alliance between Emmeline and Markie is without volition, almost fated. Markie has the *beauté du diable* Miss Bowen has mentioned in Henry Crawford of *Mansfield Park,* and the predilection for the innocent virgins attracted by this quality. Cecilia, meeting him on a train headed north to England from Italy, is able to perceive immediately in his "mobile, greedy, intelligent mouth and the impassive bright quick-lidded eyes of an agreeable reptile" a potential nemesis: ". . . in an after-world, she might deserve just such a companion: too close, glancing at her—if any shreds of the form still clung to the spirit—without sympathy, with just such a cold material knowingness" (*TTN,* 16). The diabolism that the serpent imagery here suggests is further supported by Markie's other characteristics: he is incapable of satisfaction in any relationship, opposes churches as "oppressive monument[s] to futility," and enjoys the pursuit and corruption of Emmeline far more than her passive physical surrender to him, for then he misses

> . . . that precious sense of delinquency lovers enjoy. It was in the idea of outrage, of those tender agonies of the conscience, that he was most a voluptuary: the idea of guilt so enflamed him that the form surrendered in innocence seemed as cold as marble. (*TTN,* 201)

If Markie is the devil of the novel, Emmeline is obviously its angel, a title she is given with almost annoying frequency. It is Markie's pet name for her, the basis of frequent metaphors used to describe her, and when she feels there is no way out of her relationship with Markie she becomes an angel of death. This encounter between devil and angel, linking the good and the evil, echoes the basic pattern of Elizabethan (or, better, Jacobean) tragedies, a note initially struck by the opening description of Markie quoted above. In addition to her sense of Markie's diabolism, Cecilia finds his description of Rome to evoke "the late Renaissance, with a touch of the slick mondanity of *Vogue.*"

> Though not, evidently, a son of the Church, he was on the warmest of terms with it; prelates and colleges flashed through his talk, he spoke with affection of two or three cardinals; she was left with a clear impression that he had lunched at the Vatican. As he talked, antiquity became brittle, Imperial columns and arches like so much canvas. . . . The sky above Rome, like the arch of an ornate altarpiece, became dark and flapping with draperies and august conversational figures. (*TTN,* 19)

Once the reader is aware of an Elizabethan pattern within the novel, it is easy enough to see in this language, with its metaphors of the theater, the aura of intrigue surrounding the evil churchmen of Webster and Shirley.

The melodramatic pattern is most insistently apparent, however, in the sequence of actions that accomplish Emmeline's downfall. Confrontation, seduction, fall, realization, failure of outside help, failure of outside revenge, and inevitable self-sacrificing murder are its abstract stages; and a discussion of a few of them in detail can indicate what the Elizabethan and theological levels add to a realistic modern novel.

The formal beginning of the seduction takes place, symbolically enough, in the garden of Emmeline's house where the early morning invasion by the cat from next door, "a noted *flaneur* in other gardens" and "one rippling curve of malignity" prefigures the unexpected arrival of Markie, "pale and puffy in a dishevelled white tie," still awake from the night before. His motive for coming is itself feline (curiosity) and his presence among the light and flowers, like that of the cat, is decidedly incongruous:

> Till now, she had offered to no friend her hours outside time: now the budding magnolia, plucked and discarded, breathed its unmeaning fragrance among the fumes of coffee. . . . For here Markie was: in his presence—within reach, if he cared to kiss, of his kiss, within reach, if she dared to put out a hand, of his hand—this idea of pleasure as isolated, arctic, regarding its own heart only, became desolating to Emmeline as a garden whose flowers were ice. Those north lights colouring the cold flowers became her enemies; her heart warming or weakening she felt at war with herself inside this cold zone of solitude. (*TTN,* 145)

This invasion of her private world and her unresisting acquiescence (because she "desired lowness and fallibility") are the first steps toward the downfall itself, which takes place in the hotel room in Paris, where Emmeline has gone to establish a business agreement with two Serbs who operate a continental travel agency. The arrangement, to be less formal than a partnership, they have called "interplay," and like the chess game in *Women Beware Women* or the card game in *A Woman Killed with Kindness,* the onstage discussion of interplay becomes a metaphor for the off-stage action in which Emmeline becomes Markie's mistress. Actions in this novel, indeed, are rarely to be seen as isolated events, for they can have analogues on almost any level. At the moment of Emmeline's surrender in Paris, Cecilia, at Farraways (unaware to the end of the novel of her sister-in-law's alliance), watches the sky:

> Somewhere, the moon was rising. Somewhere, clear of earth's shadow, the radiant full moon received the whole smile of the sun. Clouds hid from the earth at this bridal moment her lovely neighbour, while to the clouds alone was communicated ecstasy. . . . Clouds closed in; the moon did not appear; darkness spread over the skies again; only the lime and a wet path silver for less than a moment had known of the moon's rising. The tree and path faded; cloudbound while that tide of light swept the heavens earth less than suspected the moon's perfection and ardour. . . .
> "Perhaps," said Cecilia, "there is a moon in Paris." (*TTN*, 233)

Though her treatment of this moment may seem to justify O'Faolain's objection that "when Elizabeth Bowen is dealing with elemental things she skirts around them with too much elegance," [6] it is clear that the fall of Emmeline is being echoed, almost elegiacally, on several levels at the same time—at a business luncheon, in a hotel room, and in the heavens above the earth. The richly suggestive imagery that would be present in the language of a Webster character is, in the freer extension of the novel, presented as metaphorical action.

The second stage in Emmeline's progress toward destruction, her realization that she has no escape, is similarly presented in several metaphorically related incidents, all concerned with the dissolution of her private world. During the weekend spent with Markie at a friend's cottage (which contains a large gold harp), Emmeline's realization that her affair with Markie has become dissociated from the rest of her life is presented by a description of landscape and setting:

> A little smoke from their fire dissolved in the clear evening; the downs in their circle lay colourless under the sky. Some childish idea of kind arms deserting her mind, Emmeline said: "How alone we shall be tonight." Like a presence, this cold stillness touched the idea of their love: would they dissolve like the smoke here, having no bounds? The low roof was comforting, but the cottage door, open, showed darkness where they had been. (*TTN*, 273)

When she hears that Cecilia is to be married and that the vicar of Farraways is dead, and knows that the half of her life which had existed separate from Markie is gone, again the metaphysical coördinates of tangible property are used to suggest that disintegration is both physical and psychological:

> Timber by timber, Oudenarde Road [the house in St. John's Wood] fell to bits, as small houses are broken up daily to widen the roar of London. She

saw the door open on emptiness: blanched walls as though after a fire. Houses shared with women are built on sand. She thought: "My home, my home." (*TTN*, 278)

At the novel's least successful moments such attempts at symbolic extension become obviously linguistic, almost puns. "Falling to bits" too easily refers to houses, psyches, lives, and minds. At the same time that Markie, bored with the complete control he has over Emmeline because she loves him, reëstablishes his liaison with his former mistress Daisy, Emmeline, totally deserted, so exactly reënacts the disintegration the other girl had gone through that Emmeline's secretary can tell her that

"You should take a rest. . . . You look all to bits."

. . . .

Broken up like a puzzle the glittering summer lay scattered over her [Emmeline's] mind, cut into shapes of pain that had no other character. (*TTN*, 300)

The fluidity of this world, the fact that its essence is so conveniently controlled by the metaphors the narrator uses to construct it, makes possible the melodramatic climax. When Emmeline drives Markie toward Baldock after the dinner party to which Cecilia and her fiancé Julian have invited him under the assumption that he and Emmeline are still friends, Emmeline becomes the Elizabethan bride of death. In an entirely unreal world, she does not even bother to reject his offer to take her back, even marry her:

A sense of standstill, a hush pervaded this half-seen country. Friendly darkness, as over a pillow, and silence in which a clock striking still pinned her to time hung trancelike over this early halt in their journey. But, from beyond, the North—ice and unbreathed air, lights whose reflections since childhood had brightened and chilled her sky, touching to life at all points a sense of unshared beauty—reclaimed her for its clear solitude. (*TTN*, 323)

The scene is a corollary of the one in the garden where she deserted the "cold zone of solitude," and within the syntax of the sentences identity is lost in flux, so that darkness is "friendly," silence is "trancelike," and the abstract North performs a human action. As awareness of the inevitability of her destruction through Markie becomes clear to her, she is blinded by knowledge, and loses self. The only action, a slight one, results in destruction:

Like earth shrinking and sinking, irrelevant, under the rising wings of a plane, love with its unseen plan, its constrictions and urgencies, dropped to a depth below Emmeline, who now looked down unmoved at the shadowy map of her pain. For this levitation a total loss of her faculties,

> of every sense of his presence, the car and herself driving were very little to pay. She was lost to her own identity, a confining husk. Calmly, exaltedly rising and balancing in this ignorance she looked at her hands on the wheel, the silver hem of her dress and asked herself who she was: turning his way, with one unmeasured swerve of the wheel, she tried to recall Markie. (*TTN,* 326)

At the moment she drives the small car head-on into the large one, she experiences for the first time a completely objective awareness, and the event itself is neither Emmeline's suicide nor her deliberate punishment of a transgressor, but the translation of the irrationality of her love into the physical actions of her life. Emmeline ceases to exist personally and socially, and becomes a force. It is this inevitable, nonhuman force, the release of energy from fire burning and ice forming, that destroys both of them.

But a summary of the plot, however it emphasizes the melodramatic nature of the novel, ignores much of its more rational content. Like an Elizabethan play, the novel has its subplot, in which the practical sister-in-law Cecilia accepts the passive Julian Tower as her second husband. The marriage is rather obviously related to the social compromises of the romantic will prevalent in the other novels. Cecilia, unable to love completely, nevertheless recognizes that she has an existence only in terms of other people. Julian, whom she accepts without love, is similarly unable to form any relationship based on feeling, and like Cecilia suffers from solitude. Although both Cecilia and Julian are able to rescue themselves, they can do nothing to save Emmeline. Julian, who knows that Markie has seduced her and that he should perhaps play the brother with the whip, can feel only envy of Markie "for cutting so much ice."

Thus Cecilia and Julian, the prosaic lovers, are ironic alternatives to the passionate lovers. Cecilia refuses to take Markie seriously, seeing his roles as *âme damné* and Byronic hero as mere poses, and in Julian's adolescent niece, Pauline, the subjective innocence of Emmeline herself is parodied. Having discussed the seventh commandment and "impure curiosity" at her confirmation class, Pauline "still could not think of anything without blushing. . . . So that now flowers made her blush, rabbits made her blush excessively; she could no longer eat an egg. Only minerals seemed to bear contemplation" (*TTN,* 60–61).

The other characters who inhabit the London circles that intersect those of Cecilia and Emmeline are apparently intended to represent more bizarre disorientations of feeling. Lady Waters keeps a salon of unhappy lovers, whose lives she further complicates under the guise of being helpful; Emmeline's business partner Peter is followed by a "haggard friend," apparently homosexual; and the stenographer resigns in bitter tears because Emmeline does not return her passionate devotion.

The unification of the melodramatic main plot, the ironic subplot, and the background comedy is brought about by the predominant metaphors of traveling. A large proportion of the action takes place on something that is moving, and by which, like fate, the characters are moved. Cecilia's meeting Markie on the train from Italy, and later driving with Julian to meet Pauline at her school, illustrates the correctness of Lady Waters' comment that "Cecilia . . . never seems to be happy when she is not in a train—unless, of course, she is motoring." The more significant traveling, however, is that done by Emmeline and Markie. The plane trip to Paris during which Emmeline verbally assents to Markie's demands is made symbolic of their moral position:

> She was embarked, they were embarked together, no stop was possible; she could now turn back only by some unforeseen and violent deflection—by which her exact idea of personal honour became imperilled—from their set course. (*TTN*, 187)

And to Emmeline, as a nearsighted angel, the sky is a native element, where theory can become principle and the restrictions of the world can be ignored, where ". . . some new plan of life, forgotten between flight and flight, seemed once more to reveal itself." However, after her actual surrender in Paris, Emmeline is disturbed by movement because it threatens an idealized world where her romantic will can be realized, and she ". . . now stood still with her hands on the bark of a tree in St. Cloud . . . bark whose actual roughness blurred to the touch at the thought of so many forests, and longed to stand still always."

But of course the most significant journey of all for Emmeline (who likes Paris taxis because "they're like 'The Last Ride Together' ") is the one that is literally the last ride together for her and Markie. The description of this journey, moreover, clarifies much of the travel imagery in the rest of the novel. Although Emmeline for the first time is ostensibly in control of what is moving, she feels her actions entirely controlled by circumstance. After she has seen the sign portentously pointing "To the North" and "something [gives] way,"

> An immense idea of departure—expresses getting steam up and crashing from termini, liners clearing the docks, the shadows of planes rising, caravans winding out into the first dip of the desert—possessed her spirit, now launched like the long arrow [on the sign]. The traveller solitary with his uncertainties, with apprehensions he cannot communicate, seeing the strands of the known snap like paper ribbons, is sustained and more than himself on a great impetus: the faint pain of parting sets free the heart. (*TTN*, 325–26)

The "great impetus," Fate, the North, is basically circumstance, constructed of space and time. As she is driving, Markie stares at "the two lit dials: the clock, the speedometer."

Though it is in and through time and space that a person constructs his identity, to surrender to their abstract measures, minutes and miles, is finally to destroy oneself. In her search for permanence (whether its outward form be marriage, the house she shares with Cecilia, or the bark of a tree), Emmeline seeks an identity in something immune to time, for only in this way can she counteract the fantasy of subjectivity to which her "nearsightedness" restricts her. In her psychological concern with Emmeline, Miss Bowen emphasizes her inability—partly because of her subjectivity, partly because of the society around her—to find a permanent relationship with the members of that society or to see her identity reflected in anything that exists apart from time and motion. And as a student of society, Miss Bowen seems to be demonstrating that this dislocation is common to all (most of the characters are orphaned, widowed, unhappily married, or incapable of feeling), so that only those who suppress the romantic will and accept the outward forms of permanence as a duty that cannot be subjected to the test of the romantic will can survive.

On a moral level, the issues raised in this novel are similar to those considered in *Friends and Relations*. Emmeline, the angel of goodness, can conquer the serpent only by sacrificing herself, by cutting down the tree of knowledge which is also the tree of Jesse. The idealist, the romantic, the subjectivist, perishes: Cecilia and Julian, in their prose without passion, with their existentialist realism, inherit the earth and the last remnants of Emmeline and Markie: the forgotten white scarf and rejected gloves.

For the first time in a novel Miss Bowen dramatizes the dilemma of the romantic will in a form that takes both society and morality into account. The reader is never told whether Sydney's road did indeed lead to an empty town, what replaced the burned shell of Danielstown, or who lived along the new road pegged out by the surveyors at the end of "The Disinherited." Yet Cecilia (one is tempted to see her, like Stella in *The Heat of the Day,* as a personification of Miss Bowen's attitude) is able to give the new life a habitation and a name. The passage, though long and undramatic within its context, is significant enough to be quoted in full:

> When a great house has been destroyed by fire—left with walls bleached and ghastly and windows gaping with the cold sky—the master has not, perhaps, the heart or the money to rebuild. Trees that were its companions are cut down and the estate sold up to the speculator. Villas spring up in

> red rows, each a home for someone, enticing brave little shops, radiant picture palaces: perhaps a park is left round the lake, where couples go boating. Lovers' lanes in asphalt replace the lonely green rides; the obelisk having no approaches is taken away. After dark—where once there was silence a tree's shadow drawn slowly across the grass by the moon, or no moon, an exhalation of darkness—rows of windows come out like lanterns in pink and orange; boxed in bright light hundreds of lives repeat their pattern; wireless picks up a tune from street to street. Shops stream light on the pavements, upon the commotion of late shopping: big buses swarm to the kerb, small cars dart home to the garage, bicycling children flit through the birdless dark. Bright façades of cinemas reflect on to ingoing faces the expectation of pleasure: lovers laugh, gates click, doors swing, lights go on upstairs, couples lie down in honest beds. Life here is liveable, kindly and sometimes gay; there is not a ghost of space or silence; the great house with its dominance and its radiation of avenues is forgotten. When spring is sweet in the air, snowdrops under the paling, when blue autumn blurs the trim streets' perspective or the low sun in winter dazzles the windows' gold—something touches the heart, someone, disturbed, pauses, hand on a villa gate. But not to ask: What was here? (*TTN*, 136–37)

The casual reader might see here a tone of unabashed nostalgia, even deliberate snobbery. After all, the symbols of aristocracy and gentle living—the silence, darkness, trees, estates, obelisks, and "lonely green rides"—have been obliterated by the raucous bourgeois evils: speculators, villas, picture palaces, pink and orange lanterns, façades, garages, buses, asphalt, and wireless. But to one who reads the passage this way, the verbs at least must be vaguely puzzling, for the trappings of the new society emerge with an admirable vitality: brave and radiant, they spring up, stream, swarm, dart, flit. The ambivalence of tone is resolved finally into an attitude more of welcome than resignation, for the windows *are* gold and spring *is* sweet. Though the speaker elevates herself when she refers to the "couples [who] lie down in honest beds," there is little denigration implied and, we can assume, something does "touch the heart." "Life here is liveable, kindly and sometimes gay": for someone who *does* remember "what was here," these must be words of high praise. Such a landscape, suggesting attitudes and details from almost all the major stories and novels between 1929 and the war, is nevertheless an incomplete statement. However successfully Cecilia manages to live by limiting her vision, Miss Bowen's later heroines do repeatedly ask the destructive question, and for people with their comprehensive knowledge more complex forms of forgiveness must be found. Fortunately in the later novels the saving illusion is not merely the negative absence of memory and perception but the positive presence of knowledge and art. What Miss Bowen here accomplishes with rhetoric, she later achieves with art.

Since *To the North* does in several ways dramatize Miss Bowen's discovery of a metier, it allows, in spite of its author's later dissatisfaction, a rough evaluation of her status as a novelist at the time it was written. Placing it beside other modern novels of similar concern, a reader can at least glimpse Miss Bowen's abilities and limitations at the time. Certainly Sean O'Faolain's comment that she is a tragic obverse of Evelyn Waugh applies to this novel, for here indeed "With a sad *mouchoir* Miss Bowen waves her heroines over the cataract she has prepared for them." [7] But the novel lacks the "horrible cathartic laughter" making the cruelty of life bearable that O'Faolain praises in Waugh. The characters of *To the North* are no less driven and propelled than Brenda and Tony Last of *A Handful of Dust,* but Miss Bowen, unlike Waugh, cannot yet find terms in which (and by which) to accept this fact. No heroine as entirely passive as Emmeline can be in any useful sense tragic, and the timing and tone of the denouement similarly fail to place the fatal action. Like the burning of Danielstown, the death of Emmeline takes place at the moment when the reader is not returned to a rational social world but sees the entire world of the novel consumed, as Emmeline's world is, by fire and ice. As in a pretentious detective story he is led to anticipate significance but is dismissed with fact.

The final statement on the failure of tragedy in the novel might better be left to Miss Bowen herself. In reviewing William Saroyan's *The Laughing Matter* for the *New Republic* in 1953 she notes, in terms that immediately recall *To the North,* that

> Three appalling deaths terminate the story—which, like an Elizabethan drama, can be forced to an end in no other way. Violence evades the moral conclusion. . . . Symbolism and imagery, much used, intensify and heighten the atmosphere without fortifying the main theme. . . . For a tragedy, should not the air be purified? [8]

The fate of Waugh's Tony Last, on the other hand, is both conclusion and attitude, fact and significance, macabre tragedy and purification. To read Dickens forever to a madman in a jungle and to find a fox hunt replaced by a fox farm are fates consonant with the terms the novel sets up. Irresponsibility yields to passivity and to absurdity.

Certainly one can find a much clearer sense of direction in Waugh's novel than in *To the North,* but one can still say with assurance that Miss Bowen's novel accomplishes far more than Rosamond Lehmann's *The Weather in the Streets,* which was to appear four years after *To the North* and make use of many similar situations—the meeting on the train, the emancipated girl and her contented counterpart, even the unsuccessful attempt at reconciliation between caddish lover and sensitive mistress at a dismal borrowed cottage. To be sure, one can praise Miss Lehmann's control of dialogue, her ability to create drama by the words her characters speak to and at one another. But one can hardly retain complete faith in the writer's apparent assumption that "thoughts" are as easily expressible as conversation, that a simple interior monologue (sometimes in the first person, sometimes in the third) will put the novel's world together and establish its significance. It is difficult to accept a narrator who says, "She had a pang of love for him. It was the shake of the head, helpless looking" as effortlessly as she says, "He took out his pocket-book and by the light of the match she held, wrote down her London address and telephone number." And such assumptions about the power of language seem to be made by a narrator who is fundamentally uninterested in distinctions, willing to accept society without taking an attitude toward it, and anxious to see love and illegitimate children as parallel curses of free womanhood.

Miss Bowen's fuller recognition of the difficulties of the novelist's art is constantly implicit in her attempt to imbue the setting of her novels with significance relevant to her theme. More than once the reader of *To the North* is reminded of a much earlier and far greater novel, D. H. Lawrence's *Women in Love*. The complementary liaisons, the destruction of "will" by ice, even the symbolic cat recur in Miss Bowen's novel. Gudrun, like Emmeline, suffers "the terrible burden of this tick-tock of time"; and Celia and Julian, in much simpler form, function as F. R. Leavis sees Birkin and Ursula functioning: "In [their] married relations . . . the book invites us to localize the positive, the conceivable and due—if only with difficulty attainable—solution of the problem; the norm, in relation to which Gerald's disaster gets its full meaning." [9] Though it would be possible to go on adducing correspondences of symbol and theme, the conclusion must finally be the same: however more successful than *The Weather in the Streets, To the North* is a very pale analogue of *Women in Love*. The solution Birkin and Ursula achieve "only with difficulty" is approached with a rather vague simplicity by Celia and Julian; Gerald's "go" is both more vital and more insidiously destructive than Markie's caddishness; the relationships between characters in Lawrence's novel are created with far greater "awareness of the possibilities of life" than those in Miss Bowen's; and England itself, seen by Lawrence, has a social and intellectual complexity Miss Bowen does not approach until *The Heat of the Day*. No one in *To the North* can really, like Gerald, strive with the universe, because Miss Bowen's art, at this time, can only suggest distantly "the vast, creative, non-human mystery."

The static, thematic nature of *Friends and Relations* and *To the North* makes them particularly amenable to the approach I have been using, and the fact that they can be discussed with relatively little injustice to their art can make them seem more interesting novels than they are. Because their "framework of ideas" lies so closely under the surface, their patterns of imagery can be traced to yield meaning, passages of description can be isolated as good writing, but the heightened awareness of his world that the reader expects from a great novel is too often missing. Leavis' "reverent openness before life," after all, emerges from paragraphs and pages read in order, not from paraphrases and discussions isolated for the critic's convenience. Although most of the themes, situations, and attitudes that emerge from the second four novels are defined in the first four, literary quality is not necessarily dependent on these isolable characteristics. Only in scenes of comedy do *Friends and Relations* and *To the North* equal what Miss Bowen as an artist is able to achieve in *The Death of the Heart* and *The Heat of the Day.* A distinction between openness and containment, between diagrammatic microcosm and chaotic comprehensive macrocosm, can be seen most clearly in her fifth novel, *The House in Paris* (1935).

4 *Innocence and Experience*

Tolstoy's wild gambler Dolohov, precariously balancing on the sill of a third-story window while he consumes a bottle of rum and arrests the attention of the party of scamps, wine-sipping waiters, and dancing bear, can be read as a crude parable of the writer's impossible predicament: chaos, flux, madness, life, must somehow be brought under the controlling touch of the artist, whose success can to some degree be measured by the amount of formless life he can bring into his patterned art without losing the "balance" that Lawrence defined, the "plumb-straightness of line" that Miss Bowen mentioned in her discussion of the morality of art. Lear on the heath, or cursing his daughters, is perhaps the prototypal image of the controlling mind's failure to keep its precarious hold on the formless; Melville's Ishmael at the masthead suggests the possibility of limited success if vision is divided and the mind detached. In any case, coolness, clearheadedness, strength of vision are essential, for only a distraction prevents the impassioned Pierre Bezuhov from destroying himself by imitating Dolohov's stunt.

Miss Bowen's vocabulary for the chaos with which the artist's mind copes is a varied one. In discussing her early stories she refers to the "hazy queerness" of atmosphere; in such collections as *Joining Charles* (1929) and *The Cat Jumps* (1934) psychological aberrations, fantasy, and social chaos predominate ("Trouble now lies in the purse, not in the heart"); in *The Death of the Heart* social and moral disorganization are "frenzy," "betrayal," "madness"; in the war stories of *The Demon Lover* (1945) "hallucination" becomes an explicit subject, representing both flux and the effort to contain it. An external fate, as O'Faolain points out, drives the characters of *The Last September,* making them the passive objects of active verbs, but insofar as the novelist assumes the absolute power of such a fate, he has abdicated part of his responsibility. Civilization as a force directed against madness cannot be ignored, nor can the artist fail to assume some alliance with civilization if his art is to escape madness.

But this espousal of "civilization" can, of course, be naïve. In the mid-thirties when, George Orwell claims, "the central stream of English literature was more or less directly under Communist control," the superficial manifestations of society were rather obviously matters of concern.[1] Most of the younger writers (Dylan Thomas is an exception) in Miss Bowen's 1936 Faber collection show either political or sociological preoccupation: James Hanley, Arthur Calder-Marshall, Sean O'Faolain, William Plomer. And Miss Bowen's own inclusion (at the request of the publisher) is "The Disinherited." A comparison with the 1925 *Georgian Stories,* where Michael Arlen and J. C. Squire tend to set the tone, would suggest some of the distance traveled.

Miss Bowen's own comments on the politically oriented fiction of the thirties are infrequent but suggestive. In reviewing John Lehmann's anthology *New Writing in Europe* in 1941, she criticizes "Movement" writers for having "flattened" the storyteller by "a conscious and desired convergence between *reportage* and creative narrative act." "One finds in the prose an absence of background, a lack of power to either generalise or synthesise, that seems to come from the abnegation of social experience. There is a lack of irony, a lack of *méchanceté.*"[2] Miss Bowen calls writing of the thirties the Romantic Movement of the twentieth century and implies, as Matthew Arnold said of its earlier counterpart, that it did not know enough. Because many of its writers failed to generalize, abnegated social experience and lacked irony, they could not contain their subjects and were dominated by them. The naïf, like Bezuhov, easily loses control.

In her novels (with the exception of *A World of Love*) Miss Bowen has sought increasingly to give the inhumanity of fate a social and human form, and to use objective means for controlling it. In *To the North* madness triumphs with the death of Emmeline and Markie; Cecilia and Julian are not sufficient, by themselves, to keep the social dance from becoming frenzied riot. The early novels tend too easily to oppose social ritual to individual personal energy. The dance in *The Hotel,* the tennis party in *The Last September,* both carrying the power of an external fate, are too simply abstracted forms of civilization. But with the mocked wedding in *Friends and Relations* and the satirized house party in *To the North,* individual will is given a more appropriate opponent, a social environment as complex and fallen as itself. Although *The House in Paris* concerns itself rather with escape from society than encounters with it, *The Death of the Heart* has as its subject the failure of social ritual to order the wandering will of the individual.

Such oppositions, of course, depend on characters complex enough to give serious battle. To make characters symbols, as Miss Bowen does in *To the North,* is inevitably to reduce them. Yet the potentialities of human conduct, the indivisibility of time, the extent of space all must be distorted in the novel's compromise with reality. Whatever point the novelist focuses on for significance often is laden with more meaning than it can easily bear. The worlds of *The Hotel* and *The Last September,* limited in both time and space, are replaced by attempts at greater comprehensiveness in *Friends and Relations* and *To the North.* But the earlier novel rather crudely omits ten years, the later attempts to substitute metaphors of motion for an expression of the characters' immersion in flux. The most radical experiment with time and space is probably the one Miss Bowen undertakes in *The House in Paris.* The narrow, crowded house itself, and the intense few hours spent in it, become the narrow limits of the first and third sections of the book, while the middle third concerns itself with a year, its scene includes England, Ireland, France, and the seas between. As Graham Greene has rather generously pointed out, "unable to convey the passage of time, she has made capital out of the gap in the records." [3] Missing information engenders a sense of mystery essential to the story, and the reader must form a synthesis between what he knows of the past (presented in part II of the novel) and what he is shown in the present (parts I and III).

The pretense of reality is even further abandoned, for the house becomes a fairy-tale castle on a street which, like the roads in "The Disinherited" or *The Hotel,* "seemed, though charged with meaning, to lead nowhere." The narrative assumptions behind the middle section are no more realistic, for it is the presentation of an ideal past where "you suppose the spools of negatives that are memory . . . being unwound from the dark, word by word." But in spite of these overt tendencies toward fantasy, in spite even of the symbolic equivalence between this narrow house bursting with emotion and the image of the tree in the tomb, the novel does present a believable encounter with human reality in a way that was impossible in *To the North.* It is a novel relying on just the *"méchanceté"* she found lacking in so much fiction of the thirties.

Miss Bowen knew more than the most naïve Movement writers, and one of the things she knew best was the work of Henry James. In his novels she could easily see the use of social experience and above all the power to synthesize she found her contemporaries deficient in. *The*

House in Paris, significantly, is the only novel for which Miss Bowen has specifically mentioned a Jamesian analogue.[4] Considering technique primarily, she has noted that her own use of articulate children in *The House in Paris* fulfills the conditions James set down for such characters in the preface to *What Maisie Knew.* For both novelists, the use of articulate children allows them to dramatize the struggle to find language for perceptions beyond their vocabularies. Presumably the serious novelist, like Maisie, has "ever in her mind fewer names than conceptions." Small children, says James, "have many more perceptions than they have terms to translate them; their vision is at any moment much richer, their apprehension even constantly stronger, than their prompt, their at all producible, vocabulary." [5]

Although Leopold (and to some extent Henrietta) represents any writer's attempt to control his world by language, he also allows Miss Bowen (as Maisie allows James) to explore the values of decorum. Articulate children, talking without artifice or convention, yet influenced by these controls, give the novelist a means to approach the terror that, for adults, is hidden by decorum. It is primarily the sensibilities of these strange children that dominate the first and last sections of *The House in Paris,* and the reader is allowed to exceed them in specific knowledge only in the last third. When the children meet by chance at the house in Paris presided over by the invalid Mme Fisher and her daughter Naomi, it is, from their point of view, an occasion of terror:

> With no banal reassuring grown-ups present, with grown-up intervention taken away, there is no limit to the terror strange children feel of each other, a terror life obscures but never ceases to justify. There is no end to the violations committed by children on children, quietly talking alone.
>
> (*HP,* 25)

Although the reason for Henrietta's presence is explicit and prosaic (traveling from her married sister's home in England to join her grandmother at Mentone, she is to spend the day between trains at the Fishers' because Naomi Fisher is one of the grandmother's "sub-friends . . . whom she remembered when they could be of use"), the explanation of Leopold's presence becomes, in a sense, the subject of the whole novel: an illegitimate child usually living with "relatives by adoption" outside Spezia, he is in Paris to meet his real mother for the first time since infancy. Both children participate in the fairy-tale atmosphere in which Henrietta's meeting with Miss Fisher at the Gare du Nord is "sinister," where no questions are to be asked, where even the city seems prepared for "an immediate attack" and the red rooms of the house suggest both a prison and an operating room. But in their consequent reactions to mysterious knowledge the children are sharply distinguished. Though "the ever possible fate of little girls in Paris" is obscure to both of them, their conversations, during which Leopold too appropriately spills Henrietta's apples on the floor, are the process by which both learn more of good and evil than they can comprehend. Full comprehension is irrelevant to Henrietta, for she "knew of the heart as an organ; she privately saw it covered in red plush and believed it could not break, though it might tear." When Mme Fisher alludes to her daughter's unsuccessful engagement to Leopold's father, Max Ebhart, "she [Henrietta] knew one should not hear these things when one was only eleven." Clearly, Henrietta is destined to grow up, like her sister Caroline, covered with "an unchippable glaze."

But unlike the practical Henrietta, the romantic Leopold is insatiable in his appetite for knowledge: he fumbles constantly in an attempt to define himself, fears the future because he cannot control it, reads the letters he finds in Miss Fisher's handbag, and, when he fails to find a letter from his mother among them, composes one of his own in a day-dream of wish-fulfillment. Thus, although both children share egocentricity and define other people, death, and love by reference to themselves alone, Henrietta's egocentricity will contribute to a personality that invariably takes circumstance into account, while Leopold's is the romantic will in its formative stage. When he is told that his mother cannot meet him and that the anticipated solution to all his problems cannot take place that day, the central section of the novel, as the narrator describes it, is the unreal but ideal presentation of such a meeting:

> Actually, the meeting he had projected could take place only in Heaven—call it Heaven; on the plane of potential not merely likely behaviour. Or call it art, with truth and imagination informing every word. Only there—in heaven or art, in that nowhere, on that plane—could Karen have told Leopold what had really been. (*HP,* 67)

The story of Leopold's parents, Karen Michaelis and Max Ebhart, which is thus "unwound" to form the central section of the novel, is superficially reminiscent of *To the North.* Karen is a somewhat more aware Emmeline, Max a more responsible Markie, and their relationship assumes much of the irresponsible passion seen in the earlier novel, with the important difference that here ". . . fate is not an eagle, it creeps like a rat." Karen's visit to her aunt and uncle in Cork, an escape from the proprietary interest London society has taken in her engagement to Ray Forrestier, a young diplomat of promise, presents her alternatives, at this stage, as the polite sophistication of England or the pastoral isolation of Ireland. But Ireland, as Karen sees, can easily become a world of the past where her Aunt Violet, knowing of her approaching death, watches the activity of life from her detachment at the end of a telescope, and is, to Karen, a clock indicating the shortness of life.

To find convincing terms for the reawakening of Karen's interest in Naomi's fiancé must have been a difficult task, for the situation is almost too conventionally the stock material for a feminist romance: the unhappily engaged Karen accidentally meeting again the older "exotic" Max to whom she had been attracted five years before as a student boarder at the Fishers' in Paris. Miss Bowen avoids sentimentality by stepping back (in a way alien to Rosamond Lehmann in *The Weather in the Streets*), and the narrator calmly considers the event as both social and emotional. In such paragraphs as this Miss Bowen depends on that power to generalize, that use of irony, that advantage of social experience she found absent in so much writing of the thirties:

> She thought, young girls like the excess of any quality. Without knowing, they want to suffer, to suffer they must exaggerate; they like to have loud chords struck on them. Loving art better than life they need men to be actors; only an actor moves them, with his telling smile, undomestic, out of touch with the everyday that they dread. They love to enjoy love as a system of doubts and shocks. They are right: not seeking husbands yet, they have no reason to see love socially. This natural fleshly protest against good taste is broken down soon enough; their natural love of the cad is outwitted by their mothers. Vulgarity, inborn like original sin, unfolds with the woman nature, unfolds ahead of it quickly and has a flamboyant flowering in the young girl. Wise mothers do not nip it immediately; that makes for trouble later, they watch it out. (*HP,* 112)

But Karen is by now mature enough to recognize these demands within her, and her attempts to compromise the romantic will, to conquer it by practical will, are in harmony with the conservative mores of the London society represented by the Michaelis family:

> She had not been born Karen Michaelis for nothing; it had been on the daylit side of marriage that she liked to dwell; she had expected, even, to show her friends that there is nothing in love to get so angry about. But since the day she had walked away from Victoria [after seeing Naomi and Max off to Paris], her thoughts had bent strongly to whatever in marriage stays unmapped and dark, with a kind of willing alarm. She had now to look for Max in Ray. (*HP,* 130)

Yet when Aunt Violet's death opens a terrible possibility wherein both Karen and her mother see "the crack across the crust of life," Karen's practical will is undermined and she is ready for the telephone call from Max that summons her to the two assignations: the first, at Boulogne, where their acknowledged love takes the form of desultory conversation; the second at Hythe, where their affair is consummated and Leopold conceived. Thus Karen, like Emmeline in *To the North,* finally gives herself bodily to the "Nachtseite der Natur" in an action beyond words and logic. But the subsequent confrontation of mother and daughter in which Karen admits that "everything that could be *said* was on your side" is a departure from the pattern of *To the North.* Emmeline is never judged by the moral code of her society, nor need she ever attempt to explain irrational action. In contrast, even at Hythe Karen wakens to face implicit moral judgment. In Karen's reverie Miss Bowen presents the impossible predicament of a member of a family who retains romantic aspirations destructive to it. Because Karen (unlike Olivia in *The Weather in the Streets*) can "see" a connection between the present incomprehensible emotional moment and expressible social events in the vocabulary available to her as a member of a family, her self-criticism can be stated:

> Her life had been full of warnings; the first was: "You will get wet." They warn you because they love you and because you are theirs. Now, here she lay as it would be death to those loving warners to know she lay. Not her hiddenness now but her unhiddenness made her heart thump chokingly, as it did years ago when, playing hide and seek, she heard the steps of the seekers go by just the other side of the curtain, or heard them come into the dark room where she hid. The curtain would fall, the light would discover her before she could slip out to bolt for "Home," which used to be by the gong, at the foot of the stairs. Once you were "home" you won, you could not be caught. So sometimes you struck the gong.
>
> Being caught is the word for having a child, sometimes. Then Ray would not marry me. . . . The street would stay torn up, the trams could not begin again . . . . When do they put lamps out? This is the time of night when they say you feel most afraid. Only, I have nothing to be afraid of: no one will know. (*HP,* 164)

Although Karen's ambivalent attitude is that of a conscious member of a family and a society, we are asked to see Max's as internal, psychological, because he belongs to no society. As an Anglo-French Jew, he is, like Leopold, a self-generated force. But in spite of his obvious differences from Karen, he is faced with the same choice between security and passion. His engagement to Naomi, like Karen's to Ray, has been an escape from insecurity to an impersonal role where social identity is less necessary, where Max and Naomi "had interlocked, like two twigs on a current that, apart, would have gone on twisting perplexedly." In a world that "is in bad taste," that is no longer "history in the making," Max's attempt to abnegate his will (as Markie had utilized his) is his compensation for an inability to endure circumstance. This resignation, however, is as destructive as Markie's caddishness. When he accepts Naomi as a Martha, a sin of omission becomes a sin of commission. Because he realizes that "desire of what she gave seemed to be desire of her," she has become "ugly." Hence he can no longer feel that "to be unambitiously with her became peace" or that she offers a "place to return to," important in France because "to have no family can be more humbling than poverty." For both Max and Karen, the easier choices destroy either the self or others. Direct repression or uncritical exercise of the romantic will leads inevitably to chaos.

The marriage that Max and Karen plan after their weekend at Hythe, the rejection of their commitments to peace and society, Naomi and Ray, is their final and futile attempt to realize the romantic will in passion and to deny Max's assertion that "one cannot simply act." In Naomi's later account of Max's suicide, the controlling power of Mme Fisher is explained. Max had already told Karen at Boulogne that

> [Mme Fisher's] sex is all in her head, but she is not a woman for nothing. In my youth, she made me shoot up like a plant in enclosed air. She was completely agreeable. Our ages were complementary. I had never had the excitement of intimacy. Our brains became like senses, touching and drawing back. (*HP,* 146)

Her encouragement of the illicit romance between Karen and Max, her opposition to his engagement to Naomi, implement her perverse sexual hold over him. For Max and Naomi, Mme Fisher could only be a mother-in-law; for Max and Karen, she can be a pander. Karen has realized at Hythe that "she is a woman who sells girls" and that she thrives on Max's energy: "when he's quiet he's not hers." By returning to Paris to break his engagement to Naomi and to assert his will, Max paradoxically loses his autonomy.

Even when he slashes his wrists with a penknife in Mme Fisher's living room, Naomi insists that "It was not his will; it was a passionate act" and implies that it provides an almost sexual fulfillment for Mme Fisher: "I saw then that all her life her power had never properly used itself, and that now it had used itself she was like the dead, like someone killed in a victory." Susceptible to such power because he lacks any conventional means of identification (race, family, money), Max is thus imprisoned by someone "all mind and will" who controls even his will to escape. To both Karen and Max, life has given abundant power to live fully; for neither, in different ways, does occasion offer.

In the last section of the novel, a continued account of the day Leopold and Henrietta spend in Paris ten years later, the problem of the parents is presented anew to their child. Even at Leopold's conception, Karen had seen his potential effect on her life. He could represent the positive part of her unlocated relationship with Max and thus become an agent of destiny. And again it is Karen's interior monologue, almost too articulate, that presents the propositions by which this novel progresses, that summarizes events of the past to use them in defining the future:

> There would still be something to dread. I should see the hour in the child. I should not have rushed on to nothing. He would be the mark our hands did not leave on the grass, he would be the tamarisks we only half saw. And he would be the I whose bed Naomi sat on, the Max whose sleeve I brushed rain off: tender and guardable. He would be the Max I heard talking when I stood outside the salon, the Max I rang up: that other we were both looking for. I could bear us both lying tired and cast-off if it were for him, if we were his purpose. Paris then Twickenham, the boat train at Victoria, Boulogne, the sea-front last night—if he ran through those like a wire they would not fall apart. The boat going up the estuary, the silent mountains, the harbour the day I knew Aunt Violet would die—those would not have been for nothing. He would have been there then and then and then. (*HP,* 163)

But for the destructive alternative there is no such definitive language: "He would be disaster." The day in Paris is to determine whether, after ten years, Leopold is to be the "wire" of identity and continuity he could have been or the "disaster" she has assumed he has been.

Leopold himself is subjected, more simply (for sexuality is absent), to the temptations of his parents. When Henrietta, learning that Leopold's mother is not coming after all, accepts the disappointment calmly as further evidence that "nothing ever happens," she discovers with some superiority that Leopold cannot do the same, because "two races, in feeling, go to make up the world." But to the child of intense feeling, the reality of his mother's decision reveals the inadequacy of his romantic will; her refusal to play "her part" discredits his imaginative projection:

> He had cast her, but she refused her part. She was not, then, the creature of thought. Her will, her act, her thought spoke in the telegram. Her refusal became *her,* became her coming in suddenly, breaking down, by this one act of being herself only, his imagination in which he had bound her up. So she lived outside himself; she was alive truly. She set up that opposition that is love. (*HP,* 206)

As compensation for having suffered this first defeat of his romantic will in recognizing otherness, Mme Fisher offers Leopold the alternative to identity she had provided for the doomed romantic who was his father:

> . . . to have been born is to be present—though I find one may cease to be present before dying. For you and me, Leopold, to have been born at all is an opportunity. For you or me, to think may be to be angry, but remember, we can surmount the anger we feel. To find oneself like a young tree

inside a tomb is to discover the power to crack the tomb and grow up to any height. (*HP,* 216)

And Mme Fisher's only regret is that Leopold is too young, she too old, to make possible a recreation of her former role:

> If you were less a child, I could enjoy more fully my short time of being alive again. As it is—yes, I may still say to you frankly: rather you as you are than some grown-up sot. But it is a pity for me: I am dying too early. (*HP,* 217)

Seeing that "only purpose could flog along a sick body" in this manner, Leopold, unlike his father, is able to see that Mme Fisher too is a victim of life and the past; but Naomi, taking him away, feels she has left him with Mme Fisher too long.

When Karen's husband Ray arrives to explain her absence to Leopold, he encounters more independence than he had expected. To Ray the boy has been that part of Karen's life they must both accept, the past that Karen has rejected by trying to mold Ray into the image she had had of him earlier when ". . . Ray was my mother." When Ray decides to force Karen to adopt Leopold, it is a victory for the man and the boy, a defeat for Mme Fisher and the Karen who has tried to escape. The decision too has the effect of weakening Leopold's imperious subjectivism for he is again "made conscious of someone's consciously being other than Leopold." And although Ray determines that Leopold must be changed—

> You will not quote Mme Fisher, you will not kick me in taxis, you will not shout in houses where they are ill. You will wear a civilian cap, not snub little girls and not get under my feet. There will be many things that you will not like. There are many things that I do not like about you.

—at the same time he recognizes him as a child deserving sympathy:

> Ray had not seen Karen's child in bright light before; now he saw light strike the dilated pupils of Leopold's eyes. Egotism and panic, knowing mistrust of what was to be, died in Ray as he waited beside Leopold for their taxi to come: the child commanded tonight, I have acted on his scale. (*HP,* 255–56)

Obviously, through Ray's acceptance (of Leopold and of Karen's past), the sins of the fathers are to be mitigated by the son, and the three of them are to escape the sense of evil that permeates Mme Fisher's house (where boys as well as girls are sold). But the victory is illusory. The small world, the "rule of niceness," is finally able to control the romantic will, which appears free but is actually self-destructive. As usual, the only possible alternative is the least attractive one. The compromise between moral indifference and destructive interference involves a retreat.

Although the novel's minor characters do represent rather simple attitudes toward the impossibility of the romantic will's realization, even a summary of its plot indicates that *The House in Paris* is a more complex novel, thematically and technically, than any of the previous four, except *The Last September.* The complexity is the result of alternative attitudes toward the same situation. Naomi Fisher, for example, represses her feelings in order to assist others, while Henrietta, in spite of her youth, simply does not let her feelings take objects. The Bents, in Ireland, retreat from life and death alike, while Mrs. Michaelis, in London, accepts the moral code of a conservative society as the final arbiter of feeling. Karen, seeing the fallibility of the code and of the forms of retreat, vacillates between the passionate expression of the romantic will and the complete denial of that side of her nature. The force she worships is, in the world, unattainable. Max vacillates as well; but, lacking any retreat except Mme Fisher and his own sense of irony ("being satisfied that they should think you wrong"), he must fail. Mme Fisher herself is more a force than a character: as the personification of abstract mind and will who can direct, buy, and sell the souls of the others, but need not fear her own feelings, she, of course, gives the house in Paris its atmosphere of evil, its resemblance to a cage and an operating room. As she illustrates, both the romantic will and the practical will are capable of destructive excess.

As rescued and potential rescuer, Leopold is the little child who may lead them. Like Max in sensitivity, he is unlike him in being able to perceive unjust control (as his resentment toward his foster parents shows). As he becomes aware first of his own identity, then of the identity of others, his romantic will becomes directed toward objects that are more capable of being realized. It is seeing Leopold, apparently, that makes the nature of Ray's love for Karen clearer to him and, it is suggested, may eventually bring Karen to see that the acceptance of past *and* present, dark *and* light, is essential to human identity. Like Maisie, Leopold sows the seeds of the moral life, albeit unwittingly, among his elders. The danger that the seeds will fail to take root is a function of the world, not personality or character.

The thematic presentation of *The House in Paris* succeeds where that of *To the North* fails. Though the "evil" that infects Markie in the earlier novel is putatively the product of something outside himself, its source is obscure; though he is at one moment the serpent in the garden, he is at other times too obviously symptomatic of a general social dislocation to be considered an autonomous Satan. Although Max may be as destructive as Markie, the motives and sources of his destructiveness are more convincingly expressed. The sense of evil generated in *To the North* is blamed, rather indiscriminately, on "society"; that of *The House in Paris,* even more insidious, is ascribed to the mind and will, separated from feeling, of Mme Fisher. Finally, the problem of good and evil in *To the North* tends to disappear, rather abruptly, with the deaths of Emmeline and Markie, but in *The House in Paris* the presentation of a problem *in* one generation *through* a second suggests its permanence. Max's death is at least as tragic as those in *To the North,* but its importance is not its action (it takes place off-stage) but the repercussions and the persistence of the motives that caused it. *To the North* is both abstract and specific, *The House in Paris* concrete and general.

The technical discoveries Miss Bowen made in writing *The House in Paris* were considerable: for the first time she has been entirely successful in making a novel work as a series of dynamic propositions about the romantic will and society. The reader of most of her novels remembers them as paragraphs (a quality making them particularly amenable to quotation), and even the dialogue is carried in large units, often to the destruction of dramatic effect. By using Karen's interior monologues as statements putting together the world of the novel, Miss Bowen is able to create drama whenever subsequent events make any one of these statements inadequate. Repeatedly the reader is presented with seemingly convincing propositions about life and the world, only to be shown that these propositions are incomplete or, more often, that their terms are not as fixed as he may have assumed. Karen's statement about the romantic girl's innate love of the cad, for instance, is cool and detached enough in tone to suggest an omniscient narrator. It remains perhaps a Truth, but its assured tone becomes an example of Karen's blindness as the proposition ceases to be abstract and becomes instead an occasion of terror and death. When the reader returns to the children in the house, he can see what their innocence is—a naïve belief in propositions and a pitiable vulnerability to their inadequacy. Miss Bowen's flexibility in her use of the narrator, her willingness to accept "any trick" if it "adds a statement," approaches the subtlety and complexity it achieves in the last three novels.

The effect gained by ascribing the evil to a source in *The House in Paris* can be compared to James's accomplishment in making the abstract evil of *The Turn of the Screw* concrete in *What Maisie Knew.* If *The House in Paris* finally fails to give the same sense of what Marius Bewley calls the "fully lighted moral world" of *What Maisie Knew,*[6] the deficiency would seem to lie in the last third of it. The reader finally knows so much that the "intelligible moral framework" is destroyed, leaving pity rather than evaluation as the only possible response. Leopold seen at only one moment in time cannot, like Maisie, engage in action the reader passes judgment on; he cannot even deal with experience as a lesson as Maisie does when Mrs. Wix asks her about her "moral sense."

> It [the question] brought back to the child's recollection how she sometimes couldn't repeat on Friday the sentence that had been glib on Wednesday, and she dealt all feebly and ruefully with the present tough passage. Sir Claude and Mrs. Beale stood there like visitors at an "exam." [7]

Because there is only one day of the week for Leopold in this novel he can hardly represent, as Bewley says Maisie does, the power of *"creative* innocence." He can be a symbol of deliverance for Karen, but not its agent because he must remain an object.

But if Miss Bowen fails to realize fully the possibilities inherent in James's articulate children in *The House in Paris,* she certainly does in *The Death of the Heart.* Portia's innocence, like Maisie's, is dynamic, but its power is more destructive than creative. The narrator's language for describing Portia at first suggests James ("Portia," it should be remembered, was his generic term for the "young person intelligent and presumptuous" in his preface to *The Portrait of a Lady*), but its tone is finally bleaker and more violent than James's. The "violations committed by children on children, quietly talking alone" have been magnified to affect a far larger world:

> Innocence so constantly finds itself in a false position that inwardly innocent people learn to be disingenuous. Finding no language in which to speak in their own terms they resign themselves to being translated imperfectly. They exist alone; when they try to enter into relations they compromise falsifyingly—through anxiety, through desire to impart and to feel warmth. The system of our affections is too corrupt for them. They are bound to blunder, then to be told they cheat. In love, the sweetness and violence they have to offer involves a thousand betrayals for the less innocent. Incurable strangers to the world, they never cease to exact a heroic happiness. Their singleness, their ruthlessness, their one continuous wish makes them bound to be cruel, and to suffer cruelty. The innocent are so few that two of them seldom meet—when they do meet, their victims lie strewn all round.
> (*DH,* 128–29)

In discussing *The House in Paris* I referred to the dramatic use of propositions, the movement from paragraph to paragraph. Here the process is even more fluid, the narrator more flexible. At first, in this paragraph, he sympathizes with innocence—it is ingenuous, translated imperfectly, *we* are too corrupt. But the position subtly changes—the innocent offer sweetness, violence, betrayals, ruthlessness. The cruelty they inflict finally appears to be greater than what they suffer, for "their victims lie strewn all round." The shift is not, of course, the narrator's confusion, but a recognition that the world too has values to defend, that life and corruption can be reconciled in a way that life and purity cannot. "Singleness"—of purpose or of vision—this novel suggests is an untenable, even destructive position.

Though the violence of such confrontations of the world and the innocent remains metaphoric, as in James, they occur repeatedly in *The Death of the Heart.* Sixteen-year-old Portia Quayne, daughter of an aging country gentleman and his sometime mistress, later wife, is sent to live with her half-brother Thomas and his wife Anna at Windsor Terrace, Regent's Park, London, after the death of her mother with whom she has been living a vagabond existence in "an out-of-season nowhere of railway stations and rocks, filing off wet third-class decks of lake steamers, choking over the bones of *loups de mer,* giggling into eiderdowns that smelled of the person-before-last" (*DH,* 69). The "guilt" or experience with which Portia comes into contact in London is not as specific as the adultery Maisie finds, but it is more prevalent. The unwilling foster parents, Thomas and Anna Quayne, accept Portia grudgingly as a legacy visited upon them because of the sins of Thomas' father. Thus the World (the title, too, of the first third of the novel) that Portia enters is both mysterious and hostile.

> She had watched life, since she came to London, with a sort of despair—motivated and busy always, always progressing: even people pausing on bridges seemed to pause with a purpose; no bird seemed to pursue a quite aimless flight. The spring of the works seemed unfound only by her: she could not doubt people knew what they were doing—everywhere she met alert cognisant eyes. She could not believe there was not a plan of the whole set-up in every head but her own. Accordingly, so anxious was her research that every look, every movement, every object had a quite political seriousness for her: nothing was not weighed down by significance. In her home life (her new home life) with its puzzles, she saw dissimulation always on guard; she asked herself humbly for what reason people said what they did not mean, and did not say what they meant? She felt most certain to find the clue when she felt the frenzy behind the clever remark.
>
> (*DH,* 72–73)

It is easy, at first, to hear echoes of *What Maisie Knew* in this passage. For James's heroine, "Everything had something behind it: life was like a long, long corridor with rows of closed doors. She had learned that at these doors it was wise not to knock—this seemed to produce from within such sounds of derision." But the situations and sentences by which the society of *The Death of the Heart* is created have more contemporary echoes as well. Reference to "the frenzy behind the clever remark" and suggestions that "you felt the relentless pressure behind the small talk" emanate from the same kind of social concerns that produced, for example, the chorale in the last act of Auden and Isherwood's *Ascent of F-6* (1936), where the "wicked secret" underlies "the look of fatigue," "the croquet matches in summer, the handshake, the cough, the kiss." To be sure, the cynical acceptance of Freudian psychology is less prominent in Miss Bowen's novel, but the implication that society is a sick organism, perpetrating a malignant mystery, appears in both. What the play's world lacks is precisely what Miss Bowen's novel provides: a society that is more than an abstraction, characters that are more than symbols. The audience of *The Ascent of F-6* is continually given more synonyms to describe the same action—the abbot and Mr. and Mrs. A use different language, but the subject is unchanged. The great accomplishment of Portia's consciousness is that the referents, not the speakers, cause change.

When Portia's consciousness is absent, the hostile world does often appear in terrifying motionless vignettes. For instance, in presenting the private married life of Anna Quayne and her husband Thomas, Miss Bowen's allusion to a more famous marriage à la mode, in the "Game of Chess" section of *The Waste Land,* seems almost deliberate. Anna, "tapping about among the pots and bottles" of her dressing table after returning from Capri, engages in the same futile conversation with her husband that Eliot's unnamed woman does. Even the ironic references to revivification by water are repeated:

> With her back to Thomas, who sat raking through letters, she said: "Well, here we are back."
> "What did you say?"
> "I said, we are back again."
>
> . . . .
>
> "Did you hear me say just now that here we were, back?"
> "I did, yes. What do you want me to say?"
> "I wish you would say something. Our life goes by without any comment."
> "What you want is some sort of a troubador." . . .
> She said: "You are like one of those sitting images that get moved about but still always just sit. I like to feel some way about what happens. We're *home,* Thomas: have some ideas about home——" More lightly, less kindly, she hit at his head again.
> "Shut up: don't knock me about. I've got a headache."
> "Oh dear, oh dear! Try a bath." (*DH,* 288–89)

Windsor Terrace is a social world without opportunity for the expression of feeling. Thomas, for one, "discovered himself the prey of a passion for [Anna] inside marriage, that nothing in their language could be allowed to express, that nothing could satisfy." Sexual feeling, in this novel, remains always inexpressible, the situation for which the "corrupted" adult's mind is as inadequate as the innocent child's. Thomas' singleness in this respect is the counterpart of Portia's. Innocence is obliviousness to the absence of an adequate language, and a propensity to act from the heart without regard for social consequences. Awareness, the loss of innocence, is ultimately dependent on the discovery that social error and the absence of language are destructive to one who refuses to countenance them.

But Thomas' form of obliviousness is only the simplest alternative to Portia's innocence. As William Walsh demonstrates with *What Maisie Knew,* the child who confronts life's inadequacy to expectation is rarely the victim of a sudden despoiling. Rather, the child invests unlikely objects with a "strong bond of feeling," seeing the world "through forms which intensify the relaxed connections of events" and endowing these relationships with "a fixed and unalterable status" free of ambiguity. "The development of the child's mind, as James analyses it [one could add Miss Bowen's name as well], lies in the strengthening of the sense of implication, the quickening of doubt and the multiplication of possibilities." [8] The "strengthening," "quickening," and "multiplication" are exactly the drama of *The Death of the Heart,* and the means by which it becomes more than a statement about life in society. The "mystery" of the world that Portia enters is never dissipated, but the terms of its terror constantly change.

Portia's innocent mind is no more bewildered by London than Windsor Terrace is disconcerted by her. Her diary (which Anna has been reading) is the chaotic, uninhibited, and absolute record of her elders' lives, focused without modification on the immediate as if there were no other reality. The anger and dismay that Anna expresses in relating the diary's contents to St. Quentin Miller, a novelist friend of the Quaynes, reflect her own repressed guilt, for Anna is separated from Portia by age and experience, not nature. It is her own lost innocence that Anna sees and resents in Portia. Having failed to attain satisfaction in an early love affair, and unable to bear children, Anna has limited her aspirations to what she can succeed in. And her husband, like Hugo Montmorency in *The Last September,* compensates for his repressed romanticism and idealism, his inadequacy in the "world of telegrams and anger," by a retreat to another world, defined again by a narrator who begins with the character's perception, and enlarges that perception so that it becomes a comment on him as well as by him:

> Society was self-interest given a pretty gloss. You felt the relentless pressure behind small-talk. Friendships were dotted with null pauses, when one eye in calculation sought the clock. Love seemed the one reprieve from the watchfulness: it annihilated this uneasy knowledge. He could love with regard to nothing else. Therefore he loved without any of that discretion known to more natural natures—which is why astute men are so often betrayed. (*DH,* 109)

Only one member of the Quayne household, the housekeeper Matchett, has both the perception and the disinterestedness to qualify as a moral judge; and she alone, a combination of strictness and maternity ("The monklike impassivity of her features made her big bust curious, out of place"), befriends Portia. It is through her eyes that the love affair of which Portia is the product is shown to be different from the off-color joke that Anna sees. The story of Irene and the elder Mr. and Mrs. Quayne, presented anew by Matchett, uncovers a conflict between a woman who "had no nature"—the elder Mr. Quayne's first wife, Thomas' mother—and an innocent elderly man who was "all nature" and sought release from his wife's unsympathetic bondage in a late love affair, contaminated by the apparent encouragement of his wife. Matchett, moreover, is able to expose one missing element in the younger Quaynes' life in London: the way their life lacks any provision, in terms of tradition and moral order, for the "awkward age":

> In the home of today there is no place for the miss: she has got to sink or swim. But Matchett, upstairs and down with her solid impassive tread, did not recognise that some tracts no longer exist. She seemed, instead, to detect some lack of life in the house, some organic failure in its propriety. Lack in the Quaynes' life of family custom seemed not only to disorientate Matchett but to rouse her contempt—family custom, partly kind, partly cruel, that has long been rationalised away. In this airy vivacious house, all mirrors and polish, there was no place where shadows lodged, no point where feeling could thicken. The rooms were set for strangers' intimacy, or else for exhausted solitary retreat. (*DH,* 52)

Portia and Matchett alone are conscious of this "organic failure" and aware that Thomas and Anna lack any sense of tradition. Thus Matchett acts throughout as an "inexorable" force of morality, whose element is house-cleaning, and whose knitting needles, like those of Mme de Farge, click off the sins of the others. However, since she too seeks to violate the privacy of Portia (though in the name of morality rather than curiosity), she fails to provide a refuge for her. But her most significant weakness is that she "never was one to talk," and so makes a virtue of her failure to articulate the moral judgments she forms and Portia requires.

Alienated from a society she cannot understand, living as an exile in London as she had with her mother on the continent, Portia can only seek a desperate companionship with the victim of a similar alienation, Eddie, "the brilliant son of an obscure home," who through a campaign planned with Anna has managed to find a job in Thomas' advertising agency. To Portia Eddie is an escape from the reality of her isolation among the Quaynes to an ideal romantic isolation of love, where sex, though present, is a harmless mystery. The region of their love is a pastoral fantasy, exposed by Miss Bowen's narrator who recognizes a distance from the characters and from the landscape they project. Behind the romantic tone, just lush enough to suggest a popular song, is the almost ludicrous image of two adolescents sitting side by side, one with his eyes blinded and hands between his knees:

> Safe for the minute, sealed down under her eyelids, Portia lay and saw herself with Eddie. She saw a continent in the late sunset, in rolls and ridges of shadow like the sea. Light that was dark yellow lay on trees, and penetrated their dark hearts. Like a struck glass, the continent rang with silence. The country, with its slow tense dusk-drowned ripple, rose to their feet where they sat: she and Eddie sat in the door of a hut. She felt the hut, with its content of dark, behind them. The unearthly level light streamed in their faces; she saw it touch his cheekbones, the tips of his eyelashes, while he turned her way his eyeballs blind with gold. She saw his hands hanging down between his knees, and her hands hanging down peacefully beside him as they sat together on the step of the hut. She felt the touch of calmness and similarity: he and she were one without any touch but this. What was in the hut behind she did not know: this light was eternal; they would be here for ever. (*DH,* 104) [9]

Although Eddie is as "innocent" as Portia in being *de trop* at Windsor Terrace, he seeks escape through inconsistency rather than romantic fantasy. If the social assumptions of Eliot and Auden are echoed frequently in *The Death of the Heart,* those more recently popular are prominently anticipated in Eddie. Almost twenty years before Kingsley Amis' *Lucky Jim,* the prototype for Jim Dixon was defined by Elizabeth Bowen. The genealogy of Amis' antiheroes is perhaps unimportant, but the use made of their role is not. For Eddie who makes faces because "I can't bear people getting a line on me," for Jim Dixon and John Lewis (*That Uncertain Feeling*) who imitate Eddie, the mirror becomes an ideal romantic world where they can see reflected, albeit in reverse, the only selves they can accept. Because the man who trades his identity for anonymity can write his own lines and compose his own fiction, pantomime, burlesque, and impersonation become the healing arts. Anna imagines Eddie mentally travestying a scene between them as "he took the pose of a chap making a new start," and Eddie later, imitating Anna for Portia's amusement, finishes by looking

like an actor coming off after a big scene. At the same time he looked relieved, as though he had shot a weight off, and pious, as though a duty had been discharged. He seemed now to exist in a guiltless vacuum.
(*DH,* 127)

Only a change in the point of view differentiates Amis' Jim Dixon:

Quickly deciding on his own word, Dixon said it to himself and then tried to flail his features into some sort of response to humour. Mentally, however, he was making a different face and promising himself he'd make it actually when next alone. He'd draw his lower lip in under his top teeth and by degrees retract his chin as far as possible, all this while dilating his eyes and nostrils. By these means he would, he was confident, cause a deep dangerous flush to suffuse his face.[10]

But if the elevated social worlds of Windsor Terrace and the Merrie Englandism of a nameless provincial college are the sources of guilt, these faces of innocence are far from conventionally attractive. Jim Dixon urges the Welches' cat to "Scratch 'em . . . pee on the carpets"; John Lewis in *That Uncertain Feeling* discovers the condition in which he has kept an amorous appointment:

I was near the mirror I used for shaving and which hung above the wash-basin. I peeped in and saw the bogey. It was large and vermiform and clung to the wing of my right nostril.[11]

And in Miss Bowen's novel Eddie, with a hole in his sock, deserts Portia by holding hands in the Grotto Cinema with Daphne Heccomb, the daughter of Portia's hostess, because "I just felt matey."

To account for the elevation of such behavior to a near virtue in the works of the Red Brick writers would be irrelevant here, but Eddie's behavior in *The Death of the Heart* is explainable. The subjection of a person to forces outside himself has become, as we have seen, an increasingly complex subject in Miss Bowen's novels, and part of this complexity is due to her greater awareness of possible responses to such situations. Eddie, whose life has been consistently determined by impersonal external agents (at Oxford "he was taken up, played up, played about with, taken down, let down, finally sent down for one idiotic act"), chooses a metaphoric self-annihilation as a substitute for will and identity. Frustration is worked out in fantasy—in reality he does not even have a last name. Constantly preoccupied with his self-importance (as his letters to Portia indicate) and his appearance, he paradoxically wishes he "had no face" and seeks anonymity. Furthermore, he insists that Portia not write about him in her diary because he cannot bear to be thought of by another person. Since his existence depends on the lines he irresponsibly writes for himself, any statement made *about* him would deprive him of his freedom. In Miss Bowen's words (from her preface to the Faber anthology) he is a man who, "overlooked and dwarfed," is forced to "make himself his own theatre. Is the drama inside heroic or pathological?"

The events that make up "The World" are, outwardly, as prosaic as those in any of the previous five novels. Graham Greene, reviewing the novel for the *Spectator,* noted that, in the opening conversation between Anna and St. Quentin, Miss Bowen has used an "idealized conversation to explain complex relationships, a successful sublimation of all the butlers who ever explained matters to Edwardian theatre audiences." [12] A large proportion of the first section is made up of such idealized conversations, but an equally important part of the narrative is developed by the inserted sections from Portia's diary. This record, as St. Quentin points out to Anna, is the vehicle of the romantic will and Portia's style, in its lack of selectivity and its chaotic organization, reflects the disordered state of her mind. She can report only names and the words of conversations. Her sentences illustrate Walsh's point that the innocent mind sees only immediacy, for few of the sentences show any striving for significance and connection. Her impressions of Eddie, in particular, are as fragmentary and discontinuous as he is:

> After supper, I sat on our rug in front of Thomas's fire. I thought some of the things that Eddie had told me on this rug.
>
> His father is a builder.
>
> When he was a child he knew pieces of the Bible straight off by heart.
>
> He is quite afraid of the dark.
>
> His two favourite foods are cheese straws and jellied *consommé.*
>
> He would not really like to be very rich.
>
> He says that when you love someone all your saved-up wishes start coming out.
>
> He does not like being laughed at, so he pretends he wants people to laugh at him.
>
> He has thirty-six ties.
>
> Written down these look like the characteristics of things we have to write down at lessons. I do wonder if it would ever strike Eddie to leave a surprise for me on the table when I was out. (*DH,* 140–41)

Although the diary entries at the end of Part I indicate the failure of Portia's fumbling attempts to make connections between what she sees and what she understands, her efforts toward understanding are symbolized by the jigsaw puzzles sent her by Major Brutt, an innocent friend of Anna's former lover, "whose thought could puzzle out nothing," and who has turned up in London looking for a job only to discover that "makes of men date, like makes of cars; Major Brutt was a 1914–18 model: there was no market for that make." The puzzles he sends Portia, like Mrs. Dalloway's sewing, reflect abstract constructive activity, and the completion of a puzzle is a stage passed in Portia's development.[13]

The first third of the novel, then, has defined the World which threatens Portia's innocence: "that specious mystery the individual throws about himself, . . . Anna's smiles, Lilian's tomorrows, the shut-in room, the turned-in heart" from which she wishes to escape. But the World's reaction to Portia is similarly one of dismay and suspicion, for Anna, looking at her and thinking "how much innocence she herself had corrupted in other people" wonders, "Is she a snake, or a rabbit? At all events, she thought, hardening, she has her own fun."

The transition from the realm of the World to that of the Flesh, which forms the second third of the novel, is effected through the senses and the season. Spring, which to Anna means "They've put the deck chairs out," is an appeal to the senses for Portia. When Anna and Thomas "escape" to Capri and Portia is sent to board at Seale-on-Sea with the family of Anna's former governess, her exposure to the Heccombs, like Fanny Price's visit to Portsmouth, is an exposure to the vulgarity of life without grace, the flesh usually hidden under the veil of sophisticated manners. But when the alternative to naked flesh is pretension and a desiccated decorum, vulgarity is shown to have at least a primitive vitality in its favor. The subtleties of taste and manners are replaced by a naïve but forceful confrontation of directly experienced reality. At the Heccombs' villa Waikiki, the action takes place amid noises of plumbing (and the "clockwork" bowel movements of Dickie Heccomb), Vinolia soap, Relief Nibs, Bisurated Magnesia Tablets, and egg pie. Even the style of the novel is changed. Whereas in "The World" action is presented largely as conversation (except for the chaotic comments of Portia's diary), the style of "The Flesh" approaches a detailed naturalism. But the montage of primary sensation ("Conceivably, astral smells of tea-cakes with hot currants, of chocolate biscuits and warmed leather chairs vibrated towards them from Evelyn's home") is not a reflection of Miss Bowen's alleged snobbery or "good taste." Rather it is the expression of an alternative to the "edited" life at Windsor Terrace in London. In fact, the narrator here is very careful to avoid commitment:

> Each person at Windsor Terrace lived impaled upon a private obsession, however slight. The telephone, the door bell, the postman's knock were threatening intimations, though still far off. Crossing that springy door mat, the outside person suffered a sea change. In fact, something edited life

> in the Quaynes' house—the action of some sort of brake or deterrent was evident in the behaviour of such people as Eddie. At the same time, no one seemed clear quite *what* was being discarded, or whether anything vital was being let slip away. . . .
>
> The uneditedness of life here at Waikiki made for behaviour that was pushing and frank. Nothing set itself up here but the naivest propriety—that made Daphne shout but not swear, that kept Dickie so stern and modest, that had kept even Mr. Bursely's hand, at yesterday evening's party, some inches above the bow on Daphne's behind. (*DH,* 206)

At Waikiki "continuity dwelt in action only" and actions are real, while at Windsor Terrace desperate attempts are made to deny that "life militates against the seclusion we seek."

To evaluate this world of the senses in which crude vitality replaces edited manners, Portia depends on Eddie's weekend visit. What Portia has found to be the "real world" Eddie dismisses as "an unreal place," though he obviously belongs at Waikiki. But insofar as Eddie brings something of London and the World to the crude "pastoral" vitality of Waikiki, he is right. He still has the power to corrupt. When he dismisses his Windsor Terrace manners and betrays Portia's dependence on him by holding Daphne's hand in the movies, the scene of betrayal is heavily qualified by Miss Bowen's own sophisticated irony. Love is not a magic landscape in the sunset, but a mundane encounter followed by a tasteless action. The faint suggestions of homely adolescence that undermined (for the reader) Portia's dream are manifested in action. Any suggestion of sympathy is gradually but firmly withdrawn from the tone. Before Eddie and Portia go to the movies with the Heccombs, they

> sat down on a roll of beach and each took a shoe off. The light from the lighthouse swept round to where they sat and Portia said: "I say, you've got a hole in your sock."
>
> "Yes. That lighthouse is like the eye of God." (*DH,* 232–33)

The scene in the movie theater repeats the same situation that has been, above, the source of humor:

> Those who wanted to smoke were smoking: no one wanted a light. But Dickie, still with the flame jumping, still held the lighter out in a watching pause—a pause so marked that Portia, as though Dickie had sharply pushed her head round, looked to see where he looked. The light, with malicious accuracy, ran round a rim of cuff, a steel bangle, and made a thumbnail flash. Not deep enough in the cleft between their *fauteuils* Eddie and Daphne were, with emphasis, holding hands. Eddie's fingers kept up a kneading movement: her thumb alertly twitched at the joint. (*DH,* 236)

Obviously the disappearance of meaning can be as much a part of the loss of innocence as the discovery of new meaning. Love becomes "feeling matey" and a thumb twitching at the joint, and Eddie himself, confronted by Portia, attacks her attempt to make meaning, to "piece me together into something that isn't there." He insists on his right to inconsistency of feeling because while a "crook" he at least is not a "fake." Like an Amis protagonist he defends irresponsibility as an alternative to dishonesty.

Any resolution between Portia's innocence and this kind of worldliness can take place only outside of the life of the flesh when "in spirit the two of them rose to the top of life like bubbles" and Portia "stood in the sun by him with her eyes shut." Portia's diary, concluding "The Flesh," is now more articulate and the reference to her puzzle almost self-consciously metaphorical. Her sentences now have begun to compose and order:

> This morning Mrs. Heccomb did not say anything, as though yesterday had been all my dream. I have gone on with the puzzle, it has been knocked, so part that I did is undone and I could not begin again where I left off. Perhaps it *is* in the way in the sun porch? Daphne did not say anything more either. It is raining, but more dark than it rains. (*DH,* 268–69)

Portia's growth in experience is indicated as she turns her attention more and more to the past of memory; but rather than increase her ability to deal with experience, her days at Seale merely give her a determination to retreat to what she has known, in preference to the unknown future: "Though things have hurt me since I was left behind here, I would rather stay with the things here than go back to where I do not know what will happen."

Portia's encounter with Waikiki, then, has accomplished more for her than for the Heccombs. Though they are shocked by Eddie's "commonness," it is during Portia's frank discussion of the handholding incident that "the civilisation of Waikiki seemed to rock on its base." By ignoring the Heccomb taboo that regards "seeing" and "talking about" immorality as more serious than participation in it, Portia gains some insight into the meaning of convention: it is by subjecting itself to some sort of pattern that the complex romantic will adjusts itself to reality. And the narrator that states this discovery is now just beyond Portia, defining the direction in which she is headed:

> After inside upheavals, it is important to fix on imperturbable *things*. Their imperturbableness, their air that nothing has happened renews our guarantee. Pictures would not be hung plumb over the centres of fireplaces or wallpapers pasted on with such precision that their seams make no break in the pattern if life were really not possible to adjudicate for. These things are what we mean when we speak of civilisation: they remind us how exceedingly seldom the unseemly or unforeseeable rears its head. In this sense, the destruction of buildings and furniture is more palpably dreadful to the spirit than the destruction of human life. Appalling as the talk with

Daphne had been, it had not been so finally fatal, when you looked back at it, as an earthquake or a dropped bomb. Had the gas stove blown up when Portia lit it, blowing this nice room into smithereens, it would have been worse than Portia's being called spying and common. Though what she had said had apparently been dreadful, it had done less harm than a bombardment from the sea. Only outside disaster is irreparable. At least, there would be dinner at any minute; at least she could wash her hands in Vinolia soap. (*DH,* 250–51)

To say "Only outside disaster is irreparable" is obviously beyond Portia, but the last sentence could be hers. Her accomplishment is to have discovered the saving grace of convention. She has not, like Eddie, blindly denied its value; nor has she naïvely accepted it as a surface sign of refinement, like the Heccombs.

However, the return from "The Flesh" of self-discovery at Waikiki to "The Devil" of further human betrayal in London demolishes the equilibrium Portia has attained. The house at Windsor Terrace that Matchett has been cleaning during the absence of its owners has become "that ideal mould for living into which life so seldom pours itself"; but the devil in many guises brings pollution "with every breath that passed through the house" in this last third of the novel. Anna, rereading her love letters from Robert Pidgeon, thinks maliciously of showing them to Portia with the comment "This is what it all comes to, you little fool" and speculates with guilty pleasure about Portia's death:

But, after all, death runs in that family. What is she, after all? The child of an aberration, the child of a panic, the child of an old chap's pitiful sexuality. Conceived among lost hairpins and snapshots of doggies in a Notting Hill Gate flatlet. At the same time she has inherited everything: she marches about this house like the Race itself. They rally as if she were the Young Pretender. (*DH,* 296–97)

The most specific form the devil takes, however, is the novelist St. Quentin Miller. St. Quentin, who has many affinities with Pierre Costals in Montherlant's *Pitié pour les Femmes,* has been Matchett's mirror image, playing Satan to her Michael. But his detachment is only superficially like hers, for it extends to morals as well as behavior. A passionless Eddie, he reveals his and Anna's betrayal (reading the diary) calmly, regarding the disclosure as a form of education. His lesson for Portia is that man can make himself a novel, for fact yields easily to imagination:

Thank God, except at its one moment there's never any such thing as a bare fact. Ten minutes later, half an hour later, one's begun to gloze the fact over with a deposit of some sort. The hours I spent with thee dear love are like a string of pearls to me. But a diary (if one did keep it up to date) would come much too near the mark. One ought to secrete for some time before one begins to look back at anything. Look how reconciled to everything reminiscences are. (*DH,* 300)

To live in the present, expecting truth, is to become "God's spy" and "the loving nature in vacuo." The case St. Quentin makes is a compelling attempt to set firm rules for the world surrounding Portia. In their deceptions, he argues, exists the only life possible, for "What makes you think us wicked is simply our little way of keeping ourselves going. We must live, though you may not see the necessity."

The candor of St. Quentin's defense of deception is satanically paradoxical, but the other members of the World persist in their usual single-minded behavior. Portia's discovery that Anna and Eddie make fun of his weekend at Seale confirms her judgment that the World offers no opportunity for her assumptions, that her moral coin is worthless in it. "The sense of two allied betrayals" which have "push[ed] up to full growth, like a double tree" expresses the urgency of her predicament. To preserve her moral sense, she must try to escape the World: by fleeing to Eddie's bleak apartment with its "anti-moral colour" and, after he has rejected her because "we've got to live in the world," to Major Brutt's Karachi Hotel, built from the Kensington houses of "a class doomed from the start, without natural privilege, without grace." And Portia's flight from the World is also a flight from identity, for she reverts to the animal-like state of her arrival at Windsor Terrace, "terrified . . . like a bird astray in a room, a bird already stunned by dashing itself against mirrors and panes." In the shabby lounge among the "dregs of daylight" and later in his tiny attic room, Major Brutt, like Eddie, defends his own precarious security by fighting against the child's appeals for sympathy. Even when Portia has exposed the attitude of bare tolerance on which his welcome at Windsor Terrace depends, Major Brutt clings to the few articles of daily ritual that give a pathetic continuity to the life that is only appearance: "his own rubbed ebony hair-brushes, his stud-box, his nail-scissors," and he can answer Portia only in fragmentary clichés: "Blood's thicker—." Even when Portia desperately offers to marry him and Brutt has "the preposterous happy mirage of something one does not even for one moment desire," he still echoes Eddie's defense that "we have to live": "It's not a question of doing the best you can do, it's a question of doing the only thing possible." For both Portia and Brutt, the encounter produces the ultimate death of the heart, the emergence of a situation in which neither wisdom nor innocence is adequate, because the power of innocence ends with its discovery. As Brutt goes down to telephone Thomas and Anna,

. . . he saw her face on the pillow, and saw in a sleep-bound way how specious wisdom was. One's sentiments—call them that—one's fidelities are so instinctive that one hardly knows they exist: only when they are betrayed or, worse still, when one betrays them does one realise their power. That betrayal is the end of an inner life, without which the everyday becomes threatening or meaningless. At the back of the spirit a mysterious landscape, whose perspective used to be infinite, suddenly perishes: this is like being cut off from the country for ever, not even meeting its breath down the city street. (*DH,* 359–60)

Self-consciousness, the facing of the impossible, offers only one recourse—the forceful imposition of the practical will. The condition Portia sets for her return, that her guardians do "the right thing," is, like Maisie's demand that Sir Claude and Mrs. Beale separate, a desperate assertion of morality. However Miss Bowen, unlike James, seems to imply that a dramatization of such a moment is beyond any language, at least hers. Only the cynical voice of St. Quentin and the limited consciousness of Matchett define the novel's conclusion. St. Quentin's terms for Portia's situation are sympathetic but his metaphors reductive:

This evening the pure in heart have simply got us on toast. And look at the fun she has—she lives in a world of heroes. Who are we to be sure they're as phony as we all think? If the world's really a stage, there must be some big parts. All she asks is to walk on at the same time. And how right she is really—failing the big character, better (at least, arguably) the big flop than the small neat man who has more or less come off. Not that there is, really, one neat unhaunted man. I swear that each of us keeps, battened down inside himself, a sort of lunatic giant—impossible socially, but full-scale—and that it's the knockings and batterings we sometimes hear in each other that keeps our intercourse from utter banality. Portia hears these the whole time; in fact she hears nothing else. Can we wonder she looks so goofy most of the time? (*DH,* 374)

And Matchett, dispatched to get Portia because "she's the one who generally fetches her," thinks of herself rather than Portia. Her ride to the Karachi Hotel is presented as the interior monologue of a woman who, however "inexorable" at home, is terrified beyond familiar boundaries.

If the novel is to suggest something beyond futility (and it clearly must), and if dramatic or narrative presentation seems to the novelist inadequate, the only solution possible is a poetic one. As at the end of *Friends and Relations,* "hope" enters the novel metaphorically in the final paragraphs—the ritual of the seasons and of art suggesting a permanence immune to human frailty:

All the same, in the stretched mauve dusk of the street there was an intimation of summer coming—summer, intensifying everything with its heat and glare. In gardens outside London roses would burn on, with all else gone in the dusk. Fatigue but a sort of joy would open in all hearts, for summer is the height and fullness of living. Already the dust smelled strong. In this premature night of clouds the sky was warm, the buildings seemed to expand. The fingers on the piano halted, struck true notes, found their way to a chord. (*DH,* 384)

Though Portia's future is as ambiguous as Isabel Archer's, Maisie's, or Leopold's, this narrator (certainly these are not Matchett's conclusions) implies that Portia will come closer to sharing the authority of Matchett (who has, after all, survived the ordeal of the taxi ride) than the retreat of Anna or the romantic fantasy of Thomas.

If the methods each of the characters uses to reconcile the romantic will to reality are examined, the theme of the novel is clear. As my reading of the conclusion implied, many moments in this story can be rendered only by the intrusion of a narrator who forthrightly assigns meaning, and in one of these frequent *Sentenzen* [14] Miss Bowen comments that "illusions are art, for the feeling person, and it is by art that we live, if we do" (*DH,* 111). Each of the characters lives by some form of art, in the word's widest sense. St. Quentin, of course, most literally lives by art, and his novels contain what is "possible" but "improbable." He has no feelings, and what romantic will he does have is expressed not in the life from which he so ably dissociates himself but in the novels where, he tells Portia, "it's my game from the start." And opposite St. Quentin is Portia's schoolmate Lilian, who wantonly projects her romantic will into silly fantasies involving her body's adolescent chemistry and her memories of a Lesbian affair with a 'cello mistress.

Matchett's art, of course, is her ability to submit herself to stern morality and tradition, though she is vulnerable to jealousy (of Portia) and to ignorance away from the consoling furniture of Windsor Terrace. Thomas Quayne has found an unsatisfactory equilibrium in the illusion of passionate love, his wife in her dedication to what she can do successfully. Major Brutt, a fully confirmed innocent, lives in the daily ritual, but is dependent on the Quaynes for emotional (and occupational) sustenance. On the simplest level, the Heccombs find an art in the practice of pseudogentility.

The problem is most complicated, of course, for Eddie and Portia, who have not yet found the saving grace of an art nor finally committed themselves to an unsatisfactory illusion. Eddie, as a corrupted innocent, categorically refuses to take any role that is imposed, including that of lover, for like Karen and Max he adopts the fatal view that the romantic will can be renounced, that he can live without illusion. Eddie's virtue is to recognize that irresponsibility ("crookedness") is a lesser sin than hypocrisy ("fakery"); his fate is to learn that the world offers no solace for one with this knowledge. The consequence is a lack of identity and "a lasting state of hysteria."

Although Eddie rejects the necessity of illusion, Portia continues to search and test. The betrayals she suffers are the failures of inadequate illusions. The happiness she found with her mother was restricted to an "out-of-season nowhere," and the tentative commitments she makes within the World—to the Quaynes, Matchett, Eddie, the Heccombs, and Major Brutt—are potentially destructive to her or to them. Her final knowledge, presumably, is to realize that she must construct a world compatible with her circumstances, for an illusion can be "saving," can defend the individual against chaos, only if it be *seen* as an art—as St. Quentin, who suffers least, sees it. For St. Quentin, any action that breaks his rules, such as speaking the truth unnecessarily, "crumbles the whole scene: at once one is in a fantastic universe. Its unseemliness and its glory are indescribable really. One becomes a Colossus." One becomes, in other words, an inarticulate madman in a formless world of inarticulate power. Though all people encounter experience beyond language, Portia (St. Quentin tells Thomas) hears the "knockings and batterings" of a "lunatic" giant within her all the time, not just during moments disturbed by "love, drink, anger," and so she is able to expose the illusory nature of the appearances that some, like Anna and Major Brutt, have taken to be reality. The narrator's definition of the innocent's destructiveness could, in fact, be St. Quentin's:

> Happy that few of us are aware of the world until we are already in league with it. Childish fantasy, like the sheath over the bud, not only protects but curbs the terrible budding spirit, protects not only innocence from the world but the world from the power of innocence. (*DH*, 354)

In Portia, of course, childish fantasy has lost its ability to protect; but still to lose innocence, to suffer the death of the heart in gaining an awareness of the world is an additional and necessary step if the art the adult lives by is to be a successful one. When the alternative is to break a "pact with life" so that "the peace we seek tears right across" and "in the chaos that suddenly thrusts in nothing remains unreal except possibly love," it is evident that the only possible adult role is cautious, hesitant, self-centered, yet defiant. Even memory must distort the past, so that "we remember only in the limited way that is bearable":

> We observe small rites, but we defend ourselves against the terrible memory that is stronger than will. We defend ourselves from the rooms, the scenes, the objects that make for hallucination, that make the senses start up and fasten upon a ghost. We desert those who desert us; we cannot afford to suffer; we must live how we can. (*DH*, 179)

To read the novel in this way, to merge with Miss Bowen's observations the dialogue of her characters, is to imply that the novel is to some extent a moral tract. The implication is not entirely unjust. The more frequent sententious statements, not always immediately relevant to the action and often abstractable, help to construct the coherent moral and philosophical positions expressed by the later novels. Indeed, the paragraph above from *The Death of the Heart* could be Miss Bowen's description of the action of *A World of Love,* to appear seventeen years later. Both novels can be read as expansions of Miss Bowen's contention, in "Out of a Book," that ". . . it is not only our fate but our business to lose innocence, and once we have lost that it is futile to attempt a picnic in Eden" (*CI,* 265).

Although the existence of a dehumanized social world with unsympathetic inhabitants is a moral "evil" in this novel, Miss Bowen accepts such an evil as her donnée. If satire implies the humorous exaggeration of vices with the intent to reform them, the social worlds of Windsor Terrace and Waikiki are the objects of irony rather than the targets of satire, for the awareness of the individual, not the improvement of society, is the necessity. The social experience Miss Bowen did not abnegate (as she argues the Movement writers did) has led her to see opportunity not in actions but in the imagination's power to make inescapable events bearable. Her sense of this inevitability, almost of fatality, has determined the course of her writing, for if increased consciousness, not a reformed world, is the only change allowed, a "happy ending" is obviously impossible. As John Henry Raleigh states in "The English Novel and the Three Kinds of Time," the happy ending makes sense only "if it be regarded as a literary convention metaphorically expressing the Victorian time-sense; i.e., man projected into an imprecise but, nevertheless, happy future." In the work of later novelists (such as Hardy and James) unable to accept naïve Victorian optimism, he sees a characteristic use of the tragic or ambiguous ending, suggesting that "man's future is either dark or unsure," and a replacement of "simple historical time" with "cosmic and existential time." [15] Appropriately *The Death of the Heart* ends with Matchett's interior monologue (like Portia's diary, the literary form of existential time), and in the last paragraph the narrator turns to one of the more obvious manifestations of cosmic time, the change of the seasons, reminding the reader that the novel had opened in the brittle cold of winter. The plot is immediately responsive to the requirements of Miss Bowen's moral vision.

A detailed examination of *The Death of the Heart* should have made clear the relationship of Miss Bowen's ethos to that of Henry James (and Jane Austen). In reviewing the novel Graham Greene remarked that

> Miss Bowen's book will inevitably be compared with *The Awkward Age,* though the society it describes is more well-meaning and less corrupt than Mrs. Brookenham's circle. It can stand up to the comparison; there is

nothing in James's rather cramped novel quite so finely rendered as Miss Bowen's climax.[16]

Moreover, James's intention in *The Awkward Age* to take note of "the difference made in certain friendly houses and for certain flourishing mothers by the sometimes dreaded, often delayed, but never full arrested coming to the forefront of some vague slip of a daughter" must have been similar to Miss Bowen's. Both had "to be infinitely addicted to 'noticing' " for "under the rule of that secret vice or that unfair advantage, at any rate, the 'sitting downstairs,' from a given date, of the merciless maiden previously perched aloft could easily be felt as a crisis." [17]

Although James's use of a peculiar dramatic technique to achieve irony is very different from Miss Bowen's dependence on juxtaposed characters (Portia and Lilian) and scenes (the "eye of God" episodes), the similarity of concerns is striking, especially since Miss Bowen had not read *The Awkward Age*.[18] Both novelists show social language, as one manifestation of social behavior, to be inadequate to deal with, even recognize, the existence of terrible power beneath its "bearable film"—whether that power take the form of passion or adolescence. Nanda Brookenham has been "in the air they themselves have infected for her" and the extent of the infection is indicated by the elderly Mr. Longdon who, like Matchett, measures it by traditional, socially outmoded standards of morality. Though no attempt is made to "sell" Portia as Mrs. Brookenham attempts to sell her daughter, both novels set up an analogous contrast between the girl who is "true" and a society that jealously tries to make something of her innocence.

When Nanda leaves with Mr. Longdon at the end of James's novel, the uncertainty of her future is less important than the fact that her decision has been made clear-sightedly, when, as all those who surround her realize, finally "she knows everything." The awareness she has earned and suffered protects her from the fate of Aggie, whose innocence is artificially preserved. The tone of Mr. Longdon's admiration of Nanda is not very different from that Miss Bowen expects us to take toward Portia.[19] The fact that Nanda has the active elements of nature "for good or ill" before she is called upon to use them is what saves her from Aggie's fate. For James's heroines as for Miss Bowen's, it is the terror of imagination that it should make them sensitive to their worlds, but it is the grace of imagination that it can make possible a transcendence of those worlds.

In the novels of both writers, morality is not so much a function of the course taken as the awareness of the course taken, the extent to which it can be reconciled to "things as they are." The governess of *The*

Turn of the Screw and Aggie become evil because their innocence is blindly preserved, Gilbert Osmond because he rejects the necessity of finding an art or system, the Moreens of "The Pupil" because they assume they are "men of the world" rather than unsuccessful aspirants to that title. The successful characters are those who, going from innocence to experience, understand both states, as Maisie goes from "seeing" to "knowing" ever aware that the two activities must be distinguished and related. Miss Bowen's most successful ("finally happy") heroes and heroines follow the same path: Sydney, Lois, Janet, Cecilia, Leopold, Portia. And if Emma, Fanny, Elizabeth Bennet, Anne Elliot, and the Dashwood sisters be remembered, it can be seen that Jane Austen's heroines too see through manners to morals; when they accept a metaphorical art to live by, they see and accept both the art and the life it orders. Illusion can become madness, but only when it is accepted as the single reality.

Portia, like Nanda, avoids tragedy because she is, to some extent, already "fallen." Only the blind innocent lambs with pink ribbons, Major Brutt or James's Aggie, become the helpless victims of a society they are too naïve to see as evil. The "unexamined life" is, necessarily, the way of fakery and deceit (and one has to be aware, like Eddie, to be a crook). Innocence preserved by force, in fact, provokes appalling images in Miss Bowen's short stories: the child of "The Little Girl's Room" who "sighed acquiescence into her frilly pillow and once more slept in her prison" (*CJ,* 136); or the maiden aunt of "The Queer Heart" who "had wrapped her own rank virginity round her [niece] like someone sharing a mackintosh" (*LR,* 148). The maiden ladies of "The Easter Egg Party" who "still received intimations of immortality" personify the futility of attempting a picnic in Eden. By trying to substitute piety and militant innocence for sympathy, they bring unnecessary grief to the child they are trying to comfort after she has suffered some kind of sexual attack. But Hermione, from her "world of alien experience" finally defeats them by accusing them of "making me take an interest in things, and . . . never [taking] the slightest interest in me." She leaves them "a sort of scar, like a flattened grave, in their hearts" (*LR,* 115). Seen with Miss Bowen's complex vision, the death of the heart is part of the necessary birth of the intelligence, the achievement of civilized independence. It is a painful station on the way to the final belief.

Some of the accomplishment one senses in *The Death of the Heart* is undoubtedly produced by rather anachronistic qualities. The echoes of past writers in Miss Bowen's situations and terms give to the novel a timeless quality that the self-conscious modernity of *To the North,* for one, destroys. Though her own comments on it are rather diffident, it seems to me unquestionably her finest novel, responding to and ordering more life with greater subtlety than any of the others, and challenged closely only by *The Heat of the Day*. Perhaps *because* it so effectively defines a largely nineteenth-century concern in contemporary terms, it has no close analogues in more recent fiction. Only in its form and its use of the narrator—its most significant departure from its Jamesian analogues—does it offer qualities that can be called contemporary. Lacking James's faith (and perhaps ability) in dramatizing, Miss Bowen has given the narrator the burden of extending the dimensions of events by synthesizing, generalizing, imitating, and mimicking. Only when Portia's diary is presented is the reader left alone with the elements and characters of the novel's world, to make his own meaning. As in Proust or Joyce, motifs echo, recur, thicken, and are resolved, but the narrator who directs them into carefully composed paragraphs is protean, comprehensive, and invisible. Readers of Victorian literature are accustomed to the intrusive author; readers of contemporary fiction are certainly familiar with the characterized narrators—the Jake Barneses and Nick Carraways—who may or may not represent a novel's total consciousness; but Elizabeth Bowen's narrator in *The Death of the Heart* is one step beyond these, for in acknowledging the more open form she is abiding by her contention that any trick is justified if it contribute to the novel's poetic truth. If one senses in her earlier novels a tone committed to the destruction of what the author opposes, one finds it balanced in this novel by an inclusiveness that is far more vital. The struggle of the writer who wishes to define a world of his own and yet wishes to include faithfully all he has known can be exciting when it is unified as one voice.

In both *The Death of the Heart* and *The Awkward Age,* the novelists were dealing with a society that was "in transition," in which implicit assumptions of the past were being reinterpreted in terms of the experiences of the present. Nevertheless the narrator of *The Death of the Heart* insists, speaking of dropped bombs and bombardments from the sea, that "only outside disaster is irreparable." This assurance, in a book published in 1938, was prophetic and became ironic. In the novel that followed *The Death of the Heart* after an interval of eleven years, *The Heat of the Day,* Miss Bowen deals with a society in which exactly this "irreparable" outside disaster is constantly imminent.

5 | *Fiction and Reality*

In Miss Bowen's fiction of the late thirties the man of feeling, like Thomas Quayne, is often shown to be arrested and restricted by feminine will, the inadequacy of language, or the desiccation of his society. The montage of "A Love Story: 1939" collects three such situations: the mother who prefers her lover dead rather than interested in her daughter; the passive bridegroom who has been purchased by the wealthy father of his older, willful wife; the mistress who tries to control the natural sociability of her lover. Behind the artificial protection of the glass doors of an Irish seaside hotel in December, they work their own emotional destruction. The use of a date in the title is indicative of the greater topicality of Miss Bowen's writing during the war years. If it had been possible earlier for her to separate social content from political, private from public, any such distinctions now had to be erased. War appears in her fiction of this period with a factual immediacy far different from the hazy, almost mythical Troubles of *The Last September.* Man's fate in her fiction of this period is as political as it is personal.

The longest and most serious story of the *Look at All Those Roses* collection, "Summer Night," helps to define the relationship between war and the arrested activity portrayed in "A Love Story: 1939." Unity of time is provided by Emma's automobile drive from her home, husband, and children, to an assignation with a lover somewhere in Ireland during a summer evening in 1940. The house she has left, though in Ireland, dramatizes the aphorism that an Englishman's home is his castle. The "fortress" is guarded by Emma's husband the Major, whose unmilitary character and appearance belie his rank, and his Aunt Fran, a Victorian woman fragmentarily defined by her tasteless mementoes and clichés of the past: "photos in little warped frames, musty, round straw boxes, china kittens, palm crosses, the three Japanese monkeys, *bambini,* a

Lincoln Imp, a merry-thought pen-wiper, an ivory spinning-wheel from Cologne."

Even though the house has been carefully locked after Emma's evening departure, the darkness from which Aunt Fran retreats rises up from within as Emma's young daughter, Vivie, covers her naked body with colored chalk pictures of snakes and stars and bounces on her mother's empty bed, while "all her senses stood up, wanting to run the night." For Aunt Fran, who discovers her, the experience is a shattering revelation that public disaster cannot be seen apart from the individual.

> There are no more children: the children are born knowing. The shadow rises up the cathedral tower, up the side of the pure hill. There is not even the past: our memories share with us the infected zone; not a memory does not lead up to this. Each moment is everywhere, it holds the war in its crystal; there is no elsewhere, no other place. Not a benediction falls on this apart house of the Major; the enemy is within it, creeping about. Each heart here falls to the enemy. (*LR*, 208–9)

The house of Robinson, Emma's destination, is no less symbolic than the one she has left. The "blue china house" is regarded by the villagers as a Bluebeard's castle because Robinson has rejected the matriarchal atmosphere of the town, and the reality inside this blue china shell is ultramodern and masculine, dominated by an electric clock, cold leather chairs, tiling, chromium, and switches. Robinson himself is a man of action, alternating between a factory office and a high-powered car. His power can easily intimidate the intellectual he entertains while waiting for Emma. Justin Cavey, unlike Robinson, is a thinker who has put his faith in "the towers of Europe" and, unable to face the present, vainly seeks to cast off his self and assume power:

> I'm torn, here, by every single pang of annihilation. But that's what I look for; that's what I want completed; that's the whole of what I want to embrace. On the far side of the nothing—my new form. Scrap "me"; scrap my wretched identity and you'll bring to the open some bud of life. I *not* "I"—I'd be the world . . . You're right: what you [Robinson] would call thinking does get me rattled. I only what you call think to excite myself. Take myself away, and I'd *think,* I might see; I might feel purely; I might even love— (*LR,* 195)

Justin's attraction to Robinson's power is almost homosexual, this meeting between an impotent thinker and the almost bestial man "no more than an accident of this narrowed summer."

The disaster of the encounter between the two men is expressed when Justin returns to his hotel (after he and his sister have seen Emma "crouching in her crouching car in the dark") and writes Robinson a letter ending their friendship, condemning Robinson's illicit affair, and regretting having "attempted to enter, and to comport myself in, what might be called an area under your jurisdiction." The intellectual's defeat by the man of action takes place as Justin "smote a stamp on this letter" instead of striking Robinson.

Although the inability of the intellectual man to come to terms with the man of action is one failure of the wartime world, for Justin's deaf sister communication is a less serious problem. She "has a world to herself" as Justin says, and is "contemplative, wishless, almost without an 'I.' " In her own soundless world she can relive, in the evening she spends with Robinson, the one evening she has spent with a lover.

Though Queenie, her brother Justin, Robinson, Aunt Fran, and the Major all represent more or less static attitudes, Emma, like her daughter, is dynamic. Yielding to the animal side of her nature, she enters a conspiracy with the man of power in a setting of "fire and glass." As she drives to meet him, "her existence [is] in her hands on the wheel and in the sole of the foot in which she [feels] through the sandal, the throbbing pressure of the accelerator"; and she arrives at Robinson's house at the same time that "animals [are] rising out of ditches." She is referred to as a bat and a cat; like an animal she peers through the pampas grass at the house, and she wants to go out into the garden before they go to bed. Though she had first thought of the assignation as a romantic adventure, she finally assumes that mindless sexuality is the only medium by which a man and woman can be brought together. Yet in spite of the force and brute vitality each represents, their meeting takes place amid dryness and sterility where "there was no moon, but dry, tense, translucent darkness: no dew fell."

Much of the intellectual history rendered in *The Heat of the Day* is anticipated by "Summer Night." The incompatibility of thinking and feeling, the forms of retreat from reality, the aberrations of the romantic will that motivate both war and treachery, are all implicit concerns in this story. In an appropriately fragmentary form the story presents the destructive alternatives available in a world where values are as broken as the strings on the harp in the Major's house. The story is as close as any to what Miss Bowen has called a "pointer to futility" [1]: only for the mindlessly objective man of action and the totally subjective deaf woman can a world at war be encountered with indifference. Robinson, like Harrison in the later novel, is completely a part of war's brutality; Queenie can completely ignore it. If the story's terms were political, one could say that fascism and quietism here make their appeal to the insensitive and the uncommitted. Although the allusion to Matthew Arnold's "A Summer Night" may be coincidental, this clearly is a world where one must ask Arnold's question: "Is there no life, but these alone?

/ Madman or slave, must man be one?" The story, however, avoids the easy optimism of Arnold's answer, for the lot "left to each man still" is far from fair.[2]

The relationship between the ethos of *The Death of the Heart,* wherein individuals choose arts and patterns to cope with a hostile middle-class society, and that of *The Heat of the Day,* where war destroys not only the order of that society but its material manifestations as well, is most clearly defined by Miss Bowen's wartime short-story collection *The Demon Lover.* These stories, like "Summer Night" and *The Heat of the Day,* illustrate one important characteristic of postwar British fiction that the non-Briton can perhaps only imperfectly understand. Though prose fiction has always been dependent on assumptions about the action of men in a defined society, the second world war (and especially the Battle of Britain) emphasized the impossibility of dealing directly with men's "everyday" experience, for the regularity of behavior and the permanence of milieu on which the writer depends were quite literally shattered. Yet the war presented an overwhelming human experience that no responsible writer could ignore. Miss Bowen defines this "compulsive" quality in her postscript to *The Demon Lover* collection (1945):

> Each time I sat down to write a story I opened a door; and the pressure against the other side of that door must have been very great, for things—ideas, images, emotions—came through with force and rapidity, sometimes violence. I do not say that these stories wrote themselves—aesthetically or intellectually speaking, I found the writing of some of them very difficult—but I was never in a moment's doubt as to *what* I was to write. The stories had their own momentum, which I had to control. The acts in them had an authority which I could not question. Odd enough in their way—and now some seem very odd—they were flying particles of something enormous and inchoate that had been going on. They were sparks from experience—an experience not necessarily my own. (*DL,* 216–17)

This paradox of an inescapable but impossibly difficult subject was not easy for any writer to resolve, as the inadequacy of the "typical" war novel shows. The more successful British writers have sought rather remote objective correlatives by which they could treat the subject at one remove, and Miss Bowen's indirections took two primary forms. In *The Heat of the Day* and "Summer Night" she has conveyed the intellectual attitudes that produce (and result from) war by symbolic characters. Because they are faced with innumerable alternatives, they are not allegorical; but because they are not shown directly in contact with the physical manifestations of war they are not intended to be "realistic" and completely representative. The women on the Dublin tram in "Unwelcome Idea" and the maid in "Oh, Madam . . ." are simpler, satirically treated characters of the same kind.

The second, less rationalistic, objective correlative Miss Bowen chose is that evident in most of *The Demon Lover:* hallucination. Though Portia and Matchett found partial comfort in the order of Things (the pattern of wallpaper, the family furniture), the characters in the short stories, like the actual inhabitants of London, must substitute their own hallucination for the material comforts reduced to rubble by bombs, as Miss Bowen points out in her preface to the collection:

> People whose homes had been blown up went to infinite lengths to assemble bits of themselves—broken ornaments, odd shoes, torn scraps of the curtains that had hung in a room—from the wreckage. In the same way, they assembled and checked themselves from stories and poems, from their memories, from one another's talk. Outwardly, we accepted that at this time individual destiny had to count for nothing: inwardly, individual destiny became an obsession in every heart. . . .
>
> The search for indestructible landmarks in a destructible world led many down strange paths. The attachment to these when they had been found produced small worlds-within-worlds of hallucination—in most cases, saving hallucination. Writers followed the paths they saw or felt people treading, and depicted those little dear saving illusory worlds. I have done both in *The Demon Lover* stories.
>
> . . . .
>
> These [stories] are received impressions of happening things; impressions that stored themselves up and acquired force without being analysed or considered. . . . Taken singly, they are disjected snapshots—snapshots taken from close up, too close up, in the middle of the *mêlée* of a battle. You cannot *render,* you can only embrace, if it means embracing to suffocation-point—something vast that is happening right on top of you.
>
> (*DL,* 220–21, 223)

Throughout her description one can hear the artist apologizing for what the woman has done. When a writer "embraces" his material (one remembers Emma in "Summer Night") he presumably relinquishes the intellect and its arts, yields control and identity in exchange for passion and immediacy. Some of the stories are indeed marred by insecure narrators, but in the more successful, hallucination is both embraced and rendered.

Though these hallucinations take the form of ghosts in three of the stories ("Pinky," "Green Holly," and "The Demon Lover") and psychological obsession in several others (e.g., "The Inherited Clock"), in the more interesting stories "hallucination" refers to a complex and peculiar relationship between past and present, solid memory and fragmented identity, destiny and destruction. The child who returns as a man to Southstone in "Ivy Gripped the Steps" sees in the ivy strangling the steps of Mrs. Nicholson's empty house an intimation that a reality in both fate and nature has worked against the illusion of an artificially preserved Edwardian civilization. Like *The Death of the Heart* and *The Heat of the Day,* the story presents the danger of false illusion, art chosen without reference to reality, and implies that war itself, in 1914 or 1940, is the product of just such an aberration of the romantic will.

To consider hallucination, in many of these stories, is merely to look askance at the failure of communication as it had been presented in "Summer Night." As Miss Bowen implies, minds detached from objectivity are the corollary of "conversations" that end in futile monologues. But neither the hallucinated mind nor the collapse of human engagement are easily made into novelistic concerns. "She is mad" and "they can't talk to one another" are not, in themselves, very interesting statements. Nor, for that matter, are they very new statements. The prevalence of the first is obvious enough, and the second could be used to describe most serious twentieth-century novels. Hemingway, in *The Sun Also Rises,* had long before qualified the vitality of the drunken conversation of Jake, Harris, and Bill in Chapter XIII by setting it against the inarticulateness of Jake and Brett at the novel's end, when they too try to speak of the "good time."

The limitation of "Summer Night" (and this may be merely to say that it is a short story) is that such juxtapositions are impossible. However, when inarticulateness appears again as a major concern in *The Heat of the Day,* dramatic juxtapositions of communion and frustration, crude vital simplicity and inhibited sophistication inform the whole novel. Once glimpsed as part of the melodramatic story, such dramatic propositions about language assume a fundamental importance in the novel's structure.

To move from *The Demon Lover* stories to *The Heat of the Day* is to undergo a rather abrupt change in mood from the altitude line near poetry to the novel's prose and comprehensiveness, its obligation to supply information as well as illumination. As Miss Bowen points out in her *Demon Lover* postscript, war, as she sees it, is a territory rather than a time. The stories are momentary projections of individuals within the environment that is war, "the particular [through which] . . . in war-time, I felt the high-voltage current of the general pass." *The Heat of the Day,* published five years later, is a more ambitious project, one that Miss Bowen wished to be "enormously comprehensive." Whether or not one finally accepts Raymond Williams' judgment that "the persons exist primarily as elements in the central character's emotional landscape, and are never seen or valued in any other terms," one can agree with his implication that the struggle between "special pleading" and "careful descriptive realism" (the attempt to be "enormously comprehensive") exists throughout *The Heat of the Day.*[3]

What is most comprehensive about Miss Bowen's aim is her attempt to avoid the simplicity of blaming human disaster on Fate, Society, or any other capitalized abstraction. Though the novel's characters are passive, frustrated, acted upon—the inhabitants of London are repeatedly compared to fish shifting about in shoals—the agent that moves them is not reduced by being separated from them. In *The Death of the Heart* Portia wonders whether personality and character produce or are produced by situation, but in *The Heat of the Day* the question is irrelevant. Stella Rodney, instead, has even decided that *any* destiny, any recognizable pattern, is preferable to "freedom in nothing." She assumes that whatever she *is* has had a beginning somewhere, and that "the beginning, in which was conceived the end, could not but continue to shape the middle part of the story, so that none of the realizations along that course were what had been expected, quite whole, quite final." Although her attitude is fatalistic, although human will is assigned little responsibility for controlling the organic form of life, she is nevertheless not separated from the world whose creature she is, nor is the present moment made irrelevant; she and the world, we are told, are "fellow-sufferers," sharing "a clear-sightedly helpless progress toward disaster," arriving at "the testing extremities of their noonday." Though the phrase "one must live as one can" appears here again as "one can only live how one can," living is even less an autonomous act than it was in the earlier novels. In fact, Stella says, "one has to forget . . . if it is to be possible to live. The more wars there are, I suppose, the more we shall learn how to be survivors."

Thus the subjectivity of characters is brought into contact with the objectivity of war's territory, and the plot of the novel, the particular that embodies the general, is appropriately violent and melodramatic. Stella Rodney, an upper-middle-class divorcée working for the government in "secret, exacting, not unimportant work" is abruptly faced with a choice between human and political fidelity: the man known to her only as Harrison presents himself as a counterspy, informs her that her lover Robert Kelway is spying for the Nazis, and tells her that she must become his mistress rather than Robert's, or he will expose Robert to his superiors.

War's chaos is precisely what makes the choice a dramatic one. Stella's affair with Robert depends on ignorance, for "it was a characteristic of that life in the moment and for the moment's sake that one knew people well without knowing much about them: vacuum as to future was offset by vacuum as to past . . . ." Though the affair is beneficial in prolonging the bearable present, Stella sacrifices her immunity to disaster by being in love. Like all of Miss Bowen's lovers, she grants sovereignty to fate and the external world by engaging her emotions with something external, perishable; and in "the testing extremities of their noonday" there is no language for defining relationships publicly or privately. The urgency of her situation simultaneously requires and prevents expression or solution.

Harrison, whose proposition threatens Stella's security more severely than a bomb, is, like Stella and Robert, a creature of circumstance. However, instead of being forced to *submit* to wartime dislocation, he is a person whose ideal habitat is only then present. Stella at first imagines him a madman, then a traveling salesman, and Harrison's own description of himself shows the relevance of her guesses. He is much like Eddie, now triumphant in a world that seems to reward a distinction between crookedness and hypocrisy:

> "War, if you come to think of it, hasn't started anything that wasn't there already—what it does is, put the other lot of us in the right. . . . What you see now is what I've seen all along. I wouldn't say that puts me at an advantage, but I can't help feeling 'This is where I come in.' "
>
> "In other words, this is a crooks' war?"
>
> "I shouldn't call it that. It's a war, of course; but for me the principal thing is that it's a time when I'm not a crook. For me there've been not so good times when I did seem to be a bit out in my calculations, so you must see how where I'm concerned things have taken a better turn; everything about adds up to what I made it." (*HD,* 31)

Like Robinson in "Summer Night," Harrison is a man concerned with "getting somewhere" rather than being, and in a fatalistic decade the alternatives to verbs of action are prepositions. For Harrison, "there had never yet not been a way through, a way round, or, in default of all else, a way out." Unlike Stella, he speaks in a stereotyped language of businesslike practicality and vulgar cliché. To be in love, for him, is to be in "such and such a situation," and in his speech most significant nouns are replaced by "thing." As a creature whose native element is war and dislocation, Harrison, like Markie in *To the North,* lacks feeling and morality—his desire for Stella is an egocentric attempt to experience what he has only seen.

The distance between an innocent Portia confronted by hostile sophistication and a sophisticated Stella confounded by primitivistic violence is not so great as it might seem. The terror of both situations is that they suddenly face the sensitive heroines with the incompatibility of events and their labels, of beliefs and their names. The words Stella must forget by acting upon them are both political and emotional: what is Robert as traitor? as lover? She cannot speak the nounless argot of Harrison, but her environment offers her no other language to counter it. She must always speak in a void, lacking even the physical surroundings that reinforce the "music of the familiar": in her blacked-out apartment where even darkness cannot enter, "the senses were cut off from hour and season; nothing spoke but the clock."

As Stella will admit only much later, her choice is complicated by the fact that Harrison's obscene proposal has a dark nihilistic appeal to it. His presence as a third at least provides a terrible pattern, making Stella and Robert "two of three," and the complete amorality of his request is attractive to that side of her that wills evil, that relishes violence. What she says of herself to Harrison could apply as well to Emma of "Summer Night":

> Between you and me, everything has been impossible from the first—so, the more unseemly the better, it seems to me. With you from the very beginning I've had no face: there's nothing to lose. There's an underside to me that I've hated, that you almost make me like: you and I never had anything but impossible conversations: nothing else is possible.
>
> (*HD,* 219–20)

An inarticulate surrender to dark gods is attractive insofar as its alternative is difficult. Harrison's knowingness (the complement of Stella's knowledge) can immediately reduce her sophistication to ignorance, so that she must assume the possibility of Robert's guilt by refusing to test Harrison's assertions. To cope with Harrison's terrifying absurdity, Stella must somehow expose the false language that threatens her and attempt to form from experience a limited private language that will at least break the silence of her isolation in the void of the perpetual present.

Stella's visit to Robert's family at Holme Dene is the beginning of her education. Though Jocelyn Brooke and Edward Sackville-West have claimed to find a similarity between Holme Dene and the Heccombs' Waikiki, it is clear that the houses represent almost antithetical attitudes. The vital vulgarity of Waikiki depends on its uneditedness, yet Holme Dene, in structure and emotion, encourages lies and deceit, spying around corners, and is a "man-eating house" where the dominated, now dead, father was given only a "fiction of dominance." The sign beside its entrance ambiguously warns "CAUTION: CONCEALED DRIVE," and the "drive" that is present in Robert's mother and his sister Ernestine is one turned inward. Mrs. Kelway, like Mme Fisher, projects her own false world through mind and will:

> If Ernie's regard had held unawareness, her mother's showed the mute presence of an obsession. For, why *should* she speak?—she had all she needed: the self-contained mystery of herself. Her lack of wish for communication showed in her contemptuous use of words. The lounge became what it was from being the repository of her nature; it was the indoors she selected, she consecrated—indeed, she had no reason to go out. By

> sitting where she sat, and by sometimes looking, by sometimes even not looking, across the furnished lawn, she projected Holme Dene: this was a bewitched wood. If her power came to an end at the white gate, so did the world. (*HD,* 104)

In such an atmosphere Robert's father, like Max Ebhart, the elder Mr. Quayne, and the absent father of the house in "Look At All Those Roses," had been driven to death by relentless feminine will, of which Robert himself is a projection. The photographs of himself that decorate his room he sees as the only identity he has been allowed. When Stella asks, "But what were you doing *then*—and *then*—and *then?* . . . Or at any rate, who was doing what you seem to have done?" Robert can only reply that the pictures represent "imitation moments" and are his criminal record. "Can you think of a better way of sending a person mad than nailing that pack of his own lies all round the room where he has to sleep?" The prevailing tone of Holme Dene, then, is one of pretense, sterility, and destructive rootlessness. The family can easily consider selling out and moving elsewhere because, as Robert says,

> Everything can be shifted, lock, stock and barrel. After all, everything was brought here from somewhere else, with the intention of being moved again —like touring scenery from theatre to theatre. Reassemble it anywhere: you get the same illusion. (*HD,* 116)

As even Robert realizes, only such an illusion, a mad hallucination, bad art, could support so easily the terrible power of the will of a Mrs. Kelway. Madness and depravity are passed off as legitimate fiction, because words disguise so effectively.

Though Stella's moorings have "dissolved behind her," she is at least conscious of what she is not, whereas the Kelways, with trappings of illusion, can convince themselves and act in terms of their own hallucinatory position:

> You could not account for this family headed by Mrs. Kelway by simply saying that it was middle class, because that left you asking, middle of what? She [Stella] saw the Kelways suspended in the middle of nothing. She could envisage them so suspended when there *was* nothing more. Always without a quiver as to their state. Their economy could not be plumbed: their effect was moral. (*HD,* 109)

The distinction between Stella and the Kelways, it should be emphasized, is not a snobbish one. The statement only implies that in the one case sane life, survival, is possible; in the other it becomes perversion. The point is made clearer by the scene in which Roderick has tea at a private nursing home with his cousin Nettie, who has been driven mad by her isolation in an Irish Big House. The ritual of tea accompanied by remembered manners, decorum, an orderly language, makes possible a conversation between the adolescent and the madwoman, while Stella finds social intercourse with the hallucinated but "sane" Kelways (or the intelligent, dislocated Harrison) virtually impossible.

Stella's discovery of a sense of obligation to her son Roderick, which follows the understanding of Robert she gains at Holme Dene, is her appreciation of someone who has a richer language than her own. Roderick's verbs can have future tenses. Although he most obviously participates in the war, he paradoxically feels he is least a part of the present. The home in Ireland he has inherited is a legacy from the past that simultaneously gives him a future, and Roderick's youth gives his mother a vicarious tie with past and future. When she visits Mt. Morris as Roderick's agent, it is to realize that although the house may be an illusion of innocence (which, artificially preserved, led to madness for Cousin Nettie), nevertheless there are possibilities for extension and order in the lives of others that her own lacks. Though she has difficulty finding single words, others are capable of books:

> That her own life could be a chapter missing from this book need not mean that the story was at an end; at a pause it was, but perhaps a pause for the turning-point? There was still to be seen what came of Cousin Francis's egotistic creative boldness with regard to the future, of his requisitioning for that purpose of Roderick. A man of faith has always a son somewhere. (*HD,* 167–68)

Although Stella's discovery at Mt. Morris encourages her to confront Robert with Harrison's allegations, when she receives a hurt denial yet is told by Harrison that Robert's actions have altered enough to tell him she has told Robert, she knows she has not resolved the dilemma of guilt and love. Both words have retained their incompatible validity, and her passive surrender to Harrison's Mephistophelean proposition is celebrated in a temple of meaninglessness, an underground café identified only by a sign saying OPEN:

> She stared first at a row of backviews of eaters perched, packed elbow-to-elbow, along a counter. A zip fastener all the way down one back made one woman seem to have a tin spine. A dye-green lettuce leaf had fallen on to the mottled rubber floor; a man in a pin-stripe suit was enough in profile to show a smudge of face powder on one shoulder . . . Not a person did not betray, by one or another glaring peculiarity, the fact of being human: her intimidating sensation of being crowded must have been due to this, for there were not so very many people here. The phenomenon was the lighting, more powerful even than could be accounted for by the bald white globes screwed aching to the low white ceiling—there survived in here not one shadow: every one had been ferreted out and killed. (*HD,* 216–17)

As a descent into hell, the scene has had its prototypes in several of the other novels—the near-crash in *The Hotel,* the visit to the old mill in

The Last September. The epic motif is emphasized when, in this limbo of lost souls, Stella and Harrison meet Louie, the factory girl whose story forms a subplot in the novel. Living alone and working in London while her husband is with the army in India, the inarticulate Louie has spent her spare time picking up soldiers because she hopes to recapture vicariously the meaning her husband's absence has taken from her life by engaging in the only significant human relation in which communication without words is possible. Harrison's earlier rejection of her (with the warning that he may be "funny") now motivates Louie's exposure of Stella's weakness in associating with Harrison when she "should have had other chances."

The alliance between Louie and Stella is largely unspoken, but it is effective. Though Stella later tells Robert that Harrison rejected her, this scene suggests that she has made his rejection of her inevitable. She has waited until after she has told Robert, so Harrison's power to save is no longer operative; by joining Louie she has exposed Harrison as "funny"; her surrender has been without volition or motive. As she tells Louie, it is an inexpressible gesture asserting the values of humanity against purely mental plotting:

> "Nothing ever works out the way one hoped, and to know how bitter that is one must be a worker-out—you and I are not. This evening was to have been a celebration, the first of many more evenings. It may still be the first of many more evenings, but what will they be worth? This is the truth," she said, looking round her at all the other people apprehensively staring into each other's faces. "He cannot bear it; let's hope he will forget it—let's hope that; it is the least we can do; we're all three human. At any time it may be your hour or mine—you or I may be learning some terrible human lesson which is to undo everything we had thought we had. It's that, not death, that we ought to live prepared for." (*HD,* 231–32)

In the moral recognition between Stella and Louie, both are temporarily rescued. Louie begins to think her infidelities to her husband are wrong and chooses Stella as an ideal of virtue, though she sees her as a "soul astray." And Stella has become a soul astray, of course, by freeing herself from Harrison's domination without finding some new attachment. But unlike Sydney in *The Hotel,* she is not therefore open to all comers. When she later confronts Robert with her proof of his treason, she attempts to free herself from him as well. In his explanation of his actions are compounded Stella's dilemma and his alternative to it: he explains that his spying has been motivated by disillusion rather than a desire for money or a belief in Nazism. Both "country" and "freedom" are "dead language" to him; he can believe only in strength and law, whatever its source:

I was born wounded; my father's son. Dunkirk was waiting there in us—what a race! A class without a middle, a race without a country. Unwhole. Never earthed in—and there are thousands of thousands of us, and we're still breeding—breeding what? You may ask: I ask. Not only nothing to hold, nothing to touch. No source of anything in anything. I could have loved a country, but to love you must have—you have been my country. But you've been too much because you are not enough—are you and I to be what we've known we are for nothing, nothing outside this room? (*HD*, 263–64)

But as Stella recognizes, Robert's treachery is in effect a perversion of the romantic will, a falsely chosen illusion, an inadequate response to the failure of language: "twisted inspiration, a sort of recalcitrance in the energy, romanticism fired once too often."

In the novel's denouement, Miss Bowen undertakes a demonstration that something does exist "outside the room," that the political, intellectual, even biological questions with which she has been concerned can be resolved. Ironically Stella's attainment of precarious freedom leads Louie to license. Reading the newspaper accounts of Robert's suicide and inferring from them his affair with Stella, she returns to her promiscuous habits because

Virtue became less possible now it was shown impossible by Stella, less to be desired because Stella had not desired it enough. Why Louie should have attached her own floating wish to a face watched for an hour cannot be said: there must be faces which attract aspiration just as others focus sensuous dreams—what else had happened originally in the case of Harrison? Louie had felt herself to be in a presence. For her, therefore, now it was Stella who had fallen into the street. (*HD*, 295)

But when the birth of Louie's baby takes place (in the last section of the novel) two years after the autumn of 1942 in which Robert is killed, it is clear that the fate of the characters has, more or less, paralleled the course of the war. Montgomery's breakthrough in North Africa coincided with Stella's vision of innocence at Mt. Morris, and the opening of the second front, which assures military victory, accompanies the delineation of the characters' futures. Although Stella is to marry the "cousin of a cousin" she stays in her apartment exposed to the missiles because "prospects have alternatives": death or an indifferent marriage are equally desirable futures to one who has finally rejected meaning. For Roderick at Mt. Morris the future is to be quite different. There he can acknowledge the legacy left him by his three fathers—"the defeated Victor, the determining Cousin Francis, the unadmitted stepfather Robert"—and recognize with chagrin that he and his mother should have amounted to something more as a result of the "unapprehendable inner wills of the dead."

The continuum of past and present into the future, that Stella fails to find and that Roderick imagines, is realized on a lower level (socially and morally) by Louie. With the baby she returns to Seale-on-Sea and the bombed-out ruins of her parents' home. In the absence of "meaning," nature boldly asserts itself as a value:

> Just after six o'clock in the evening, Louie wheeled the perambulator some way out of the town, along the canal path, towards the marsh. Reeds grew out into the still water; ahead, there was distance as far as the eye could see—a thoughtless extension of her now complete life. Across the canal the hills rose, bare, above the other bank's reflected oak trees. No other soul passed; not a sheep, even, was cropping anywhere nearby. A minute or two ago our homecoming bombers, invisibly high up, had droned over: the baby had not stirred—every day she saw him growing more like Tom. But now there began another sound—she turned and looked up into the air behind her. She gathered Tom quickly out of the pram and held him up, hoping he too might see, and perhaps remember. Three swans were flying a straight flight. They passed overhead, disappearing in the direction of the west. (*HD,* 319)

In this last paragraph of the novel, as in *The Death of the Heart,* the unpredictable future of the young and the predictable future of cyclical nature are brought into harmony. The symbolic swans flying west point up, of course, an absolute that is superior to human material illusions, bombed out of existence in man-made London, and the fragile moral code Louie found herself too weak to follow. Like the "arbitrary vulgar fate lines" of ivy in "Ivy Gripped the Steps," nature attempts a repossession where human will has failed. Even Robert's "crime," as Stella saw it, had been partly a denial of a nature as dominant (if not as affirmative) as Wordsworth's:

> He might have been right in saying she could not have loved him had there been in him no capacity other than love, but his denials of everything instinctive seemed now to seal up love at the source. Rolled round with rocks and stones and trees—what else is one?—was this not felt most strongly in the quietus of the embrace? (*HD,* 265)

But as in Miss Bowen's other novels, the most positive solution is found only by the least complex characters, too naïve to know alternatives to "everything instinctive."

Although *The Heat of the Day* is more dependent on incident and melodrama than the other novels, it is, not less than they, thematic. The Faust motif, suggested by the encounters between St. Quentin and Portia in *The Death of the Heart,* is echoed when Harrison, like St. Quentin, first meets his quarry in a graveyard: "Stella's first view of him, glancing back, had been of someone stepping cranelike over the graves." Moreover, Harrison and Robert, both fighting for the possession of Stella's soul, are merely aspects of the same force: both regard morals as illusions and deny their validity as feelings. Louie at first assumes it is Harrison who has fallen from the roof, and Harrison has sympathy for Robert because they are alike. Stella explicitly recognizes the similarity shortly before Robert kills himself: "It seemed to her it was Robert who was Harrison." Both, it is finally revealed, have the same Christian name, and at Mt. Morris Harrison is remembered as "Robertson." As Vernon Young, reviewing the novel for the *Hudson Review,* pointed out, "The circumstantial subject of Miss Bowen's novel is the dilemma of Mrs. Rodney, exposed between a love dedicated to the destruction of her environment and a love that would save her environment by violating her personality." [4] Both Harrison and Robert, as Stella finally sees, are the destroyers: of law, of morality, of personality. But neither, of course, is wholly and separately evil. Harrison manages to accomplish good though willing evil when he takes Stella to the underworld, and Robert, as Roderick realizes, "must have been pretty brave." The fact that they cannot be finally distinguished, even by name, is Miss Bowen's bitterest comment on the moral chaos she explores.

By such means, the relatively static situation of "Summer Night" is given motion in *The Heat of the Day*. In a city at war, without a past (most of its usual inhabitants have left), without a predictable future, without even an "elsewhere" to provide escape from "the enemy within," only the values of force are operative. Insofar as any one of the characters "thinks" in Justin Cavey's sense, or puts trust either in the "towers of Europe" or his own identity, he is vulnerable. To object that Robert's Nazism is unmotivated is to introduce a new set of irrelevant terms. The attraction of fascism in this novel is that it offers to the weak the double satisfaction of a group identity with strength and an escape from the dangers and struggles of trying to sustain a personal identity. Robert's Nazism is as believable as Harrison's crookedness, though Harrison's way is easier because he has no identity which he must either preserve or escape. As he tells Stella, war is "a time when I'm not a crook." But Robert, more sensitive and more complex, has neither time nor place in which he can be at home. It is in this sense that Robert tells Stella that she alone, as his mistress, has been his country.

Set between the innocent (e.g., Roderick and Hannah) and those capable only of a single-minded evil (e.g., Mrs. Kelway and Ernestine), Stella, Robert, Louie, and Harrison try to find meaning in a world where they are creatures of circumstance, moving in shoals. Harrison, for example, eats "pretty much what there is where I am, according of course a certain amount to when." And Stella and Robert, though they are in love, cannot separate themselves from the world in which they are creatures of history, whose coming together was of a nature possible in no other day—the day was inherent in the nature. Which must have been always true of lovers, if it had taken till now to be seen. . . . Could these two have loved each other better at a better time? At no other would they have been themselves; what had carried their world to its hour was in their bloodstreams. . . . In dwelling upon the constant for our reassurance, we forget that the loves in history have been agonizingly modern loves in their day. War at present worked as a thinning of the membrance between the this and the that, it was a becoming apparent—but then what else is love? (*HD*, 187–88)

It is partly as love, then, that war enters this novel as a force and elevates its concerns beyond the topical to the "enormously comprehensive." The Shakespearean theme of love and war (as in *Antony and Cleopatra, Troilus and Cressida, Coriolanus*) was the basis of *The Last September* as well, but the war in Ireland, like the one outside Troy, was presented as an apathetic, mythical one. However, the second world war, in this novel, threatens not only the individual's life but his integrity; "dry cerebration" attacks the heart. Some time after Harrison has made his proposition, and the reader has watched Stella gradually compromise by talking to him, she makes just this distinction.

To her, tonight, "outside" meant the harmless world: the mischief was in her own and in other rooms. The grind and scream of battles, mechanized advances excoriating flesh and country, tearing through nerves and tearing up trees, were indoor-plotted; this was a war of dry cerebration inside windowless walls. No act was not part of some calculation; spontaneity was in tatters; from the point of view of nothing more than the heart any action was enemy action now. (*HD*, 136)

By talking of language in attempting to account for the action of this novel, I have merely extended a metaphor Miss Bowen has used implicitly to inform the whole. Looking at "real events" as a novelist, seeing the war as the tattered remnants of stories made about it, she finds a triumph of bad art. Indeed, when words take over completely, the art that depends on its distinctness from the life it orders is denied. Destructive action, she suggests repeatedly, is the implementation of a belief in easy language, and even the innocent Roderick knows that ". . . conversations are the leading thing in this war! . . . Everything you [Stella] and I have to do is the result of something that's been said." And Stella herself lives "at the edge of a clique of war, knowing who should know what, commanding a sort of language in which nothing need be ever exactly said." Although Louie is inarticulate, her contact with war is also made through language. Until her dictatorial friend Connie forces her to read newspapers, Louie has no "ideas," but "after a week or two on the diet [Louie] discovered that she *had* got a point of view, and not only *a* point of view but the right one." Her weakness is that as a kind of universal reader, any words define her:

> Dark and rare were the days when she failed to find on the inside page of her paper an address to or else account of herself. Was she not a worker, a soldier's lonely wife, a war orphan, a pedestrian, a Londoner, a home and animal-lover, a thinking democrat, a movie-goer, a woman of Britain, a letter-writer, a fuel-saver, and a housewife? She was only not a mother, a knitter, a gardener, a foot-sufferer or a sweetheart—at least not rightly. Louie now felt bad only about any part of herself which in any way did not fit into the papers' picture; she could not have survived their disapproval. They did not, for instance, leave flighty wives or good-time girls a leg to stand on; and how rightly—she had romped through a dozen pieces on that subject with if anything rather special zest, and was midway through just one more when the blast struck cold. Could it be the papers were out with *Louie?*—she came over gooseflesh, confronted by God and Tom.
>
> (*HD,* 146)

Louie loves newspapers because they give her a ready-made identity and a preformed means of ordering experience; but when such a medium is absent, as it is when she meets Stella, Louie finds it impossible to organize experience, to connect concrete feelings and abstract ideas. When she attempts to tell Connie about Stella, language fails her:

> It's the taking and taking up of me on the part of everyone when I have no words. Often you say the advantage I should be at if I could speak grammar; but it's not only that. Look the trouble there is when I have to only say what I *can* say, and so cannot ever say what is really. Inside me it's like being crowded to death—more and more of it all getting into me. I could more bear it if I could only say. (*HD,* 237)

Louie's inability to express her reaction to the experience in which she is immersed; Robert's inability to feel anything, including danger, except as an abstraction; and Harrison's "out-of-the-straight" eyes ("black little condensations of a world too internal to know what expression was"), are all symptomatic of a world where language dominates yet communication is impossible. Between the abstract war conducted by conversations and the concrete private world of the individual falls the fatal separation. Some can, of course, retreat to the private subjectivity of the madhouse to live in a happy perpetual present as Cousin Nettie does, or escape from England to Ireland where tradition and social order seem to extend the present backward into the past, forward into the future. But only the very simple, like Louie, can find happiness in England and the cycle of nature. For the others, who are too decidedly the sophisticated products of their civilization to find escape by these methods, the alternatives are less promising. Robert, whose devotion to absolute abstract power fails him, chooses death; Harrison, like Eddie in *The Death of the Heart,* chooses anonymity and discontinuity but will never be loved; Stella resigns her will to act and to live.

"Communication" is central to both the theme and the aesthetic of *The Heat of the Day.* Each character tries to connect his private anguish with the public disaster, the romantic will with external circumstance, in a meaningful way. And Miss Bowen herself, who acted as an air raid warden in London while defending the neutrality of Eire in the *New Statesman and Nation,*[5] used the public prose of her novel to try to communicate and define her own private and complex response to the war years. The novel discusses the methods by which individuals connect prose and passion and is itself a vehicle for connecting private "passion" and public "prose."

In discussing communication, and in pointing out the necessity for finding a rational or metaphorical connection between public London and personal identity, Miss Bowen often echoes E. M. Forster in *Howards End;* but the distance between their final attitudes can suggest a great deal about the forty-year period that separates the two novels. Although Forster's 1910 London is not threatened by external disaster, it does symbolize an impersonal, almost antipersonal flux that "one visualizes . . . as a tract of quivering grey, intelligent without purpose, and excitable without love; as a spirit that has altered before it can be chronicled; as a heart that certainly beats, but with no pulsation of humanity." [6] When Miss Bowen describes the London of September 1940 in *The Heat of the Day* similar notes are struck (see, for example, pp. 85–86). Both novels, of course, treat the city as a dynamic force, organic, capable of change. Forster's London could be "religion's opportunity"; Miss Bowen's London, to which religion is irrelevant, changes from a positive to a negative organic force by the autumn of 1942 when "faith came down to a slogan" and "you breathed in all that was most malarial."

In *Howards End* the impersonal force of flux is opposed by the microcosmic private life of the individual, the illimitable romantic will confined by circumstance. This disparity between public and private life, as Margaret Schlegel sees it, emphasizes the inadequacy of language, for

> . . . in public who shall express the unseen adequately? It is the private life that holds out the mirror to infinity; personal intercourse, and that alone, that ever hints at a personality beyond our daily vision.[7]

Especially in Margaret's romantic sister Helen the private life fights for recognition. Like Karen of *The House in Paris* or Emmeline in *To the North* she was "over-interested in the subconscious self. She exaggerated the Punch and Judy aspect of life, and spoke of mankind as puppets whom an invisible showman twitches into love and war." Helen's affair with Leonard Bast, like Karen's with Max and Emmeline's with Markie, involves a rejection of society's restrictions on sexual behavior that removes her from her sister's comprehension because "morality can tell us that murder is worse than stealing, and group most sins in an order all must approve, but it cannot group Helen."

The spirit of compromise, the "coming to terms" with environment that Helen rejects and Margaret (like Cecilia in *To the North*) more realistically accepts, is implicit in Margaret's marriage to Henry Wilcox, a commitment to a future determined by prose rather than romance. The Wilcoxes, to be sure, are inadequate; but unlike Robinson in "Summer Night" or Harrison in *The Heat of the Day,* they are vaguely aware of the identities they lack, so that Charles can wish "that something had been different somewhere . . . that he had been taught to say 'I' in his youth." Though the strength the Wilcoxes represent has been necessary to the building of England, their abstractness, their denial of personal responsibility (like the Nazism Robert adopts) is now a threat to England. Helen's explanation virtually defines the Kelways:

> There's a nightmare of a theory that says a special race is being born which will rule the rest of us in the future just because it lacks the little thing that says 'I'. . . . That there are two kinds of people—our kind, who live straight from the middle of their heads, and the other kind who can't, because their heads have no middle. They can't say 'I'. They *aren't* in fact, so they're supermen. Pierpont Morgan has never said 'I' in his life.[8]

As in *The Heat of the Day,* the answer to the dilemma is not innocence, as Margaret recognizes, nor extreme subjectivity, for "we recognize that emotion is not enough, and that men and women are personalities capable of sustained relations, not mere opportunities for an electrical discharge." The ideal is the third force that connects the poles. Margaret's attempt is in the right direction, but is an action impossible in the world of *The Heat of the Day:*

> . . . the building of the rainbow bridge that should connect the prose in us with the passion. Without it we are meaningless fragments, half monks, half beasts, unconnected arches that have never joined into a man. With it love is born, and alights on the highest curve, glowing against the grey, sober against the fire.
>
> . . . .
>
> Only connect! That was the whole of her sermon. Only connect the prose and the passion, and both will be exalted, and human love will be seen at its height. Live in fragments no longer. Only connect, and the beast and the monk, robbed of the isolation that is life to either, will die.[9]

Since Wilcox, of course, is not sufficiently freed from his isolation of pure action, the ideal is one that can be realized only in the future. Margaret's possession of Howards End, symbolic of England, is only a trust for Helen's illegitimate son. Lionel Trilling, whose thorough discussion of the novel makes further treatment of it here superfluous, suggests that *Howards End* has a Faustian theme, that the child is the Euphorion.[10] Like Louie's illegitimate child, he is held forth as the hope of England.

I have, of course, strongly emphasized the parallels between *The Heat of the Day* and *Howards End,* and I have ignored much of Forster's novel—especially his treatment of the class struggle. Nevertheless both novels, in analyzing the status of English civilization at two separate but important periods in modern intellectual history, ascribe the failure of the romantic will to the same basic source. Since the status of public life must be accepted as a necessary condition, whether it be manifested in evolutionary flux or violent war, the solution lies in the individual. The "connection" that the individual must make, moreover, is based on awareness: by living "straight from the middle of their heads," accepting both the romantic passion and the necessary prose, acknowledging the inseparability of good and evil, individuals presumably can find a *modus vivendi.* Roderick can "connect" past and present; the child of Helen Schlegel and Leonard Bast quite literally unites opposing forces. *The Heat of the Day,* far from denying the argument of *The Death of the Heart* that we live by an illusion that is art, reaffirms that position in an even more chaotic world. In the tradition of the novel, both Forster and Miss Bowen have reëxamined the lesson of "awareness" suggested by Jane Austen and Henry James, applying it to life in a modern and physically threatening London.

While the "solutions" presented by these novels have become far more complex with the passage of time, they have, as well, become less assured. Fanny Price, of course, can live happily ever after in the undeniable future, and even Isabel Archer acts positively, decisively, autonomously in choosing to return to Osmond. For the Schlegel sisters, a symbolic equilibrium is attainable, apparently, in the next generation; and Margaret, by accepting her sister, can perform a consequential action, a choice seen as "right" according to the moral assumptions of the novel. However, even though Stella Rodney has a choice that is melodramatic in explicitness, and even though she discovers and accepts a duty toward her son, her future has no direction. Neither she nor her creator has language adequate to deal with the future the novel has made inevitable. Far from conquering herself or others, Stella becomes increasingly aware of the impossibility of anyone in her generation accomplishing anything through the will. An almost Calvinistic sense of predestination forces her to sit back and watch the meek, the innocent, and the simple inherit the earth. Because a distinction between Robert and Harrison is finally impossible, there can be no question of "connecting" the prose and passion. The absolutes in *Howards End* implied by the metaphor of the rainbow bridge are qualified by Forster's irony, but for Miss Bowen "here" and "there" do not exist as separable points. The neat halves on which Forster depends have become a blurred, formless Now. In fact, the solution suggested by the concluding section of *The Heat of the Day* is deceptive: Stella's pointless future is rather ignored in the optimism applied to Louie and the swans. Once the reader's attention is turned to nature, the novelist has begged the question, since whatever pattern is found there clearly has little relevance to Stella Rodney as a passive creature subject to a society that is organic only in the metaphors Miss Bowen uses to describe it. Only here perhaps does she fail to be "enormously comprehensive," for to comprehend is finally to include these diverse worlds within a world of art, giving them a relationship that is more than rhetorical. Arnold, in "A Summer Night" and "Dover Beach," achieved some sort of artistic order by including love and man in the same vocabulary as the incomprehensible heavens, in the same metaphor of battle. But that was at another time, and his civilization, for Miss Bowen at least, is dead.

It is tempting to locate that death in the forty years between *Howards End* and *The Heat of the Day*. The tone of Forster's novel certainly is admonitive, almost didactic and political. Yet the image of Stella Rodney passively exposing herself to death in her London apartment is nearly a dramatization of what George Orwell defines as quietism, the only honest political attitude he will allow a writer of the forties. The serious writer, he says, is a liberal, and the destruction of liberalism in the modern world leaves him without a language:

> It seems likely, therefore, that in the remaining years of free speech any novel worth reading will follow more or less along the lines that [Henry] Miller has followed—I do not mean in technique or subject matter, but in implied outlook. The passive attitude will come back, and it will be more consciously passive than before. Progress and reaction have both turned out to be swindles. Seemingly there is nothing left but quietism—robbing reality of its terrors by simply submitting to it. Get inside the whale—or rather, admit you are inside the whale (for you *are,* of course). Give yourself over to the world-process, stop fighting against it or pretending that you control it; simply accept it, endure it, record it. That seems to be the formula that any sensitive novelist is now likely to adopt. A novel on more positive, "constructive" lines, and not emotionally spurious, is at present very difficult to imagine.[11]

Orwell's prediction (and prescription) of 1940 seems valid for most serious English novelists. At least the tendency toward increasing topicality in Miss Bowen's novels came to an end with *The Heat of the Day.*

Between 1931 and 1949 all of her novels, with the exception of *The House in Paris,* were set in England, and the London of *To the North, The Death of the Heart,* and *The Heat of the Day* is geographically specific. However, the bulk of Miss Bowen's postwar work (one novel, one play, several short stories) has been set in Ireland. Such a shift in subject matter and setting is not easy to account for. But even though writers, like other individuals, respond to an infinitely complex combination of internal and external stimuli and are not merely the products of the few trends and "influences" that can be documented, certain general directions in the mass of contemporary literature are charted by Orwell's statement. Disillusionment with sociology and politics has accompanied a preference, especially in England, for the less "realistic." Although no single word indicates the direction taken by Apocalyptics and New Romantics in poetry, or the work of Rex Warner, William Sansom, P. H. Newby, Ivy Compton-Burnett, V. S. Pritchett, Iris Murdoch, and Henry Green in prose fiction, it is clear that the years since 1939 produced, or forced into prominence, many writers whose attitude merges realism and fantasy. In the work of many of these novelists, the settings and "assumptions about life" are realistic, the action fantastic. Both Newby's *The Retreat* (1953) and Henry Green's *Caught* (1943), for example, ostensibly deal with the second world war; yet in both novels the immediate aspects of war—bombs and battles—are replaced by hallucination and near madness. In *Caught* (which deals with London in exactly the same months as *The Heat of the Day*) incest and other sexual aberrations become more important to London firemen than the less symbolic fires they are called upon to cope with. In Newby's novel, the protagonist is involved in a love affair with an almost illusory woman for reasons unclear to himself; the landscape is permeated with the odor of a vixen in heat. Such distortions of realism, often subtle, combined with an ironic tone, characterize many English attempts to deal with the more extensive distortion of the "everyday" that war and its after-effects bring about.

Although a trend is so vague a concept that it is almost useless, by returning from all English literature to the works of Miss Bowen this tendency can be illustrated if not explained. Unlike many of the other writers mentioned here, she moves geographically as well as psychologically in her increasing concern with the subject of illusion until, in *A World of Love,* the theme of illusion is set in an illusory landscape, with only a practicality of tone saving the novel's world from complete unreality.

One brief attempt at complete objectification, and Miss Bowen's only venture into drama (with John Perry as co-author), anticipated *A World of Love.* Although *Castle Anna* uses Ireland exclusively as its setting, and in several other ways served as a preliminary exercise for *A World of Love,* it gave Miss Bowen the least appropriate form for what then seems to have concerned her.[12] The play is as simple and forthright in its presentation of a problem as *The Hotel* was. The first act, dramatizing the battle between the practical will and the heart for possession of a son and a country house, takes place at the turn of the century and defines the area of conflict: Castle Anna, a house in the south of Ireland inhabited by its owner, Richard Castlevance, his English bride Cecilia, and his unmarried sister Teresa. Richard, who does not appear, is killed in an accident, leaving the house in entail to his as yet unborn son John, with the provision that Cecilia may live at Castle Anna and act as John's guardian as long as she does not remarry. Otherwise, possession and guardianship pass to Teresa.

The will, it becomes clear, has been written under the influence of Teresa, who is jealous of Cecilia, covetous of Castle Anna, and aware that Cecilia and Nicholas Bell, the "stormy-petrel" heir of neighboring, decaying, Bell Grove, are attracted to one another. The second act, which takes place twenty years after Richard's death, brings the latent conflict to the surface. John, returning from the first world war to receive his inheritance, enters a Castle Anna which has passed to Teresa (since Cecilia has just married Nicholas). As Teresa has planned it, the future is secure: she and John will live at Castle Anna, his mother and Nicholas at Bell Grove. However, several factors prevent the realization of Teresa's will. Cecilia for twenty years has accepted Nicholas as lover rather than husband simply to keep John and Castle Anna; and although Teresa has blackmailed Cecilia into marrying Nicholas by threatening to expose them to John, Cecilia still is determined not to relinquish her claim on John as a mother. Furthermore, John has returned from the army with a will of his own, and undecided whether to remain at Castle Anna or become manager of a London garage because ". . . having come through the War . . . makes you expect . . . to cut some ice in the world," he bases his final decision on his evaluation of Teresa and Cecilia.

The third act is the series of revelations that force John's decision. Teresa, learning that Nicholas in operating Castle Anna has used its profits for Bell Grove and that John intends to write off Nicholas' misappropriation as salary, breaks her promise to Cecilia and reveals to John the nature of his mother's twenty-year affair with Nicholas. Forced to choose between a mother who has disregarded conventional morality to preserve her own heart and protect his interests, and Teresa, who has used him as a tool of her possessive will, John chooses his mother and accepts his duty as heir. He banishes Teresa and decides to remain in the house alone because

> It's easy to like things the way they ought to be. It's easy to love people—the way one imagines them. But to cope with things as they *are,* to take people as they *really* are—I suppose that's what one's put here to learn to do? I suppose, to be able to do that *is* living?

But as Bridget the maid tells John, "Still, in the end of it all, it's for the heart that you'd love her [Cecilia]—the sweet, good heart. Yes, the heart's the thing you can't imitate—though there be many who'd like to try."

Bridget's defense of the heart is familiar enough, and the play's relationship to the novel that preceded it clear. John Castlevance repeats Roderick's actions, preserving the tradition of his inheritance in an isolated society by ignoring the temptation of more material prospects in London. But the time is not the present, and Ireland in the play has few connections with England. Any danger of "constructive" suggestions has been eliminated, for John, like Jane Danby of *A World of Love,* is the victim of another *person's* will to power, which he must reject in terms equally personal. Teresa, at the end of the second act, winds a home-knit scarf around John's neck as she sings him to sleep; Cecilia, at the end of the third act, proudly allows John, as host, to pour out her tea.

The simultaneous presentation of inner states of mind and the external expression of them that Miss Bowen's complex narrator in *The Heat of the Day* made possible was, of course, missing in the play. But if an unsuccessful development toward objectivity can be seen by regarding *Castle Anna* as a product of one aspect of her art in the novel that preceded it, an even clearer case for a concern with hallucination and fantasy can be made by linking *A World of Love* with "Summer Night" through *The Demon Lover* stories. Perhaps it is misleading to see "Summer Night" as the seminal work from which so much of Miss Bowen's postwar writing grew, but it does illustrate several of the directions her writing took. In Justin's deaf sister Queenie the isolated, hallucinated mind is first seen as a symptom of wartime dislocation. In *The Demon Lover* the most complex story, "The Happy Autumn Fields," defines memory not as an individual's recollection of his own past but as a projection by which a woman enters a past explicitly not her own. Vignettes of a Victorian family are alternated with scenes presenting a woman waking and sleeping in the bomb-damaged London flat she is about to leave. Since the story begins directly with the Victorian family, the reader, like the dreamer, assumes the dream to be the reality. Only in its manner of presentation is artificiality suggested: the Victorian family, walking in the autumn fields, is subtly presented as a series of tableaux. The progress through the fields, led by the father, is orderly until two of the daughters, breaking off from the group to walk with the lover of one of them, form a new tableau. In the final and most explicitly artificial scene of the first section—when the family comes to rejoin Henrietta, Sarah, and Eugene —the reader hears a narrator who has assumed the role of museum guide and travelogue commentator:

> We surmount the skyline: the family come into our view, we into theirs. They are halted, waiting, on the decline to the quarry. The handsome statufied group in strong yellow sunshine, aligned by Papa and crowned by Fitzgeorge, turn their judging eyes on the laggards, waiting to close their ranks round Henrietta and Sarah and Eugene. (*DL,* 114)

Most of the dream is presented from Sarah's point of view, but the dreamer who has assumed her identity is revealed to be Mary, who wakens suddenly in modern London to hear "someone . . . playing Tchaikowsky badly in a room without windows and doors" and to see her lover, "a man she knew to be 'Travis' but failed to focus. . . ." Freeing herself from Travis' demand that she move before the house collapses, Mary gains two hours from him in which to return from "the unreality of this room" and from "the story . . . which like a book once read she remembered clearly but with indifference," to the arranged reality of the dream. When the transition, aided by the box of letters she has discovered, is effected, she escapes again to the past and to a new tableau. In the first dream she, as Sarah, was divided between a passionate attachment to her sister and a more conventional love for Eugene. The second dream brings the family from the fields to the drawingroom, and the landscape with figures becomes a Victorian group portrait. In the dark red shadows of the sunset Eugene leans against the white marble mantelpiece and "she [Sarah] looked at him as though he, transfigured by the strange light, were indeed a picture, a picture who could not see her."

Sarah's dilemma reflects that of Mary in the present: "How could she put into words the feeling of dislocation, the formless dread that had been with her since she found herself in the drawingroom? The source of both had been what she must call her dream." When the second dream ends with Eugene's departure (he still has not formally proposed) her problem remains unsolved. At the end of the first section she had failed to speak the word of comfort that would save the doting Henrietta; at the end of the second she "could not speak" after Henrietta, in the presence of the family, demanded that she tell Eugene that "whatever tries to come between me and Sarah becomes nothing!"

When Mary wakens from the second dream to find she has survived the falling of her ceiling, "the one way back to the fields was barred. . . . Sarah was right in doubting that there would be tomorrow: Eugene, Henrietta were lost in time to the woman weeping there on the bed, no longer reckoning who she was" (*DL,* 127). As she tells Travis when he comes to take her away, these excursions into the past have been the only way she can know feeling, because in the present "all we can do is imitate love or sorrow." The only pattern possible is the dream; its alternative is a loss of identity:

> She continued: "What has happened is cruel: I am left with a fragment torn out of a day, a day I don't even know where or when; and now how am I to help laying that like a pattern against the poor stuff of everything else?—Alternatively, I am a person drained by a dream. I cannot forget the climate of those hours. Or life at that pitch, eventful—not happy, no, but strung like a harp." (*DL,* 127–28)

Travis, who has taken the letters away to read them, tells Mary that her illusion of being related to Sarah is false: both Sarah and Henrietta apparently died young and unmarried while Fitzgeorge in a letter refers to "some friend of their youth [Eugene] who was thrown from his horse and killed, riding back after a visit to their home. . . . Fitzgeorge wonders, and says he will always wonder, what made the horse shy in those empty fields."

The story, in spite of its brevity, is most revealing. Like "Ivy Gripped the Steps" it renders an individual's attempt to establish his identity in a patternless present, for Mary's dreams are Miss Bowen's most explicit portrayals of the "saving hallucinations" she mentions in her postscript. But even in the art of the dream events resist a pattern, and it is not so much the lack of blood relationship as her knowledge of the unexpected death of Sarah's lover that destroys Mary's illusion. The story suggests that the aberration of feeling (Henrietta and Sarah) and its accompanying private anguish are as destructive in the order of the Victorian world as the public disaster of a dropped bomb would be in the more fragile present.

The juxtaposition of historical periods tends to extend the meaning of "The Happy Autumn Fields." As in the Tennyson poem to which the title alludes ("Oh, Death in life, the days that are no more"), the past in the story is at first idyllic, finally destructive. Mary's search for identity, like Quentin Compson's (his "very body was an empty hall echoing with sonorous defeated names," a "commonwealth" rather than an "entity"), confuses hallucination and history, so that the life of enhanced possibilities she creates merely increases her anguish. Quentin's active investment in the past, bringing to life "from that forgotten chest

. . . the words, the symbols, the shapes themselves, shadowy inscrutable and serene, against that turgid background of a horrible and bloody mischancing of human affairs," does not save him from its chaos or help him to define his own in the present. When the words, symbols, and shapes become, in Faulkner's words, more than "the conventional family group of the period, with formal and lifeless decorum," they become part of a story he can neither tell nor live. Though it would be misleading to compare Miss Bowen's vision in this story with Faulkner's in *The Sound and the Fury* and *Absalom, Absalom!* (her imagination is both surer and more limited), the writers share, for this moment at least, a common concern with the distorted mind's futile attempt to allay present anguish with a past soothed by narrative.

The reader who turns to *Bowen's Court* with this story in mind is apt to see a biographical connection. In her history Miss Bowen quotes at length from the Bowen family diary for 1876, written by the children Sarah, Annie, Mary, and Charles Bowen. The Victorian family and its occupations, even Sarah's style, suggest the dream of Mary in "The Happy Autumn Fields." And Miss Bowen makes clear in her "Afterword" that the Bowen's Court of the past has been a sustaining illusion of peace to her as she writes the second half of its history in London when she "returned to [it] on curious mornings when the smoke and smell of raids still hung in the air." But unlike the Mary of her story, she emphasizes that such illusions must be used with caution, that "the scene [from the steps of Bowen's Court] is a crystal in which, while one is looking, a shadow forms." Though both the fictional Mary and her creator have "the experience of living more than my own life," the "bits of self" the photographs and diaries represent are allowed to become the sole agents of destiny only by the mind that dreams or the mind that goes mad. The distinction between fiction and reality, mad illusion and saving hallucination, implicit in the style of the story, is easily made by introducing scenes without giving the reader a temporal position, and suggests that the dreams of the past are the reality for the troubled Mary. Yet the deliberately pictorial quality of those scenes (as tableaux) reminds the reader that the events of the past, objectively and sanely considered, are art, not nature.

The story's distinctions are easily made, of course, because the narrator moves abruptly from surveying the landscape of Mary's dream to another position, outside Mary, with Travis, where, like Travis, he can comment definitively on the "meaning" of the hallucination. The two narrative positions, indeed, are so distinct that it would be more accurate to say that hallucination and reality are "yoked by violence together," that the story has in effect two separable narrators.

In *The Heat of the Day,* to be sure, there are "hallucinated" characters, but their interior landscapes are presented by a narrator whose basic position is clearly in a saner world. The strangeness of *A World of Love* is that much of the material of *Castle Anna* (which, as a conventional play, can present *only* exterior events) is recast, reordered by a narrator who sees several interior landscapes and categorizes *no* landscape as real. The novel helps to indicate where the "rising tide of hallucination" Miss Bowen saw in her wartime fiction was heading, and how desperate a narrative position this "tide" made necessary.

The rather simple "problem" set up in *Castle Anna* is made considerably more complex and subtle in the novel. By using the first definition of love from Thomas Traherne's *Centuries of Meditations* as both epigraph and theme, Miss Bowen apparently intends the novel to be a metaphysical, not a social, statement about love and illusion:

> . . . So is there in us a world of Love to somewhat, though we know not what in the world that should be. . . . Do you not feel yourself drawn with the expectation and desire of some Great Thing? [13]

No reader who has seen love take the form of possession in *The Hotel,* a "large imposture" in *The Last September,* "overruling disaster" in *Friends and Relations,* fiery destruction in *To the North,* adolescent hysteria in *The Death of the Heart,* or an analogue of war in *The Heat of the Day,* will be tempted to equate the simplicity of the epigraph with Miss Bowen's position. Traherne, of course, included his statement as a definition of Christian love in a book of instruction, while Miss Bowen, relying on his vocabulary, uses it to make a very different novelistic statement about human love and secular illusion. But several of Traherne's concepts, removed from their religious context, point out directions in the novel. When he postulates two worlds—one "great and beautiful made by God" and the other "a Babel of Confusions" made by men—he defines the Christian's duty as leaving the second to join the first, the "voluntary Act of an obedient Soul" made possible by a sort of transitional world (a "Thought of the World, or the World in a Thought") within the human imagination. This world of imagination given by God, or as Miss Bowen redefines it, the world of love, is essentially a subjective state that one first enters by enjoying and participating sensuously in the beauty of nature. As "awareness" has been presented as a necessary first step for moral existence in Miss Bowen's novels, so here Traherne argues that awareness is a necessary prerequisite for participation in the world of love, for "he is most like God that is sensible of everything."

The prelude to awareness, the loss of innocence that such novels as

The House in Paris and *The Death of the Heart* dramatize, is also implicit in Traherne's concept of *felix culpa.* He even insists that a knowledge of hell is essential to the understanding and appreciation of heaven, that innocence preserved can lead to damnation, since "they that look into Hell here may avoid it hereafter. . . . Hell itself is a part of God's Kingdom, to wit His Prison. It is fitly mentioned in the enjoyment of the world. And is itself by the happy enjoyed, as a part of the world" (I, 48).

The final benefit to be gained by the sort of mystical consciousness Traherne urges is a victory over finite time and death. Through love the soul evades all the restrictions of the "outside" world, temporal or spatial; and other people become something "created to entertain us."

> One soul in the immensity of its intelligence, is greater and more excellent than the whole world. The Ocean is but the drop of a bucket to it, the Heavens but a centre, the Sun obscurity, and all Ages but as one day. It being by its understanding a Temple of Eternity, and God's omnipresence, between which and the whole world there is no proportion. (II, 70)

Thus, regarded from a secular point of view, Traherne postulates a world of illusion, or love, which exists side by side with the finite world of time, space, and circumstance; and he offers to the person who accepts the duality an escape from finite limitations. By using religious terms, Traherne solves the dilemma of the romantic will by defining for it an ideal illusory goal. A similar assumption, heavily qualified by an irony of which Traherne is innocent, informs both theme and technique in *A World of Love.*[14]

Since the setting of Elizabeth Bowen's eighth novel is as essential to its theme as its epigraph is, it too deserves preliminary explanation. Arriving in New York for her first visit after the war (in March 1950), Miss Bowen told John K. Hutchens of the *Herald Tribune* that she had abandoned a plan for four long short stories about the seasons in favor of a novel: "The novel will be of Ireland, but not specifically Irish." The use of Ireland as an exclusive setting for the first time since *The Last September* is significant, especially in the light of her uses of Ireland in *The House in Paris* and *The Heat of the Day.* In both of these novels, Ireland was the region of escape, where the Bents could ignore life and death and where Roderick could hope to find a future. The use of Ireland in *A World of Love* intensifies these qualities by making them an exclusive reality. Montefort, the decaying home of the Danbys, is as isolated from the outside world of action as the County Mayo village in *The Playboy of the Western World.* The narrator's descriptions of the surrounding topography strongly suggest the imaginary scenes projected by the innocently romantic adolescents in the other novels. When Portia in *The Death of the Heart* dreamed of Eddie, she

> saw a continent in the late sunset, in rolls and ridges of shadow like the sea. Light that was dark yellow lay on trees, and penetrated their dark hearts. Like a struck glass, the continent rang with silence. The country, with its slow tense dusk-drowned ripple, rose to their feet where they sat. . . . This light was eternal; they would be here for ever. (*DH*, 104)

Here, of course, the topography is explicitly a metaphor for innocence. But in *A World of Love* the pastoral setting, equally vague and idyllic, is presented forthrightly by the narrator as objective description, the words "painted" and "empty" alone suggesting qualification:

> The sun rose on a landscape still pale with the heat of the day before. There was no haze, but a sort of coppery burnish out of the air lit on flowing fields, rocks, the face of the one house and the cliff of limestone overhanging the river. . . . This light at this hour, so unfamiliar, brought into being a new world—painted, expectant, empty, intense. The month was June, of a summer almost unknown. (*WL*, 9)

Disturbance is brought to this pastoral isolation primarily by one who is entirely immersed in it. Jane Danby *can* be described as a character: a twenty-year-old girl, she has (like Sydney of *The Hotel*) completed her formal education and is ready for adult experience; but (unlike Sydney) she is victim of a rather complex environment and heredity. Her English mother, Lilia, had been engaged to Guy, owner of Montefort. After his death in battle in 1918 Montefort passed to his first cousin Antonia who took charge of Lilia, married her to Fred Danby ("Antonia's illegitimate cousin, bye-blow son of a roving Montefort uncle"), and established the two of them at Montefort as her tenants. Jane, the product of the short-lived passion of this arranged marriage, has spent her winters in London with Antonia, a professional photographer, but in the decisive summer presented in the novel has returned with her to Montefort.

But to describe Jane only in this way is to falsify her role in the novel, for she becomes a force as well as a person. Both innocent and romantic, she projects a subjective world around her that she prefers to the sense of the past she feels oppressing her at Montefort:

> . . . she had an instinctive aversion from the past; it seemed to her a sort of pompous imposture; as an idea it bored her; it might not be too much to say that she disapproved of it. She enjoyed being: how could it not depress her to realize that the majority of people no longer were? Most of all she mistrusted the past's activity and its queeringness—she knew no one, apart from her own contemporaries, who did not speak of it either with falsifying piety or with bitterness; she sometimes had had the misfortune to live through hours positively contaminated by its breath. (*WL*, 48–49)

But Jane's discovery of the collection of love letters from Guy to an anonymous girl makes possible the recreation of a past that is not *the* past, and her introduction to a literary love. Both expose her to the power of nostalgia and the security of an illusory Destiny. When she finds that the letters describe the very trees and rocks around her, she is transported in time: reality becomes art, a past transforms the present, and things are altered by the incantation of their names. Thus

> . . . the landscape became a vision and Jane could hardly believe it was still before her. But it was, and not only still here but poetically immortal; and better still it had comicalities which his eye had noted. . . . And here, three paces from where she lay, was the thorn tree; also part of the story, for that it grew wickedly crooked he had perceived, passing for a minute into its shadow then out again into the golden-yellow beyond. But all this he had been beholding not for its own sake only; through it he was seeking a speaking language—he was in love. *"I thought,"* he wrote, *"if only YOU had been here!"*
>
> A thread lay dropped on the grass, for Jane to pick up. "But here I am. Oh, here I *am!*" she protested. (*WL*, 69)

Thus infected by an illusion of love she takes to be reality, Jane resents anything that intrudes to remind her that her fantasy must be restricted to moments of solitude or anonymity. Because she can see justice in the mockery of others, her moment of vision becomes for her a "caricatured hour."

But all her hours are caricatured. The intrusion of the letters on Jane's imagination is paralleled by what at first seems a more material intrusion. The chauffeur who arrives at Montefort to summon Jane to a dinner party to be given by Lady Latterly, the sophisticated, *nouveau riche* purchaser of the nearby castle, is an emissary from the underworld. At the dinner, Jane (and the reader) is faced with two opposing perceptions that cancel out her sense of "reality" almost entirely. The castle and its "finish," where Jane watches Lady Latterly manufacture her beauty at the dressing table, Jane can dismiss as a theater. But the standard for "reality" is the fantasy created by the letters. She can echo Alice in mocking the artificiality of the dinner guests:

> "You're nothing," she thought of the company, "but a pack of cards!"—but the cards were stacked, and against her. (*WL*, 89)

Yet the "real" person present for her is the absent dinner guest, in whose place at the table Jane projects Guy.

> Guy was among them. The recoil of the others—she did not for an instant doubt it was a recoil—marked his triumphant displacement of their air. She saw the reflection of crisis in each face, heard it in loudening, dropping then stopping voices. Dinner had been announced; but it was not, could not be simply that—the butler vanishing from the door had no more than offered an alibi or afforded cover for a single, concerted movement of disarray on the part of these poor ghosts on whom the sun had risen, to whom the cock crew. (*WL*, 95)

When Jane is removed from the party by Antonia, she has lost all sense of time and has been completely possessed by the illusion of the past and of an imaginary love. But the details, Cousin Antonia's jealous words, and occasionally the narrator ("The cards were stacked, and against her") are there to remind the reader that his position is not as simple as Jane's appears to be, that his standards of "reality" have almost been eliminated. He can accept the social judgment brought against the guests by Jane, her dismissal of them as displaced rich, "men of a world that doesn't exist"; and he can see that they are as artificial as the house party in "The Disinherited," the mad dinner guests in "Her Table Spread," the Edwardian civilization in "Ivy Gripped the Steps." But the reader can hardly accept as completely valid the consciousness of an adolescent who, after three martinis, sees as more real than the guests a ghost across the dinner table. The joke on the reader that begins in the first pages of the novel—he does not know until the mention of the packet of Gold Flake that the girl in the Edwardian muslin is not herself Edwardian—is complicated, and part of the novel's strength lies in this "Babel of Confusions." As in "The Happy Autumn Fields," the legacy from the impassioned past, worked up by susceptible imaginations, blurs the distinction between dream and reality. "Hallucination," obliterating reality, is a pattern that can be laid "against the poor stuff of everything else." Travis' explanation to Mary (in the short story) can be applied as well to the characters of this novel: "You don't like it here. Your self doesn't like it. Your will keeps driving your self, but it can't be driven the whole way—it makes its own get-out: sleep" (*DL,* 116). But in *A World of Love,* of course, there is no Travis to stand aside and explain. Even the narrator hesitates to separate fantasy from reality.

As Miss Bowen has emphasized, it is misleading to read the novel as a story of adolescence, or to make any distinction between the characters and the theme. Jane's discovery of the letters is also the means by which Guy's illusory importance is brought back to Antonia and Lilia. To Antonia, who had been in love with her cousin and lost him first to Lilia, then to death, the unfinished story of a young man apparently destined for greatness is still a vital action though it has no agent. His uncompleted destiny has a future in which she can invest, and so lose her impotence. Before the discovery of the letters Antonia is incapable of sustaining any illusion except that artificially supplied by liquor, and even then she can control only the surface of her experience. Her devotion to Lilia and Jane, it becomes clear, is her homage to the past she imagines; and when she discovers that Jane is "possessed" by Guy, it is her opportunity to reassert her will by yielding to the past. The world is transformed by Antonia into a mystical voice, and by the narrator (deliberately) into a metaphorical chaos:

> No part of the night was not breathless breathing, no part of the quickened stillness not running feet. A call or calling, now nearby, now from behind the skyline, was unlocatable as a corncrake's in uncut grass. A rising this was, on the part of two who like hundreds seemed to be teeming over the land, carrying all before them. The night, ridden by pure excitement, was seized by hope. All round Montefort there was going forward an entering back again into possession: the two, now one again, were again here—only the water of their moments had run away long since along the way of the river; the root-matted earthiness and the rockiness were as ever their own, and stable. (*WL,* 113)

And through this resurrection of the illusion of Guy, Antonia imagines she can control time, so that "tonight was a night which had changed hands, going back again to its lordly owners: time again was into the clutch of herself and Guy. Stamped was the hour, as were their others" (*WL,* 114). This power regained Antonia apparently intends to use to seduce Fred, as she had exercised it before in buying Fred for Lilia and in buying him back after he once forced Lilia out. The illusion of Guy, which had existed as an end in itself for Jane, adds force to Antonia's will to power over the others.

Lilia can be victimized by this power because her own memory of Guy is not nearly as compensatory as Antonia's. Guy's death and the fact that he had been looking for someone else (beside Lilia or Antonia) at the station after his last leave, have left her no role ("if not the Beloved, what was Lilia?") and only her jealousy of Antonia gives any support to her life at Montefort where "animosity itself had become a bond." But the bond depends on their equal strength. Antonia's assertion of power forces Lilia back on her own emptiness, and her journey to Clonmore, her symbolic surrender to Antonia, removes the veil of illusion from the world to reveal a hell as shadowless as the subterranean café in *The Heat of the Day:*

> There on the kerb outside Lonergan's, Lilia braced her shoulders as though facing reality—looking up then down the Clonmore straight wide main street at the alternately dun and painted houses, cars parked askew, straying ass-carts and fallen bicycles. Dung baked on the pavements since yesterday morning's fair; shop after shop had insanely similar doorways, strung with boots and kettles and stacked with calicoes—in eternal windows goods faded out. Many and sour were the pubs. Over-exposed, the town was shadeless—never a tree, never an awning. Ice cream on sale, but never a café. Clonmore not only provided no place to be, it provided no reason *to* be, at all. So, but for the heat, was the place at all times—but the glare today stripped it of even its frowsty mystery, flattened it out, deadly glazed into a picture postcard such as one might receive from Hell. (*WL,* 130–31)

But as Traherne reminds us, the glimpse into hell is essential. The illusion of the past flickers briefly back into life when Lilia thinks she hears Guy, but the sudden appearance of Fred introduces the novel's first conversion of black magic into white. Miss Bowen's presentation of moments such as these has especially troubled the critics of this novel. One can see easily enough what Miss Bowen intends here: by countenancing Guy's infidelity, as she is forced to do by the presence of his letters to someone else, Lilia makes possible her frank discussion with Fred; it is as if the love freed in the exorcism of Guy could now take Fred as its object. To ask a reader to accept such a transition is a bold demand, and Miss Bowen qualifies her demand only by insisting that the world is not magnified into something rich or strange, but reduced to a crude conflict between man and his circumstance. As it was for Stella Rodney in *The Heat of the Day,* living is merely surviving:

> Impossible is it for persons to be changed when the days they have still to live stay so much the same—as for these two, what could be their hope but survival? Survival seemed more possible now, for having spoken to one another had been an act of love. (*WL,* 156)

But the young in all Miss Bowen's novels exceed their elders in enjoying possibilities that are not merely a matter of the arithmetic of life expectancy. The absence of an adult language brings Portia suffering and bewilderment, but it is also her opportunity to help create the language that will define her. "Survival" is hope when "the days [and language] they have still to live stay so much the same," but innocence can still yield to the power of imagination. To lose the letters on which her illusion depends, to be kissed by Lady Latterly's lover Peregrine, are events that magically change the nature of Jane's world. The loss of the letters is at first part of a resurrection—"In the sultry-scented inside of the elder, there the stone was, nothing at all to show it had been disturbed till she came to lift it . . ."—yet Guy has not risen but fallen, first to become "the packet upon her mother's lap," finally to thrill the kitchen maid who burns the letters. Similarly Peregrine's kiss gives a new reality to what had seemed a mere illusion. Jane can see her experience with the letters and at the dinner as a "game,"

> Though which of them, dead man and living girl, had been the player, and which the played with? Either way, Jane seemed doomed to know that this dallying and being dallied-with had gone on long enough. (*WL,* 179)

For Lilia, for Jane, and finally for Antonia, "reality" exorcises illusion. "Reality" in the novel is never finally defined—it exists only as events, facts, inexorable verities such as sex, time, and laughter. When Jane, disillusioned, fears that the world may be laughing at her, it does. From the radio (Montefort's tie with a larger world) "out came blood-up laughter, which, thanks to the force of the new battery, blasted its way round and round the room, bringing the instant look of a quarry, terror, mortification, to Jane's face." The same device punctuates the end of Antonia's illusion as well. The return of sense to Lilia and Jane ends Antonia's power over them, and the mystical voice she had heard calling over the fields is replaced by the radio's blare. *"It is going . . . to be Nine O'Clock,"* says Maud as she tunes in Big Ben to satisfy a childish passion of her own, and the tones become Time, Age, Fate, Reality:

> At the full, the first of the whanging blows struck down upon quivering ether, the echo swelling as it uprose. Repetition, fall of stroke after stroke where stroke after stroke had already fallen, could do no more than had been done: once was enough. From the first, the room was a struck ship—hither, thither slithered the thoughts and senses; the windows, like portholes careened over, appearing actually to fill up. The sound of Time, inexorably coming as it did, at once was absolute and fatal. Passionless Big Ben.
>
> The reminder, after so long, came with an accumulation of all force, and eloquence more than could be borne, demanding finally the reckoning. One was hearkening to an ultimatum. The term had been set, and the term extended, again, again and again, while useless the fate of nations went on preparing; and for what culmination, and for what? Rubbed-weary passions had had their say, leaving nothing said. But now came Now—the imperative, the dividing moment, the spell-breaker—all else was thrown behind, disappeared from reality, was over. Time swooped as it struck—and Antonia, hearing each felling blow, flinched once: who can flinch nine times? (*WL*, 193)

This banishment of false illusion by the harsh fateful sound of the present is both the exposure of Guy's falsity ("he had scattered round him more promises as to some dreamed of extreme of being than any one man could have lived to honour") and an attack on all uses of the past in which memory becomes nostalgia and unjustified expectation. The danger lies, the narrator suggests, in a failure to recognize that the dead, "being left behind in their time caused estrangement between them and us, who must live in ours."

> Life works to dispossess the dead, to dislodge and oust them. Their places fill themselves up; later people come in; all the room is wanted. Feeling alters its course, is drawn elsewhere or seeks renewal from other sources. When of love there is not enough to go round, inevitably it is the dead who must go without: we tell ourselves that they do not depend on us, or that they have not our requirements. Their continuous dying while we live, their repeated deaths as each of us die who knew them, are not in nature to be withstood. (*WL*, 63)

Though the false illusion that Guy generates among the "obstinate rememberers of the dead" is rightly dispelled, according to the assumptions of the novel, some sort of illusion is necessary if the hell of unmasked circumstance and fate is to be avoided. The "blood-up laughter" and the strokes of Big Ben may be real, but they are unbearable except for a child. There must be (in Rosa Coldfield's words in *Absalom, Absalom!*) "that might-have-been which is the single rock we have to cling to above the maelstrom of unbearable reality." Imagination can be the curse of the naïve and sensitive, but it is the only salvation of the wise. Wisdom is the knowledge, finally, of imagination's limits. The vision of love with which the novel ends defines the nature of saving illusion. Jane's journey to Shannon to meet Richard Priam, one of Vesta Latterly's ex-lovers who is to arrive "out of the blue" from Colorado, begins as a "blind bridal rush" and ends, as Miss Bowen has explained, with the convergence of fate on the individual (just as Antonia's "apparent will" in uniting Fred and Lilia had "done no more than implement waiting nature"). Insofar as this novel is committed to *any* cosmology, it is this fluid mysterious order of elements:

> The air, of which the flatness allowed for much, seemed if anything harder than the land—birds as though labouring flew through it, under the influence of the hush, and one could imagine with what effort anything larger than a bird must have to continue to forge its way; though at the altitude out of sight at which the airliner anxiously must be hastening in order to converge upon the van at the given time, at the given spot, all might be otherwise—one could not say. The passengers, unable to see down, might all the same be looking down, just as Jane, unable to see up, was looking up—her forehead out of the window. (*WL*, 216–17)

If the ending of the novel is to merge fate, or circumstance, with illusion, the world of love in individuals, some complex form must be found to define the boundary between the "what might-have-been" that is destructive illusion, the "what-must-be" that is fate, and the "what-will-be" that is constructive faith in the imagination. A first reading of the novel's final paragraphs may suggest (and indeed did suggest to most of the novel's reviewers) that Miss Bowen is naïve or irresponsible enough to dismiss the problem by a change of terms. Out of context, the ending would seem to be part of a silly fantasy:

> Richard Priam's gait marked him as not being a transit passenger. . . . She [Jane] seemed, too, in the act of turning away, of indeed fleeing, but had not yet done so. She wore the air of someone who cannot help knowing she must be recognized; her not yet willing but lovely gaze rested, accordingly, upon nothing; or rather upon a point in the diminishing nothingness between him and her.
>
> He swerved nearer the rail, crying "Hullo!" as though to somebody behind her. There was, as she knew, no one. Their eyes met.
>
> They no sooner looked but they loved. (*WL*, 224)

If the novel is read only as a series of incidents showing the progress of a young girl from innocent adolescence to sophisticated maturity, the ending is false and Priam no more than the *deus ex machina* reviewers have called him.[15] However, if the rest of the novel's direction is assumed, if the narrator's position has been understood, the ending is perfectly appropriate. The sudden "love at first sight" is an illusion, but one we are asked to see as taking fate and circumstance into consideration. It is not, like the initial blindness of Jane, her mother, and Antonia, an attempt to live in an idealized past, but an acceptance of the present and future, the merging of Now and later.

Yet, to a reader familiar with the novel that precedes *A World of Love,* the great silver bird that brings Priam becomes a bitter joke about the buzzbombs that threaten Stella's existence and the birds that promise Louie a future, for it replaces them with an image of a mechanical, fateful obscurity. And the tone of the novel's conclusion reminds us, indeed, that no moral terms are to be taken too solemnly. Miss Bowen, like Traherne, has acknowledged the primacy of a "real" world, the source of the laughter that brought chagrin to Jane, outside the illusory isolated world of love. And within the frame of the novel is the novel's caricature, Jane's twelve-year-old sister Maud, whose activities closely parallel those of her elders on an absurd, childish level. Gay David, her invisible companion, is obviously Guy's caricatured counterpart. Though Maud can explicitly compare her own form of "pretending" to Jane's during the "caricatured hour" by the river, she simultaneously lives in an Old Testament universe of her own projection and imagines she can destroy Montefort and her enemies by calling down vengeance. As Jane (like Portia) is God's spy in Lady Latterly's drawingroom, Maud is Judgment at Montefort: by constantly casting the ridicule and criticism of absolutism on the nostalgic activities of her elders, Maud helps to define the final reality. Though the others too often measure time by the apparently timeless obelisk on Montefort's front lawn (later revealed to have been erected by a forgotten man to his own memory), Maud worships instead the inexorable sound of Big Ben, the present and the outside world: " . . . it was only Maud who ever shook or poked at the defective clock or ran round plaguing to know what the time could be."

To be sure, Maud is not present in the novel's last paragraphs, but the consciousness that produced her is. The narrator Miss Bowen has created for *A World of Love* is her most elusive and complex voice. Repeatedly its tone reminds us by indirections that Montefort and Jane's imagination do not exhaust the world, and that the worlds beyond, any worlds put into words, are literary artifacts. Jane, for instance, is ironically compared to Ophelia and Cleopatra; her trials are recounted in biblical language; and the dinner party at Lady Latterly's is rendered with allusions to *Alice in Wonderland, Macbeth,* and *Hamlet.* Even Lilia had first met Guy in the fairyland of *A Midsummer-Night's Dream:* "Ill met, since this was the outcome, had Guy been by the ballroom-blue moonlight of Maidenhead." Thus, in the context of the novel, the tone with which the meeting of Jane and Richard Priam (his last name, like both of Vesta Latterly's, a literary joke) is described can hardly be called, as one reviewer did, "Dantean finality." [16] The final sentence is directly from *As You Like It,* its original speaker was Rosalind, and the love referred to there was that of Oliver and Cecilia. Rosalind's mocking tone sets the pattern for Miss Bowen's:

> *Rosalind:* O, I know where you are: nay, 'tis true: there was never any thing so sudden but the fight of two rams and Cæsar's thrasonical brag of "I came, saw, and overcame:" for your brother and my sister no sooner met but they looked, no sooner looked but they loved, no sooner loved but they sighed, no sooner sighed but they asked one another the reason, no sooner knew the reason but they sought the remedy; and in these degrees they have made a pair of stairs to marriage which they will climb incontinent, or else be incontinent before marriage: they are in the very wrath of love and they will together; clubs cannot part them. (V, ii) [17]

The last page of *A World of Love* could easily be used as a *locus classicus* for defining the most recent art of Elizabeth Bowen. To call the consciousness that emerges most fully here a "voice" is somewhat misleading. *A World of Love* is the kind of novel reviewers often call "poetic," and one measure of the "poetic" quality of this prose is its distance from the normal speaking voice. Miss Bowen once said that the critical remark that pleased her most was one that characterized her as a "muffled poet," and the peculiarities of the prose of *A World of Love* can be called "muffled poetry." [18] Even without Miss Bowen's statement that she finds the short story just short of poetry and prefers it as a form to the novel, the rhetoric in this book would hint at some suspicion on her part of the novel's discursiveness. To be sure, her rhetoric changes from novel to novel, but is usually idiosyncratic enough to be recognizable. Although an early work like *The Last September* is heavily dependent on extravagant metaphor, in *Friends and Relations* such extravagance is used with irony: "The Tilney connection . . . bright woof to a sober warp, shuttled their way to and fro through the Studdart connection." *To the North,* as I suggested earlier, used metaphor to construct an underlying symbolic statement. But obvious metaphor becomes much less obtrusive in the later novels. In *A World of Love* appears that condensed use of metaphor in which a comparison is suggested briefly by an unexpected adjective or verb: "Blight had cut short her early beauty; apathy mildewed what might have remained," "wilderness sheathed in hostility," or the "crouching room with its smoky ceiling."

Even more evident has been the development in Miss Bowen's use of sentence structure and rhythm. Jocelyn Brooke, in 1952, noticed that

> ... her prose has become, with each new book, more elaborate, as though the pressure of her material demanded a more complex and comprehensive form for its perfect expression.... The prose [of *The Heat of the Day*] has an extraordinary tautness and intensity, the syntax seems often to be stretched, like elastic, to near breaking-point; and here, again, one recognizes Miss Bowen's deliberate intention to fashion a style which shall correspond with the overstrained, strung-up condition of men and women in war-time London. At times, indeed, this tautness gives the effect of some neurotic impediment, a kind of stammer; and occasionally it may lead to actual obscurity.[19]

However, since such "convolutions" are even more evident in *A World of Love,* to which "war-time London" is irrelevant, Brooke's explanation cannot be complete. Even random selections from this novel demonstrate how often inversion, double negatives, and alliteration enter the prose. To gloss the sentences would almost exhaust a rhetorician's vocabulary:

> ... shocking was it to her that there should be so much ignominy, perhaps infamy.
>
> Mush for the chickens, if nothing else, was never not in the course of cooking ...
>
> The bedroom gained still more unreality by now seeming trapped somewhere between day and night—this marvel of marbling and mirror-topping, mirror-building-in and prismatic whatnots being at the moment a battleground of clashing dazzling reflections and refractions.
>
> Bowers of flowers cascaded fern mist from the piano top; jaded late green heat came in at the open windows. (*WL,* 37, 27, 82, 84)

Context can perhaps explain the function of the last two selections: they are deliberately artificial descriptions of the rococo castle of Lady Latterly. But all the distortions cannot be explained away as parts of a literary joke. Although Brooke is undoubtedly right in ascribing some of this stylistic idiosyncrasy to Henry James, Miss Bowen rarely uses (in her later novels) his method of relying on indefinite pronouns and abstract nouns defined by lengthy contexts. The unexpected diction of *A World of Love* far more often results from the substitution of a gerund or a participle for a noun, a concrete word for an abstract one. Thus

> All round Montefort there was going forward [rather than *occurring*] an entering back again into possession [rather than *repossession*]: the two,

now one again, were again here [emphasis by repetition]—only the water of their moments [rather than *events of the past*] had run away [rather than *disappeared*] long since along the way of the river; the root-matted earthiness and the rockiness were as ever their own, and stable. (*WL,* 113)

And the double negatives are necessary in creating a world in which every action must be accompanied by its more usual alternative, in which one occasion is to be seen simultaneously with others—"Antonia, not ungently [though she is usually ungentle] putting aside the tumble of hair, looked down . . ." At other moments, inevitability must be suggested, like the signal from Guy to Antonia (or vice versa) that never failed "for not come it could not and never did." Such deliberate trials of the reader's patience Miss Bowen has defiantly announced in her "Notes on Writing a Novel": "Any trick is justified if it adds a statement."

The "statement" added to *A World of Love* by these "tricks" is the same assumption that justifies the novel's conclusion, and that makes it possible to try to find in those paragraphs a culmination of Miss Bowen's ethos and aesthetic. At this point the reader, if he is to find sense, is finally forced to hold two opposing views at the same time. He must accept the necessity of illusion to life in the world at the same time that he distinguishes between illusion and the world. In other words, he must accept the novel's tribute to the power of love's illusion and simultaneously recognize that the finite limitations of language cannot directly express that power. The style, the ironies, the allusions constantly ask him to look at words and art, to be conscious of himself as a reader seeing the form he expects broken before him. Yet he must also be absorbed by the form that is being broken. As Robert M. Adams has defined them, such effects are the literary analogues of the painter's *trompe l'oeil,* the use of an open form.[20]

The position the reader is forced into by such a technique is hardly, as Adams demonstrates, a new one. The power of Shakespeare's late comedies depends of course on such ambiguities. Illusion, power, and absolute judgment hold sway on Prospero's island where the "insubstantial pageant" is as real, and as artificial, as "the great globe itself." Though *A World of Love* is like *The Death of the Heart* in stating the necessity of finding an illusion reconciled to circumstance, it goes beyond this ethical and moral concern to attempt a metaphysical one: the novel, like the late comedies, almost makes possible a statement about the nature of reality and the interrelationship of nature and art.

Both the novel's events and its style reflect Traherne's metaphysics, yet repeatedly turn the reader's attention to other more literary precedents. Within the sentences one even glimpses Faulkner, whose use of oxymoron, says Adams, is his grammatical counterpart of open form. The substitution of gerunds and participles for nouns, the fine distinctions made in the forms of "to be" (a Faulknerian device as well) simultaneously turn the reader's attention to "style," "muffled poetry," and act as the smaller equivalents of interests writ large throughout the novel—in the nature of Guy, who is seen as both being and becoming, in the nature of time, and in the tenuousness of "reality."

But in discussing the novel, I have substituted my assumptions about Miss Bowen's intentions for an account of her achievement. *A World of Love* is probably her most intellectually ambitious novel, but artistically one of the least convincing. In stating her preference for the short story as a form, she has particularly objected to the novelist's obligation to indicate the future of his characters and to provide narrative bridges from one scene of importance to another.[21] In this novel she tries to avoid such bridges by distorting syntax and word order to control the reader's attention, by directing him to important statements and forcing him to devote the kind of close attention to the words that he would give to a short story or poem. As she has indicated, *A World of Love* is a "condensed" novel from which many scenes were discarded. Like Henry James, Miss Bowen has been influenced, rather unhappily, by her preference for another genre. James's interest in the drama is reflected clearly enough in his reliance on dialogue in the novels, and his ability to write essential dialogue gives his plays substance when language is separated from scene. However Miss Bowen's preference for the self-contained, "realized" incident of the short story, her reliance on scene and "atmosphere" (significantly she finds dialogue the least difficult part of a novel to write[22]), were severe handicaps in her one attempt to write for the stage, and often limit the success of her novels. This lack of flexibility is presumably responsible for what T. C. Worsely meant in saying that the "idiosyncratic Elizabeth Bowen light" was missing from *Castle Anna*.[23] Wit and art are found more often in the stage directions than the dialogue. The lighting directions are heavily impressionistic; and the instructions to actors, though amusing, must have been impossible to objectify: "eyes Barney with a gloomy realism"; "with the agonised impatience of the man not happy in love"; "sexy pause all round."

When Henry James and Elizabeth Bowen attempted novels in which their nonnovelistic preferences could be realized, the results were not entirely successful. *The Awkward Age,* presented almost entirely in dialogue, reflects James's conviction that the drama's objectivity could be imposed upon the novel's discursiveness and extension. *A World of Love,* in this sense alone, is Miss Bowen's *Awkward Age*. The short timespan, the unity of theme, the concentration on atmosphere, the distortion of syntax to command attention are all qualities more often associated with the short story than the novel. The length of *A World of Love* makes it a novel, but its technique places it at that point just short of poetry that Miss Bowen points to as the territory of the short story.

The discrepancy leaves the reader vaguely uncomfortable. Somehow he expects more of a novel. This is hardly the place to argue, as John Holloway has done so convincingly,[24] that the last thirty years of literary criticism, with their emphasis on local analysis, have paralyzed our ability to talk about novels, nor is it the place to argue a private conviction that *longueurs* are functional in extended prose fiction. Nevertheless it is apparent that *A World of Love,* however fine a tour de force of Miss Bowen's literary and critical assumptions (about which more will be said in the next chapter), loses its power as art in the confusion of genres, in the imposition of one form upon another. In her preface to *Ann Lee's* she recalls that, in first starting a novel, she feared she could not sustain her vision over the necessary length of time. The recognition of this difficulty presumably accounts for the severe time limits she imposes in many of her novels (the single day framing *A House in Paris,* the three days of *A World of Love*), but it cannot be used to excuse an abdication of responsibility to the art of the novel. It does not seem naïve to expect richness of world from the one genre that can supply it, or to retain anticipations for a story. It is in lyric poetry, after all, that Keats, as Adams puts it, "calls attention to his writing as writing in order to emphasize that it is a comfortable fraud, and only partial and temporary and perhaps not very comfortable at that." [25] What he calls "discoveries made by the mind on itself," extended to the novel, can too easily lead to fiction that is predominantly formula. The continued attention that a novel, by its length, demands, should be repaid with more than exposure.

6 *Craft and Relevance*

"It is a truth universally acknowledged . . ." begins Jane Austen, and if the statement had been final and complete, if it had been immune to continual redefinition, there could have been no *Pride and Prejudice*. In fact, there seem always to have been novelists who compose by propositions, the art of whose fiction is generated and controlled by exploring the significance both expressed and hidden by a statement of condition. Such propositions need not be expressed moral and social maxims—James's prefaces repeatedly define his novels as attempts to see what would happen and what could be said about it "if." That is, according to his own testimony many of his novels began as dramatic propositions. There can, of course, be fiction dependent on inherent propositions that are aesthetic (Huxley's *Point Counter-Point*), religious (Greene's *The Heart of the Matter*), philosophical (Iris Murdoch's *Under the Net* or Virginia Woolf's *To the Lighthouse*). To attempt any such distinction may seem crude and factitious, but it is one way to define a particular kind of talent and to distinguish its products from those of a different vision. Certainly there is something about the way the world of a Faulkner novel is created that distinguishes it as an example of composition from the more self-consciously "intellectual" world of a novel by Conrad, say, or Wright Morris.[1] And the difference is not only a function of Faulkner's more extensive genius and an underlying interdependent structure for an entire canon. As "contained" a work as Eudora Welty's *The Golden Apples,* for instance, achieves its fullest success in events, in the presentation of situations for which a perceiver must order "things divined and endured, spectacular moments, hideous things . . . [that] seemed . . . to be by their own nature rising . . . and crossing the sky and setting the way planets did." And drama in this case is provided by ways of looking and ordering, alternatives to "roll[ing] back your head and feel[ing] their rays come down and reach your eyes." Great art can consist even of isolated, fragmentary attempts to find a language to talk about "moments [that] double upon themselves, and in the doubling double again, amending but never taking back." [2] A novel can be the product primarily of an extensive historical vision, or "each venture" (in Eliot's words) can be "a new beginning, a raid on the inarticulate / With shabby equipment always deteriorating / In the general mess of imprecision of feeling . . ." Obviously all these terms fit most novels worth reading, and I may merely be repeating Miss Bowen's distinction between the intuitive novelist and the one who depends on a "framework of ideas" (though her implication about the novelist's self-consciousness and education is irrelevant here). My only desire is to separate, briefly and crudely, a third category, that I have called novels of proposition, from the rest of the mass.

In all the previous chapters I have assumed that "propositions" are valid abstractions in a discussion of Elizabeth Bowen's fiction; that she herself relies on them; that they are responsible for the form and structure of her novels, even the rhythms of her sentences; that their content (not their significance or operation) is expressible. When, on the twenty-fifth page of her first novel Miss Bowen's narrator comments that "Sydney professed herself . . . a Realist, and it was perhaps because of this that her imagination, which she dealt with austerely, was able to revenge itself obliquely upon her," a pattern of language is set up. Like any pattern, its virtue is that it can be extended to define the form of other "materials"—the events of this novel, or the more extensive patterns of other novels. Within the sentence are philosophical abstractions ("Realist," "imagination"), an attitude toward them and their adherent (the capital "R"), and terms predicting dramatic action ("dealt with austerely," "revenge itself obliquely"). The example is a conveniently simple one (others are abundant among the quotations in my earlier chapters), but it may serve to point to a form of fiction. Robert Penn Warren is able to make a similar extraction from Conrad, whose "propositions" are not that different, in nature or use, from Miss Bowen's. Extending a gloss on Stein's speech about the destructive element from *Lord Jim* in order to apply it to *Nostromo* Warren finds that

> Conrad's skepticism is ultimately but a "reasonable" recognition of the fact that man is a natural creature who can rest on no revealed values and can look forward to neither individual immortality nor racial survival. But reason, in this sense, is the denial of life and energy, for against all reason man insists, as man, on creating and trying to live by certain values. These

values are, to use Conrad's word, "illusions," but the last wisdom is for man to realize that though his values are illusions, the illusion is necessary, is infinitely precious, is the mark of his human achievement, and is, in the end, his only truth.[3]

It is not because Conrad is a "philosophical" or didactic novelist that Warren can make this statement, nor is it merely Warren's speculation about values implied vaguely in Conrad's art. The form of Warren's statement is valid because it is gloss on a particular passage within a novel, and because Conrad's novels often "move" by the juxtaposition and dramatic dialectic of just such propositions as Stein's.

Apparently the novel of proposition is largely characteristic of English writers, and the American writers who look to the English tradition. Pamela Hansford Johnson, discussing modern English fiction, defines a phenomenon that, though certainly not a cause of the characteristic I have been proposing, is at least its correlate: the emergence of understatement as a predominate mode in English fiction of the present century.[4] The quality of English understatement is not the tone one hears in the voice of a Hemingway narrator, whose distrust of language centers on the words one man speaks to another. English understatement is correlative with the novel of proposition because it depends, rather, on a distrust of final paragraphs—of definitive formulations of meaning and significance—combined with a conviction that the *search* for final statement is imperative. The writer of understatement (Miss Johnson adduces Anthony Powell, Evelyn Waugh, E. M. Forster, and C. P. Snow) protects himself from the sins of hypocrisy and dishonesty by refusing to commit himself to any equation of words and experience. But the attitude, it seems to me, is not necessarily as defensive as Miss Johnson implies, for in the novel of proposition understatement is one technique that makes movement possible, that keeps propositions from closing down and destroying both drama and truth.

Miss Bowen's use of propositions is at once more explicit and more misleading than that of James or Conrad. As I have pointed out, her narrators can assume mysterious unidentified voices that simultaneously confide in the reader, predicate an action, predict future events, and mockingly imitate a character. If he is to remain anonymous, such a narrator must be complex indeed to be able to report economically on the status of a proposition and at the same time indicate the events and persons by which the proposition is to be tested.

The limitations implied by such a technique are probably obvious. The richness and "reverent openness" that the novel *can* provide are often reduced when the world of any one novel depends so heavily on the propositions that can be made about it. Expansions of that world, transcendence of the propositions' terms, are difficult. The danger is that when propositions fail, the novel's world can collapse, as it does in *To the North,* leaving only consciousnesses inadequate to the task of containing it. Or the narrator can lose control of language, letting anything happen because words seem to allow it; and again the best example would be that point in *To the North* at which metaphoric propositions about fire and ice are allowed to determine events that are not in the same way metaphoric. A complementary form of the same failure occurs in *A World of Love,* where the narrator's faith in the power of words and simultaneous recognition of their inadequacy leads to a kind of rhetorical *jeu d'esprit.* So far above the product of his art that he can joke about its magic, this narrator is almost self-congratulatory. Prospero unbalanced by a Caliban can be annoying.

Yet the novel of propositions can be an exciting and responsible art, especially if the protagonist too be a maker of propositions, if his efforts parallel those of the narrator who contains him. In *The Death of the Heart* and *The Heat of the Day* Miss Bowen's use of this technique approaches its fullest realization, as it might have in *The House in Paris,* had more attention been given to Leopold's consciousness. Portia Quayne's attempts to secure meanings, to find adequate ways to express what she encounters within and around her, are paralleled by the anonymous narrator just beyond her who is able to place those attempts. This narrator disappears to allow Portia's own consciousness to take over (when the diary is presented); frequently reappears to indicate Portia's actions in language no more complex than hers but from just beyond her point of view ("Portia instinctively looked at the tree to see if it were still vertical"); can restate Portia's perceptions in terms Portia might almost use if she were as articulate (the "landscape in the sunset" vision quoted in Chapter Four above); can comment with omniscient wisdom on any immediate situation in order to relate it to a world larger than the novel's seemed to be ("Illusions are art . . .").[5] In a novel concerned with a child's growth from speechless innocence to articulate maturity, such a technique is obviously dramatic and organic. But to prove that such a narrative position can be vital, contributes to meaning, and does not result in a static omniscience, one would have to quote an entire novel. An extensive quotation from a less "significant" scene can at least indicate how such shifts create, not destroy, drama. When Major Brutt calls at Windsor Terrace, the event itself is certainly prosaic, yet it embodies far more action than many of the outwardly climactic scenes in the earlier novels. When Major Brutt, acting in innocent good faith on an invitation that was extended only from politeness, rings the doorbell, many things happen:

Almost unremitting solitude in his hotel had, since his last visit, made 2 Windsor Terrace the clearing-house for his dreams: these reverted to kind Anna and to that dear little kid with fervent, tender, quite sexless desire. A romantic man often feels more uplifted with two women than with one: his love seems to hit the ideal mark somewhere between two different faces. Today, he came to recover that visionary place, round which all the rest of London was a desert. That last night, the Quaynes, seeing him out, had smiled and said heartily: "Come again." He took it that people meant what they said—so here he was, coming again. Thomas's having added "Ring up first" had made no impression on him whatever. They have given him *carte blanche,* so here he was, dropping in. He judged that Saturday should be a good day.

. . . .

This [the Quayne's privacy being protected] being so, even Phyllis, with all her aplomb, her ever-consciousness of a pretty cap, had forgotten how to cope with a plain call. She well knew the cut of "expected" people, people who all but admitted themselves, who marched in past her without the interrogatory pause. Some smiled at her, some did not—but well did she know the look of someone who knew the house. And, except for a lunch party or a dinner, nobody ever came who did not.

So, directly she opened the door and saw Major Brutt, she knew it was in her power to oppress. She raised her eyebrows and simply looked at him. For him, that promising door had opened on something on which he had not reckoned. He knew, of course, that people have parlourmaids—but that last time the hall had been so full of light, of goodbye smiles, of heaps of women's fur coats. He faltered slightly at once: Phyllis saw the drop in his masculine confidence. Her contempt for humility made her put him down as an ex-officer travelling in vacuum cleaners, or those stockings that are too shiny to wear.

So it was with snappy triumph that she was able to say Mrs. Quayne was not at home. Modifying his expectant manner, he then asked for Mr. Quayne—which made Phyllis quite sure that this person must be wanting something. She was quite right: he was—he had come all this way to see a holy family.

"Mr. Quayne? I couldn't say," Phyllis replied pursily. She let her eye run down him and added, "sir." She said:—"I could inquire if you like to wait." She looked again—he did not carry a bag so she let him in to a certain point in the hall. Too sharp to give Thomas away by looking into the study, she started downstairs to ring through on the room-to-room telephone. As she unhooked the receiver at the foot of the basement stairs, intending to say, "Please, sir, I think there is someone—" she heard Thomas burst open his door, come out and make some remark. Now Mrs. Quayne would not have allowed that.

In the seconds before Thomas came to his door, Major Brutt may have realised this was a better house to be brought back to in triumph than to make one's way into under one's own steam. While he looked up the draughtless stairs behind the white arches, some aspirations faded out of his mind. He glanced at the console table, but did not like to put down his hat yet: he stood sturdily, doubtfully. Then a step just inside that known door made him re-animate like a dog: his moustache broadened a little, ready for a smile. (*DH,* 105–7)

Even though I have omitted a paragraph in which Thomas' questioning reaction to the bell is presented, the action here is still extremely complex. Within the context of a thematic situation in which the *de trop* innocent approaches a household of sophistication and "edited" life where callers phone ahead, within the "story" where Portia's ally visits her enemies (just after Portia has alienated Matchett), an event occurs. At one remove, the expectations of Major Brutt and Phyllis are played off against each other. He expects welcome, smiles, light, and finds instead a contemptuous parlormaid. Phyllis, however, expects and at first finds a despicable salesman toward whom one can be "snappy," to whom one can reply "pursily"; and even when she realizes her error ("he did not carry a bag") she calls upon set methods of operation: she delays the "sir," allows him to advance only to "a certain point in the hall," and is "too sharp" to give away Thomas' presence.

Between the two points of view, of course, there is a conflict, a test of power. Because Brutt is caught off guard, Phyllis can "oppress" and he must "falter"; Phyllis has a "snappy triumph" as a result of which Brutt must "modify" and then "may have realised this was a better house to be brought back to in triumph than to make one's way into under one's own steam." Finally, as "some aspirations faded out of his mind," Brutt is defeated: he fears to put down his hat and, at Thomas' approach, is re-animated "like a dog." On both sides there have been shifts of position, even a minor setback for one of the victors (when Thomas dashes out), yet an event has happened with finality: a pilgrim has become a dog, innocence and faith have been defeated by suspicion and coldness.

However the reader, whose position has been established well above the conflict, is able to see the battle ambivalently. He is far enough separated from both participants so that he can recognize their language when it appears without quotation marks: "kind Anna and . . . that dear little kid" or "those stockings that are too shiny to wear." Any sympathy the reader may feel for the victim is qualified by the emphasis put on Brutt's silliness, his absurd notion that 2 Windsor Terrace is "a visionary place" enclosing a "holy family." Nor is Phyllis entirely to be blamed for her brusqueness, for she too is partially a victim of a society that no longer gives her a chance to take rightful advantage of her "pretty cap" and aplomb. Only the reader and the narrator here are completely capable of common sense, know that the event so exaggerated by all its participants is, finally, a "plain call." Because he can see so much, the narrator is solidly on the side of sense, plainness, honesty, but knows at the same time that these virtues, in this situation, do not exist, that they have been obliterated by necessary illusions, meant to be saving, which here conflict. It is a measure of Miss Bowen's success as a novelist that the viewpoints and attitudes of her characters, however complex and flexible, can be contained within a literary style great enough to organize and comment on them.

I have deliberately made much of a relatively minor event to illustrate Miss Bowen's extensive awareness, her ability to turn the *longueurs* of the novel into an advantage. Only a writer as skillful as Jane Austen or Henry James could probably have done more than she has done with the opening of a door. Her success in dealing with such a moment recalls what Virginia Woolf found to be one of Jane Austen's important achievements:

> Jane Austen is . . . a mistress of much deeper emotion than appears upon the surface. She stimulates us to supply what is not there. What she offers is, apparently, a trifle, yet it is composed of something that expands in the reader's mind and endows with the most enduring form of life scenes which are outwardly trivial.[6]

The expanding "something" that Mrs. Woolf does not define is responsible for Miss Bowen's success as well. Seen in the terms I have been using, it is the writer's ability to create a narrative consciousness flexible enough to echo the living tones of her characters, and inclusive enough to place by comment the tones she imitates. Propositions—"the romantic man often feels more uplifted with two women than one"—are given almost immediate qualification by their realization as voices and acts—"he came to recover that visionary place"; "a step . . . made him re-animate like a dog." The irony of the proposition that opens the first chapter of *Pride and Prejudice* and the apparently definitive comment on Mrs. Bennet that closes it are similarly modified by the events and living tones that separate them.

The task that Miss Bowen sets herself in *The Heat of the Day* is probably her most difficult one, for Stella Rodney's consciousness, the terms of her world, her tone (but not, obviously, her experiences) are perilously close to those of the narrator and, presumably, to those of the narrator's creator. Certainly the significant propositions placing Robert, Harrison, and Roderick could be appropriately assigned either to the narrator or to Stella. Only Louie is outside the range of Stella's language, and Louie is defined by a self-conscious writer, almost a literary critic. When Stella herself must be placed by a consciousness outside her own, there are voices enough different from hers that they seem to say something, but so inferior to hers that their comment is the irony of their inadequacy. Louie can call Stella a "soul astray" (words that, suspiciously, appear by magic, reach her "imperatively" when "her lips seemed bidden"), but for the most part, as Louie herself says, she can't speak grammar and has no words. Harrison too is a commentator, but when he meets Stella after Robert's death he is much more articulate about himself than Stella. His consciousness of her is reflected in rather inadequate questions—"Here, you're still fairly snug?"—and for anything like a final statement about Stella, the reader has only the narrative equivalent of her passivity and quietism: silence.

A careful reading of almost any single page, even out of context, from a late novel by Elizabeth Bowen would seem to make inescapably obvious the self-consciousness of her fiction and its creator's awareness of what she had read and what she is doing. Yet the nature of Elizabeth Bowen's contribution to the tradition of English literature has been rarely understood, considering the fairly frequent comments on her work. Unfortunately her achievement has been least understood by those who have admired it most extravagantly. Particularly misleading are the critics who see in her the image of the romantic feminine sensibility, the advocate of feeling and love, a kind of sophisticated Marie Corelli. "Elizabeth Bowen is the most feminine of contemporary novelists," begins E. D. Pendry in his chapter on Miss Bowen in *The New Feminism of English Fiction,* thereby limiting the possibility of his responding to the toughness inherent in her intellect and essential to her art.[7] And one can only wonder how a competent novelist like Jocelyn Brooke can admire her work while he underestimates the almost cruel alternate vision undermining the "good taste" he finds so admirable.[8] The only possible conclusion is that, aside from a violent devaluation by Elizabeth Hardwick and the laudatory chapter of Sean O'Faolain, her work has had almost no sustained critical attention that can be called responsible.[9]

Miss Hardwick's essay in the *Partisan Review* can at least be praised for its uncompromised honesty. Responding to the "fine writing" and romantic feminism other critics have lavishly praised, she finds these qualities a deplorable screen that hides simple gothic melodramas embodying a codified snobbery. What Miss Hardwick overlooks is precisely what O'Faolain finds: not a disparity between manner and moral assumption, but a "kind of *farouche* note" behind her "civil façade." This quality, which O'Faolain rather awkwardly calls "bifrontine," is basically a radical irony of vision, by which "she exposes the brittleness of romance by soliciting it ruthlessly." [10] Though Miss Hardwick perceptively saw that the romance solicited was very brittle indeed, she rather surprisingly failed to see its exposure:

As in an opera libretto you must take the roles on faith—a grunt of satire or a shiver of common sense on the spectator's part, would be enough to disrupt the performance and bring the pretty scenery down upon the soprano's head.[11]

As I have pointed out in previous chapters, the grunt of satire, the perception of common sense, are constantly invoked, are in fact essential to all the novels. For instance, the caricaturing understudies (Cordelia for Sydney, Livvy for Lois, Theodora for Janet, Lilian for Portia, Louie for Stella, Maud for Jane) expose romance by echoing the heroines' behavior in exaggerated (but simpler) form at the same time that they succeed in the society the heroines reject. More than foils, they often play the Fool. The truly gothic novelist cannot afford such falsetto mockery of her soprano's role, nor the explicit recognition of fakery implied by it. Paradoxically, Miss Bowen's role must be that of the novelist who possesses absolute confidence in her craft at the same time that she distrusts its reality. Her own synonyms for art and tradition, it must be remembered, are "dishonesty" and "debt."

Her confidence in treating the illusions she creates is most evident at those moments when her assumptions about the novel arise as particular sentences that define the narrator's role. Like E. M. Forster she willingly subjects her fabric to severe and unusual tests by rejecting the strictures on narrative point of view adhered to by James and legislated by Lubbock. In her own "Notes on Writing a Novel" she explicitly recognizes the illusory nature of fiction:

Plot is story. It is also "a story" in the nursery sense = lie. The novel lies, in saying that something happened that did not. It must, therefore, contain uncontradictable truth, to warrant the original lie. (*CI,* 249)

In using frequent sententious generalizations (what Forster calls "taking the reader into your confidence about the universe"), in speaking aside to the reader, in establishing the "ideal memory" of *The House in Paris,* she repeatedly reminds her reader that art is not, should not be, life.[12] Once he is placed on this level of detachment above the characters with their creator, the reader can hardly participate in what Miss Hardwick calls "the satisfaction of unabashed tears, an emotional evening in which love retains all its old sovereign rights, and the final pleasure of witnessing the bad end to which the inconstant come." Nostalgia may be invoked, but only to be derogated, for illusion in her novels does not approximate reality, it is set off against it.

Even in the subordinate craft usually called "description" Miss Bowen is neither the inspired romantic defined by her intemperate admirers (L. A. G. Strong finds her consciousness of light a peculiarity of

Irish writers [13]) nor the uncritical naïf implied by her tougher-minded detractors (Herbert Gold calls the weather in *A World of Love* symbolic, "just like Taylor Caldwell" [14]). The use of light and scene within her novels is symbolic, but as her early essay on "Modern Lighting" makes clear, the symbolism is neither simple nor obvious. Events are marked by the weather in which they occur (as in the assignation at Hythe in *The House in Paris*), and the opening paragraphs of *The Death of the Heart* show how scene, season, and character are often interwoven. Here, although the details have no previous context to define them, their meaning is immediately, richly clear:

> That morning's ice, no more than a brittle film, had cracked and was now floating in segments. These tapped together or, parting, left channels of dark water, down which swans in slow indignation swam. The islands stood in frozen woody brown dusk: it was now between three and four in the afternoon. A sort of breath from the clay, from the city outside the park, condensing, made the air unclear; through this, the trees round the lake soared frigidly up. Bronze cold of January bound the sky and the landscape; the sky was shut to the sun—but the swans, the rims of the ice, the pallid withdrawn Regency terraces had an unnatural burnish, as though cold were light. There is something momentous about the height of winter. Steps rang on the bridges, and along the black walks. This weather had set in; it would freeze harder tonight.
>
> On a footbridge between an island and the mainland a man and woman stood talking, leaning on the rail. In the intense cold, which made everyone hurry, they had chosen to make this long summerlike pause. Their oblivious stillness made them look like lovers—actually their elbows were some inches apart; they were riveted not to each other but to what she said. Their thick coats made their figures sexless and stiff as chessmen; they were well-to-do, inside bulwarks of fur and cloth their bodies generated a steady warmth; they could only see the cold—or, if they felt it, they only felt it at their extremities. Now and then he stamped on the bridge, or she brought her muff up to her face. Ice pushed down the channel under the bridge, so that while they talked their reflections were constantly broken up. (*DH*, 9–10) [15]

As Dorothy Schneider has pointed out, the scene is presented cinematically—the camera begins with a panoramic survey and finally focuses on two individuals (as it does in the opening paragraphs of *The Heat of the Day*).[16] But of course verbal description is far more selective than photographic representation, and allows the writer to sort out and merge impressions and senses for his own purposes. The "bronze" cold of January, suggesting both brilliance and coldness, is to be found in the man and woman (Anna and St. Quentin) as well as in their environment. Warmth, conveniently a quality both of temperature and human feeling, is prevented from escaping, and cold, again an ambiguous quality (as in "cold fact"), is kept at one remove by "bulwarks." The swans, isolated in the coldness, are used as symbols of romanticism and innocence throughout the novel and, like Portia, they have an ability the others lack: with "slow indignation" they can swim in the channels of dark water. Anna and St. Quentin, though removed, are at the same time part of winter's coldness and subject to it: "their reflections were constantly broken up." The seasons change, of course, as Portia's relationship to the society changes; but the "height and fullness of living" that summer represents at the end of the novel, though an optimistic sign to Matchett, still paradoxically brings Portia back to the coldness of Windsor Terrace. Contrast, paradox, conflict are metaphorically prefigured by the "summer-like pause" (in January) of two figures who look like lovers, though they are apart and their figures are sexless.

I have isolated one of the more obvious examples of Miss Bowen's craftsmanship to demonstrate its deliberateness. Such self-consciousness of artistry, her unremitting ability to look at herself as a writer, her express belief that "any trick is justified if it adds a statement," has made her particularly perceptive in criticizing the local successes (and failures) of her own short stories and novels. However, "tricks," techniques, expanded metaphors do not make a novel. Even in her criticism of other writers, her impressionistic insights, often extremely illuminating, tend to be static. Her sympathy for "tricks," for example, has led her to overvalue minor novels wherein, as she admits, she sees solved a problem she herself has struggled with. She is most successful as a critic when she is able to translate her particular experience of a work into metaphorical terms from which the reader can derive insight. The remark that D. H. Lawrence has the form of naturalism within which "every bush burns" is one such perception, as is her evaluation of Ben Jonson's sensuousness:

> The sensuous element is immense. This is Renaissance theatre: in those days one had a world at the fingertips, and the fingertips had not thickened. Immediacy of sensation comes through the language—concrete, and with an exact touch. The boom was at its height; wealth came in at every port. Magnetic new precious objects were on the market; each brought a world with it; luxury meant sublimation, not just dull expenditure. Learning, with its range of subtle experience, Latin elegance, outlandish mystery all struck the English shore. The world was not yet mapped; experience had no limits; a new mistress was an America. Intellect quickened love. The table soared into art, above the levels of subsistence or gluttony. (*CI,* 117)

It might be argued that this is no more than an expansion of Eliot's statement that, in a world without dissociation of sensibility, intellect was at the tips of the senses, but Miss Bowen's statement of a similar perception must be praised for its wealth of expanding images.

Even though Miss Bowen's prefaces to her own work are often

amazingly objective, and her "Notes on Writing a Novel" bring art from the plane of ethereal speculation to the situation of a human being sitting with pencil poised above a sheet of paper, she tends to overlook both in her own work and in that of other writers the most important quality contributing to the novel's uniqueness—its ability to move through a story, assigning meaning and importance. Although she sees that a novel must give shape, she is less explicit in defining the peculiar kind of moving shape it must give. Action she sees as essential, more important than characters (who "must only be so created as to give his or her . . . contributory part in the novel's action verisimilitude"), but she has few terms other than those of causality and change with which to discuss this "advance."

In three talks delivered for the BBC Home Service in 1956 Miss Bowen returned to the subject of the novel as a genre and a craft. Classifying the elements of a novel statically—as story, theme, situation, people, time, period, and reality—she implicitly defines the dilemma faced by a critic who must talk specifically yet generally, without a vocabulary that can, like a calculus, comprehend the two modes at the same time. On the one hand, the novel must on every page present an undeniable immediacy so that "the present moment [will] grip us and hold us, so that while we read it is as important—more important—than the moment in the room where we are in our chair." But, on the other hand, there must be a constant precipitation of events, so that "we are . . . conscious of a clock that strikes from hour to hour and leaves of a calendar which turn over." The result of this double requirement, immediacy and motion, is, in a "good story," the "succession of effective Nows—call them scenes if you like—and those Nows are linked together by intermediate action." [17] However, Miss Bowen concentrates on openings and "stage-setting" techniques, partially ignoring the more difficult case in which a scene operates in the midst of a sequence, simultaneously result and cause. She admits that she "would still stand by the first two pages" of most of her own novels, and the reader can largely agree that the satiric vignettes initiating *The Hotel* and *Friends and Relations,* or the cinematic isolation of mysterious activity from the midst of a panoramic scene at the beginning of *The House in Paris, The Death of the Heart,* and *The Heat of the Day,* do provide "situations which hold promise" even though they do not necessarily define the quality of the whole novel. In her discussion of dialogue Miss Bowen comes closer to defining complex action, for here she sees that "all good dialogue perhaps deals with something unprecedented." "Unprecedented," however, is a rather misleading word, for any scene must necessarily be precedented by the events and characters as they appear earlier in the sequence, and we can perhaps only say that the characters who have taken part in a scene are in a new position, are now able to make "unprecedented" statements about themselves and their "circumambient universe." And presumably, in a good novel, this change from one image of the world and self to another has an intrinsic relevance to other situations, actions, themes, propositions (in Miss Bowen's case) within a novel. In this sense, then, her definition of speech in "Notes" as "what the characters *do to each other*" is more applicable: "During dialogue, the characters confront one another. The confrontation is in itself an occasion. Each one of these occasions, throughout the novel, is unique" (*CI,* 255).

The differences between Miss Bowen's assumptions about the novel as they appear in her 1945 "Notes" and those underlying the 1956 talks on "Truth and Fiction" can be seen as regrettable by those who value her novels. The greater emphasis on "theme" and "idea" at the expense of "scene" is reflected too clearly in the transition, mentioned earlier, from *The Heat of the Day* to *A World of Love.* The attempt to condense the discourse of the novel to the metaphor of the short story seems to have been detrimental. Yet the motive for such a change has been inherent in Miss Bowen's aesthetic from the beginning. Her repeated insistence on fatality, circumstance, predestination is overtly paralleled by her apparent conviction that character is inevitably determined by action and that the social individual is subordinate to his circumstance. This conviction, as a social philosophy and as an aesthetic, reaches its fullest expression in *A World of Love,* a novel born of an abstract metaphysical concept and narrated from a position of remote detachment.

To be sure, in quoting the incident of the dead cat from *Howards End* Miss Bowen warns that the characters in such a situation "must be close up to the eye, close to one's feelings the whole time, otherwise *Howards End* could have been an abstract tract." Nevertheless she deliberately moves away from action and people in *A World of Love* and, in her BBC talks, seems to welcome this form of ironic removal as a necessary trend in contemporary fiction. Noting the lack of verisimilitude in the dialogues of Henry Green and Ivy Compton-Burnett, she asks if

> this change in the manner and use of a dialogue denotes or symbolises some change in the form of the novel, and still more in the intentions of the novel in our day? Does it mark the ending of a study of individualised character, the individual for his own sake, as a theme? Are we going back to the symbolic, the masked speaker? Is this turning away from naturalism a lapse or suspension of interest in single people and a greater sense, on our part, of the importance of crisis or the meaning of group emotion and group feeling? Do we think more of *kinds* of people? [18]

Her answer to these questions, as many of her short stories and *A World of Love* illustrate, is apparently a willing "yes." This quality of detachment, and its variation that V. S. Pritchett has called "anthropological," certainly pervades much contemporary British fiction.[19] However much the narrator in Anthony Powell's "Music of Time" series owes to Fitzgerald's Nick Carraway, his Nicholas Jenkins, amusedly watching both himself and society as a sequence of social images, through decade after decade, is certainly the product of an assumption similar to Miss Bowen's. Whether stories told at such removes, fiction created by minds so ruthlessly self-deprecating and self-conscious, can still be called novels may be an unimportant question. But the ultimate demands such arts make upon the reader's expectations—and Miss Bowen warns the reader that he must provide "more attention and more response and more comeback"—are considerable. They may be part of what she calls a seeking for a language "that shall be unique to our age and yet hold in it the elements of all time," or they may simply be reflections of a loss of faith in fiction. Indeed, a literary historian might find in the development and shift of Miss Bowen's concerns a paradigm useful in describing the disappearance of serious novels dealing comprehensively with middle-class, urban life. But Elizabeth Bowen does not deserve to be put with Virginia Woolf in an eccentric tradition of "sensibility," apart from whatever more relevant "mainstream" may be seen emanating from D. H. Lawrence, precisely because she has always known what and where her novels were. Only a most superficial reading could lead anyone to see her novels as apologies for a decadent Establishment or exhausted Civilization. The intellectual and cultural awarenesses expressed by *The Heat of the Day* made necessary the abstraction of *A World of Love*. Her knowledge of her own time and the possibilities for her fiction in it are expressed by that change. Like Stella Rodney's final silence, it is articulate, not oblivious. For the honest and intelligent nonrebel, it is rebellion's alternative.

As all of my comments have been intended to suggest, Elizabeth Bowen's fiction at its best is conscious, intelligent, even austere. One can say relatively little about the relationship of her art to that of her contemporaries, for her debts to them are either explicit and self-evident, or so oblique as to be nonexistent. She has always read widely in literature (poetry as well as prose) of all periods, and is fully aware of the debts she owes to past and present for the body of literary experience on which her own art draws. It is pointless to draw attention to the concerns her fiction does *not* dramatize, in domestic and professional life, in social classes other than her own. The world one could construct from all her novels and stories would seem "narrow" indeed, compared with that of almost any other major novelist. As O'Faolain notes, for instance, anything "elemental" is usually circumscribed—not for the sake of "elegance" (as he implies) or prudery—but simply because she has always been cognizant of what any writer's language cannot do, and of the limits of her own powers.

It is certainly a measure of Elizabeth Bowen's stature as a novelist that these powers are used unremittingly in the dramatization of events that are important, in giving a unique form of life to propositions that are essential. What is at stake in her fiction one must call, for lack of less pompous terms, a sense of reality: in any world, the intelligent, imaginative person cannot make things of people and survive with integrity, cannot crudely substitute art for life and live with sanity. Yet one must in some way (her novels consider many) make art of life in order to live, for to deny the risk of imagination, inherent in its ability to expose the sensibility, is to abandon one's self to imagination's revenge as chaos and fantasy. This moral proposition her art repeatedly sets; but because these terms, like those of a parable, are extensive, her fiction is rarely repetitious.

To speak of any writer's success "within limits" usually implies denigration, even if one adds that the limits are "deep if not wide." Spatial metaphors used for evaluation too often introduce irrelevant nonsense. What a reader *can* say of Miss Bowen's achievement in the art of the novel can only be said of the greatest: that she has kept going a worthwhile continuity without submitting to nostalgia; that she has attempted honestly to assign importance to the elements of the world she and her readers share, without resorting to clichés of material or attitude; that she has given to her age and to her culture an image of art within which life can go on with relative fullness and sanity. Because she accepts and comprehends the work of those who have preceded her, thus giving her own art a role in a tradition, and because she has adapted what has gone before to a contemporary world, Elizabeth Bowen's novels, at their best, have the quality she herself has called (in a different sense) the most difficult to achieve: relevance. It is as great a demand as can be made of a writer that his art be relevant to the work of the past, that his technique be relevant to his theme, that his theme be relevant to the reader and his world.

* *Notes*

Chapter One

1 Miss Bowen's account of her arrival in London is number 6 in John Lehmann's *Coming to London* (London, 1957), pp. 74–81. Other contributors to the collection of fourteen include V. S. Pritchett, J. B. Priestley, John Middleton Murry, Rose Macaulay, and Edith Sitwell.
2 "Out of a Book" (1946), reprinted in *Collected Impressions* (London, 1950), p. 269. This selection of Miss Bowen's essays will hereafter be cited in the text by the abbreviation *CI.*
3 "The Big House" (1942), *CI,* p. 197.
4 Virginia Woolf, *A Writer's Diary* (London, 1953), p. 365.
5 *Coming to London,* p. 75.
6 *Ibid.,* p. 76.
7 *Why Do I Write? An Exchange of Views between Elizabeth Bowen, Graham Greene, and V. S. Pritchett* (London, 1948), p. 23.
8 *The House in Paris* (1935; London, 1949), p. 216. All references to Miss Bowen's novels and collected short stories are to the Jonathan Cape collected edition, except for *Encounters* (1923), republished by Sidgwick and Jackson in 1949, and *A World of Love,* published in 1955 by Cape, but not in the collected edition. All references to these works are cited in the text with the following abbreviations (the first date is that of original publication, the second that of the collected edition):

CJ — *The Cat Jumps* (stories: 1934; 1949)
DH — *The Death of the Heart* (novel: 1938; 1948)
DL — *The Demon Lover* (stories: 1945; 1952)
E — *Encounters* (stories: 1923; 1949)
F&R — *Friends and Relations* (novel: 1931; 1951)
H — *The Hotel* (novel: 1927; 1950)
HD — *The Heat of the Day* (novel: 1949; 1954)
HP — *The House in Paris* (novel: 1935; 1949)

JC — *Joining Charles* (stories: 1929; 1952)
LR — *Look at All Those Roses* (stories: 1941; 1951)
LS — *The Last September* (novel: 1929; 1948)
TN — *To the North* (novel: 1932; 1952)
WL — *A World of Love* (novel: 1955; —)

Other abbreviations used for Miss Bowen's nonfiction are:

BC — *Bowen's Court* (1942)
CI — *Collected Impressions* (1950)
EN — *English Novelists* (1946)

9 Also quoted by Mario Praz, *The Hero in Eclipse in Victorian Fiction* (London: Oxford University Press, 1956), p. 323.

10 J[erome] D[avid] Salinger, "Zooey, *New Yorker,* XXXIII (May 4, 1957), 32–42; "Seymour: An Introduction," *New Yorker,* XXXV (June 6, 1959), 42–111.

11 Robert M. Adams, *Strains of Discord: Studies in Literary Openness* (Ithaca, N.Y.: Cornell University Press, 1958), pp. 52ff.

12 Northrop Frye, "Towards Defining an Age of Sensibility," *Eighteenth Century English Literature: Modern Essays in Criticism,* ed. James L. Clifford (New York: Oxford University Press, 1959), pp. 311–18.

13 "Contemporary" (review of *In My Good Books* by V. S. Pritchett), *New Statesman and Nation,* XXIII [N.S.] (May 23, 1942), 340.

14 "Books in General," *New Statesman and Nation,* XLII [N.S.] (October 21, 1951), 438–39.

15 *Why Do I Write?,* p. 24.

16 Preface to *The Portrait of a Lady* in *The Novels and Tales of Henry James* (New York: Scribner's, 1907–9), III, xii.

17 D. H. Lawrence, "Morality and the Novel" (1925), reprinted in *D. H. Lawrence: Selected Literary Criticism,* ed. Anthony Beal (New York: Viking Press, 1956), pp. 109–10.

18 T. S. Eliot, "Tradition and the Individual Talent" (1917), *Selected Essays: 1917–1932* (New York: Harcourt, Brace, 1932), pp. 4–5.

19 "Sponge of the Present," *Saturday Review of Literature,* XXXVI (June 20, 1953), 44.

20 "Mental Annuity," *Vogue,* September 15, 1955, pp. 108–9.

21 F[rank] R[aymond] Leavis, *The Great Tradition* (London: Chatto & Windus, 1950), p. 9.

22 D. W. Harding, "The Character of Literature from Blake to Byron" in *From Blake to Byron,* "Pelican Guide to English Literature," ed. Boris Ford (London, 1957), V, 51–59.

23 *Portrait of a Lady, Novels and Tales,* III, 273–74.

24 *Ibid.,* p. xv.

25 "The Function of Criticism at the Present Time," in *Essays in Criticism: First Series.*

26 A case could probably be made for including *Daniel Deronda* in the tradition defined here, but a discussion of that very special book would require a disproportionate amount of space.

27 Quoted by Harvey Breit, "A Talk with Miss Bowen," *New York Times Book Review,* March 26, 1950, p. 27.
28 John K. Hutchens, "On an Author" (interview with Elizabeth Bowen), *New York Herald Tribune Book Review,* March 26, 1950, p. 3.

Chapter Two

1 ". . . the ideality of hotel life as a stage for [a novel] came to me, one afternoon, in a flash. The Italian Riviera, on which I had spent one winter in a hotel, offered—with its social futility, pretty backdrop, and dramatic change of weather—propitious climate for a first novel of mine." Preface to *Ann Lee's* in *Early Stories* (New York, 1950), p. xviii.
2 This assumption, made by Lionel Trilling in *E. M. Forster* (Norfolk, Conn.: New Directions, 1943), p. 97, is confirmed by Forster himself in an interview for the *Paris Review.* See *Writers at Work,* ed. Malcolm Cowley (New York: Viking Press, 1958), p. 31.
3 See F. W. Dupee, *Henry James* (New York: William Sloane Assoc., 1951), p. 128. Dupee also (p. 113) notes the particular advantages of using women as protagonists in such novels: because of their "relatively greater freedom from material pressures" they can be used to typify "human possibilities in general."
4 *Forster,* p. 12.
5 E. M. Forster, *A Room with a View* (1908; New York: Alfred A. Knopf, 1953), p. 194.
6 To label such scenes as this "existentialist" may be misleading, but the pattern is prevalent enough in novels to deserve some label: a despondent protagonist anticipating his own death finds sudden release and a sensuous appreciation of his universe. Meursault is soothed by the summer night air and feels for the first time the benign quality of the universe's indifference: "De l'éprouver si pareil à moi, si fraternel enfin, j'ai senti que j'avais été heureux, et que je l'étais encore"—*L'Etranger* (Paris, Gallimard, 1953), p. 171. And both protagonists have followed similar paths in reaching their awareness. Meursault, like Sydney, has until this moment been perceiving but dimly the static lifeless world from which he has felt detached. The connection, surely not one made by the writers, would be merely pedantic if it did not point up in Miss Bowen's moral assumptions an "existential irony" that, implicit here, reaches fuller expression in the later novels, especially *The Heat of the Day.* Only in presenting Stella Rodney does Miss Bowen dramatize her apparent conviction that the future, for one who attains Sydney's knowledge, is irrelevant.
7 As Karl E. Zink points out (in "Flux and the Frozen Moment: The Imagery of Stasis in Faulkner's Prose," *PMLA,* LXXI [June 1957], 285–301), Faulkner's *tableaux vivants* are both "a means of dramatizing or heightening the significance of an event" and "a moment of insight into true meaning." They become narrative reflections of Faulkner's conviction that "it is in the consciousness that [man] transcends the limitations of

both time and space." Like the account of Sydney descending the mountain, this too is a device of which Miss Bowen in *The Hotel* has not taken full advantage. In a short story like "The Happy Autumn Fields" or novels like *The Heat of the Day* (the subterranean café) and *A World of Love* (the Clonmore street), the ambivalence in such descriptions—events and objects become comprehensible, but dead—is reconciled to the total meanings of their contexts.

8 Sean O'Faolain, *The Vanishing Hero: Studies in Novelists of the Twenties* (London, 1956), esp. pp. 173–75. In spite of many factual errors (some dates and titles are inaccurate, characters are confused), O'Faolain's chapter is by far the best essay on Miss Bowen's work. See also O'Faolain's *The Short Story*, London, 1948.

9 Preface to the 1952 reissue (by Knopf) of *The Last September*, pp. vii–ix.

10 *LS*, 1952 ed., p. xi.

11 "Autobiography as an Art," *Saturday Review of Literature*, XXXIV (March 17, 1951), 10.

12 "The Writer's Peculiar World" in *Highlights of Modern Literature: A Permanent Collection of Memorable Essays from the New York Times Book Review*, ed. Francis Brown (New York, 1954), pp. 34–35.

13 "Modern Lighting," *Saturday Review of Literature*, V (October 27, 1928), 294.

14 John Lehmann, *The Whispering Gallery: Autobiography I* (New York: Reynal, 1955), p. 202.

15 George Orwell, "Inside the Whale" (1940), in *A Collection of Essays* (New York: Doubleday, 1954), p. 217.

16 Mark Schorer, "With Intellectual Iron," *New Republic*, CXXVII (November 3, 1952), 18.

Chapter Three

1 "Twenty-five Years of the Novel," in *The Craft of Letters in England*, ed. John Lehmann (London, 1956), pp. 46–47.

2 Miss Bowen's most recent definition of the short story is almost the same, except that the sociological language is entirely eliminated. See *Stories by Elizabeth Bowen* (New York, 1959), p. x.

3 Christopher Morley, "Their Untouchable Selves," *Saturday Review of Literature*, IV (April 7, 1928), 740; Carlos Baker, "Death of a Ghost," *Nation*, CLXX (February 21, 1955), 123.

4 *Mansfield Park, The Novels of Jane Austen*, ed. R. W. Chapman (Oxford University Press, 1933), III, 203.

5 Lionel Trilling, "Mansfield Park" (1954), *The Opposing Self: Nine Essays in Criticism* (New York: Viking Press, 1955), p. 220.

6 O'Faolain, *Hero*, p. 188.

7 *Ibid.*, p. 182.

8 "In Spite of the Words," *New Republic*, CXXVIII (March 9, 1953), 18–19.

9 F. R. Leavis, *D. H. Lawrence: Novelist* (New York: Alfred A. Knopf, 1956), pp. 212–13.

Chapter Four

1 Orwell, "Inside the Whale," *Essays,* p. 239.
2 "Advance in Formation," *Spectator,* CLXVI (January 17, 1941), 65.
3 "The Dark Backward: a Footnote," *London Mercury,* XXXIII (October 1935), 564.
4 Miss Bowen made this connection in a lecture delivered at the University of Wisconsin in November 1955.
5 Preface to *What Maisie Knew, Novels and Tales,* XI, viii–ix.
6 "Appearance and Reality in Henry James," *Scrutiny,* XVII (Summer 1950), 113.
7 *Maisie,* p. 313.
8 William Walsh, *The Use of Imagination: Educational Thought and the Literary Mind* (London: Chatto & Windus, 1959), pp. 148–63.
9 This fairy-tale landscape is both an image and a metaphor. When Major Brutt's fidelities to the Quaynes are betrayed, "that betrayal is the end of an inner life, without which the everyday becomes threatening or meaningless. At the back of the spirit a mysterious landscape, whose perspective used to be infinite, suddenly perishes . . ." (*DH,* 360). Leopold's failure to control his mother's actions with the force of his imagination brings a similar destruction to the symbolic landscape of his romantic will: "She [Henrietta] could not know how sharply Leopold realised everything that at this moment perished for him—landscapes, his own moments, hands approaching making him unsuspicious. She had seen the country he had thought he would inherit—her certainty of it made it little, his passionate ignorance made it great—trees rounded, standing in their own shadow, spires glittering, lakes of land in light, white puffs from the little train travelling a long way" (*HP,* 209).
10 Kingsley Amis, *Lucky Jim* (London: Gollancz, 1955), p. 8.
11 Amis, *That Uncertain Feeling* (London: Gollancz, 1955), p. 158.
12 "Two Novels," *Spectator,* CLXI (Oct. 7, 1938), 578.
13 See Reuben A. Brower, "Something Central which Permeated: Virginia Woolf and 'Mrs. Dalloway,'" *The Fields of Light: An Experiment in Critical Reading* (New York, 1951), pp. 123–37.
14 This ungraceful German word is used to avoid the derogatory connotation of "sententious" and the disconnected quality usually associated with "aphorism." I have used the word here to refer to the technique of generalizing from particulars, often involving a shift from the third to the second person, or from the personal "he" to the impersonal "one."
15 John Henry Raleigh, "The English Novel and the Three Kinds of Time," *Sewanee Review,* LXII (Summer 1954), 436.
16 "Two Novels," p. 578.
17 Preface to *The Awkward Age, Novels and Tales,* IX, vi–vii.

18 See note 4 above.
19 Cf. *Awkward Age,* pp. 238–39.

Chapter Five

1 *Why Do I Write?,* pp. 24–25.
2 The echoes of nineteenth-century poetry in Miss Bowen's fiction, especially her short stories, deserve some mention. The "two cities" of the Arnold poem appear again in "Mysterious Kôr," though the title and lines quoted in the story are from Andrew Lang's "She," prefixed to the H. Rider Haggard novel. Yet in conversation Miss Bowen said that she had not realized, until she read Peter De Vries' parody in the *New Yorker* (Jan. 26, 1952), how often she relied on Victorian poetry for her titles (e.g., "Tears, Idle Tears," "The Happy Autumn Fields," etc.).
3 Raymond Williams, "Realism and the Contemporary Novel," *Partisan Review,* XXVI (Spring 1959), 209.
4 Vernon Young, "Hell on Earth: Six Versions," *Hudson Review,* II (Summer 1949), 316.
5 "Eire," *New Statesman and Nation,* XXI (April 12, 1941), 382–83.
6 E. M. Forster, *Howards End* (1910; London: Edward Arnold, 1924), p. 105.
7 *Ibid.,* p. 78.
8 *Ibid.,* p. 231.
9 *Ibid.,* pp. 183–84.
10 Trilling, *Forster,* pp. 134–35.
11 Orwell, "Inside the Whale," *Essays,* p. 255.
12 I am indebted to Mr. John Perry for generously lending me the typescript prompt copy of *Castle Anna.* The play deserves to be considered as a part of Miss Bowen's work since Mr. Perry wrote only one or two sections of it. However, since it is unpublished, since its text is uncertain (the ms. contains many changes, some of them in Miss Bowen's handwriting), and since the extent of Mr. Perry's influence on its structure and dramaturgy is uncertain, no evaluation of it is included here.
13 Thomas Traherne, *Centuries of Meditations,* ed. Bertram Dobell (London: Dobell, 1908), I, 2. Further references to the meditations are by "century" and section.
14 Literary secularizations of a similar religious and metaphysical position are frequent enough among twentieth-century writers and critics. Andrew H. Wright in *Jane Austen's Novels: A Study in Structure* (London: Chatto & Windus, 1954), p. 24, discussing Jane Austen's irony, finds a useful definition in Kierkegaard's statement that "irony is an existential determination, and nothing is more ridiculous than to suppose that it consists in the use of a certain phraseology, or when an author congratulates himself upon succeeding in expressing himself ironically. Whoever has essential irony has it all day long, not bound to any specific form, because it is the infinite within him." The most familiar modern

definition of irony (though he calls it "wit"), Eliot's "recognition, implicit in the expression of every experience, of other kinds of experience which are possible," has its source of course in the practice of Andrew Marvell and the metaphysical poets of the seventeenth century (*Selected Essays,* p. 262). The concept reaches its fullest secularization probably in Fitzgerald's statement in *The Crack-up* that "the test of a first-rate intelligence is the ability to hold two opposed ideas in the mind at the same time, and still retain the ability to function" (discussed by Wright Morris, "The Ability to Function," *New World Writing,* XIII [1958], 34–51), or in Wallace Stevens' statement used as an epigraph for this book ("Adagia," *Opus Posthumous,* ed. Samuel French Morse [New York: Alfred A. Knopf, 1957], p. 163).

15 E.g., *Time Magazine,* LXV (Jan. 17, 1955), 96.

16 Charles A. Brady, *Buffalo Evening News,* Jan. 15, 1955.

17 I am indebted to Miss Bowen for calling my attention to this allusion.

18 "Miss Bowen on Miss Bowen," *New York Times Book Review,* March 6, 1949, p. 33.

19 Jocelyn Brooke, *Elizabeth Bowen* (London: Longmans, Green, 1952), p. 26.

20 Adams, *Strains of Discord,* pp. 52ff.

21 Breit, "A Talk with Miss Bowen," p. 27.

22 "Elizabeth Bowen at her Typewriter," *Listener,* XLII (Nov. 24, 1949), 890.

23 T. C. Worsley, review of *Castle Anna, New Statesman and Nation,* XXXV (Mar. 6, 1948), 193.

24 John Holloway, "The New 'Establishment' in Criticism," *Listener,* LVI (Sept. 20 & 27, 1956), 429–30, 473–74.

25 Adams, *Strains of Discord,* p. 72.

Chapter Six

1 The "propositional" quality of Morris' *The Field of Vision* is represented by its epigraphs: Milton's "The mind is its own place . . ." and Lawrence's distinction between the "old stable *ego* of character" and "another ego, according to whose action the individual is unrecognizable . . ." And in spite of the contrasting and separated points of view Morris uses, the novel's propositions are as quotable as Miss Bowen's: e.g., the child, to Boyd, is a

> jigsaw loose in its box, the bullfight one of the scarlet pieces, but he would not know its meaning until the pattern itself appeared. And that he would not *find*. . . . The pattern—what pattern it had—he would have to create. . . . The problem? In an age of How-to-do-it, the problem was how not. . . . How to live in spite of, not because of, something called character. To keep it open, to keep the puzzle puzzling, the pattern changing and alive—*The Field of Vision* (New York: Harcourt, Brace, 1956), pp. 154–55.

2 Eudora Welty, *The Golden Apples* (New York: Harcourt, Brace, 1949), pp. 51, 234.

3 Robert Penn Warren, preface to Modern Library edition of *Nostromo* (New York: Random House, 1951), p. xxiii. The "central passage" Warren quotes is from ch. 20 of *Lord Jim:*

> A man that is born falls into a dream like a man who falls into the sea. If he tried to climb out into the air as inexperienced people endeavor to do, he drowns—*nicht wahr?* . . . No! I tell you! The way is to the destructive element submit yourself, and with the exertions of your hands and feet in the water make the deep, deep sea keep you up.

4 Pamela Hansford Johnson, "Modern Fiction and the English Understatement," *Times Literary Supplement,* August 7, 1959, p. iii.

5 At first the simple immediacy of Portia's diary would seem to be analogous to that of Benjy's narrative in *The Sound and the Fury.* Certainly Faulkner's novel depends on expansions of the world as the story moves from one section to another. But the "placing" of the sections is largely done by the reader who gives Benjy's narrative, for instance, the temporal context it lacks. The novel of proposition, and the use made of Portia's diary, depends on the continuity of a more self-conscious narrator who faces always the same basic puzzle. The sections of *The Field of Vision,* for example, in spite of their separation into characters' points of view, do contain a consciousness explicitly larger than the consciousness of the characters; Faulkner, restricting his narrators more severely, separates them. This distinction, of course, is a matter of technique, not value.

6 Virginia Woolf, "Jane Austen," *The Common Reader* (New York: Harcourt, Brace, 1925), p. 197.

7 E. D. Pendry, *The New Feminism of English Fiction: A Study in Contemporary Women-Novelists* (Tokyo, 1956), p. 120.

8 Brooke, *Elizabeth Bowen,* pp. 9, 10, 23.

9 As Miss Hardwick points out, the source of Miss Bowen's literary reputation is difficult to trace. Her most enthusiastic proponents have been V. S. Pritchett, Graham Greene, Edward Sackville-West, writers of pamphlets for the British Council (including Walter Allen and P. H. Newby), and the popular reviewers. Many of these writers, it should be noted, are either popular essayists or fellow novelists who too often share her uncritical generosity. *Scrutiny* essayists, whose considerations of contemporary literature are at least based on a consistent standard, have condemned her works by omission, but she shares this banishment with Dylan Thomas, W. H. Auden, and Graham Greene. (H. A. Mason, in 1949, referred to the novels of Miss Bowen, Greene, and Pritchett as "productions," their criticism as "critical journalism.") The essays by Daiches, Miss Snow, Harkness, and Miss Seward, although they appeared in "academic" periodicals, do not go far beyond the book reviews.

Miss Snow and Harkness are primarily descriptive, Miss Seward rather sentimental, Daiches rather vague. None of them attempts a full critical analysis of any one novel. Other shorter notices are briefly described in the bibliography below.

10 O'Faolain, *Hero,* p. 171.

11 Elizabeth Hardwick, "Elizabeth Bowen's Fiction," *Partisan Review,* XVI (November 1949), 1121.

12 Cf. Forster, *Aspects of the Novel* (1927; London: Hogarth Press, 1949), pp. 75–77, 79, *et passim.*

13 L. A. G. Strong, *Personal Remarks* (New York, 1953), p. 133.

14 Herbert Gold, "Random Dreams, True and False," *Hudson Review,* VIII (Spring 1955), 154.

15 This passage has become a kind of "set piece" to illustrate Miss Bowen's style. For instance, May Sarton in her autobiography describes watching Miss Bowen's husband Alan Cameron ". . . walk up and down that room [at Clarence Terrace], a glass in his hand, and recite the first page of *The Death of the Heart,* breaking off to shout in his rather high voice, 'That's genius!' "—*I Knew a Phoenix* (New York, 1959), p. 217.

16 "The Novels of Elizabeth Bowen," unpubl. M.A. thesis (Washington University, 1952), pp. 78–79.

17 "Truth and Fiction" (III: "Time, Period and Reality"), *Listener,* LVI (Nov. 8, 1956), 751.

18 "Truth and Fiction" (II: "People: the Creation of Character"), *Listener,* LVI (Nov. 1, 1956), 706.

19 Pritchett, "Prospects for the English Novel," *New York Times Book Review,* April 17, 1949, pp. 21–22, claims that modern British novelists are making "anthropological" explorations, looking at the actions and behavior of a society as if they were exotic rites, in preparation for a new "tradition" of the novel. He specifically mentions both Henry Green and Elizabeth Bowen.

* Bibliography

This bibliography has been limited to those books and articles (cited or not) containing significant statements about Miss Bowen's work, and to those works by Miss Bowen that can be considered literature or relevant to literature. No attempt has been made to list collected essays and short stories separately, to itemize American editions, to give full bibliographical information about first editions and first appearances, to list "occasional" reviews and nonliterary essays, or to mention the many translations of her work.

Allen, Walter. "Fiction," *The Year's Work in Literature: 1949*. London: Longmans, Green for the British Council, 1950. [includes a brief discussion of *The Heat of the Day*]

Baker, Carlos. "Death of a Ghost," *Nation,* CLXX (Feb. 21, 1955), 123. [review of *A World of Love*]

Bogan, Louise. *Selected Criticism: Prose, Poetry*. New York: Noonday Press, 1955. [includes review of *The Death of the Heart*]

Bowen, Elizabeth. "Advance in Formation," *Spectator,* CLXVI (Jan. 17, 1941), 65. [review of *New Writing in Europe,* ed. John Lehmann]

———. *Ann Lee's: & Other Stories*. London: Sidgwick and Jackson, 1926. [short stories included in *Early Stories* (New York: Alfred A. Knopf, 1950)]

———. "Jane Austen," in *The English Novelists: A Survey of the Novel by Twenty Contemporary Novelists,* ed. Derek Verschoyle. London: Chatto and Windus, 1936. [essay]

———. "Autobiography as an Art," *Saturday Review of Literature,* XXXIV (Mar. 17, 1951), 9–10.

———. "The Bend Back," *Cornhill,* CLXV (Summer 1951), 221–27. [essay on the use of children and childhood experience in fiction]

———. "Books in General," *New Statesman and Nation,* XLII (Oct. 20, 1951), 438–39. [essay-review of *Mr. Beluncle* by V. S. Pritchett]

———. "Elizabeth Bowen at her Typewriter," *Listener,* XLII (Nov. 24, 1949), 890. [brief unsigned interview]

———. "Miss Bowen on Miss Bowen," *New York Times Book Review,* Mar. 6, 1949, p. 33. [unsigned interview]

———. *Bowen's Court.* London: Longmans, Green and Co., 1942. [family history]

——— [and John Perry]. *Castle Anna.* [play, unpublished, first performed in London in March 1948]

———. *The Cat Jumps.* London: Victor Gollancz, 1934. [short stories, published in Cape Collected Edition in 1949]

———. "Claimant," *Vogue,* Nov. 15, 1955, pp. 122–23, 167–68. [short story]

———. *Collected Impressions.* London: Longmans, Green and Co., 1950. [essays, reviews and prefaces]

———. *Coming to London.* London: Phoenix House, Ltd., 1957. [contains an autobiographical account by Elizabeth Bowen, pp. 78–81]

———. "Confessions," *Saturday Book,* IX (1949), 108–9. [answers to questionnaire]

———. *Consequences: A Complete Story in the Manner of the Old Parlour Game in Nine Chapters Each by a Different Author.* Waltham Saint Lawrence, Berkshire: The Golden Cockerell Press, 1932. [The chapter called "She Gave Him" is by Elizabeth Bowen. The edition of this curious book consists of 200 signed, 1000 unsigned copies.]

———. "Contemporary," *New Statesman and Nation,* XXIII (May 23, 1942), 340. [review of *In My Good Books* by V. S. Pritchett]

———. "The Cost of Letters," *Ideas and Places* by Cyril Connolly. London: Weidenfeld and Nicolson, 1953.

———. "The Cult of Nostalgia," *Listener,* XLVI (Aug. 9, 1951), 225–26. [essay]

———. "A Day in the Dark," *Botteghe Oscure,* XVI (Autumn 1955), 85–94. [short story]

———. *The Death of the Heart.* London: Victor Gollancz, 1938. [novel republished in Cape Collected Edition, 1948]

———. *The Demon Lover.* London: Jonathan Cape, 1945. [short stories republished in Cape Collected Edition, 1952; published by Knopf in 1946 as *Ivy Gripped the Steps*]

———. Preface to *Doctor Thorne* by Anthony Trollope. New York: Houghton Mifflin, 1959.

———. "Eire," *New Statesman and Nation,* XXI (Apr. 12, 1941), 382–83. [essay on the neutrality of Ireland]

———. *Encounters.* London: Sidgwick and Jackson, 1923. [short stories republished with a preface, 1949; included (with *Ann Lee's*) in *Early Stories*—New York: Knopf, 1950]

———. "English Fiction at Mid-Century," *New Republic,* CXXIX (Sept. 21, 1953), 15–16. [essay]

———. *English Novelists.* London: Collins, 1946. [literary history; part of the "Britain in Pictures" series]

———. "Flavia," *The Fothergill Omnibus: for which Eighteen Eminent Authors have written Short Stories upon One and the Same Plot,* intro. by John Fothergill, *et al.* London: Eyre and Spottiswoode, 1931, pp. 59–70.

———. *Friends and Relations.* London: Constable, 1931. [novel republished in Cape Collected Edition, 1951]

———. "Gone Away," *Listener,* XXX (Jan. 3, 1946), 13–15. [short story]

———. *The Heat of the Day.* London: Jonathan Cape, 1949. [novel republished in Cape Collected Edition, 1954]

———. *The Hotel.* London: Constable, 1927. [novel republished in Cape Collected Edition, 1950]

———. *The House in Paris.* London: Victor Gollancz, 1935. [novel republished in Cape Collected Edition, 1949]

———. "I Died of Love," *Choice: Some New Stories and Prose,* ed. William Sansom. London: Progress, 1946. [short story]

———. "I Hear You Say So," *Pleasures of New Writing: An Anthology . . . from . . . New Writing,* ed. John Lehmann. London: John Lehmann, 1952. [short story]

———. "In Spite of the Words," *New Republic,* CXXVIII (Mar. 9, 1953), 18–19. [review of *The Laughing Matter* by William Saroyan]

———. *Joining Charles.* London: Constable, 1929. [short stories republished in Cape Collected Edition, 1952]

———. "Just Imagine," *Best British Short Stories of 1927,* ed. E. J. O'Brien. New York: Dodd, Mead, 1927, pp. 72–84.

———. *The Last September.* London: Constable, 1929. [novel republished in Cape Collected Edition, 1948]

———. "A Living Writer," *Cornhill,* CLXIX (Winter 1956–57), 120–34. [This essay on Katherine Mansfield appears in substantially the same form as the introduction to *Stories by Katherine Mansfield*—New York: Alfred A. Knopf (Vintage Books), 1956.]

———. *Look at All Those Roses.* London: Victor Gollancz, 1941. [short stories republished in Cape Collected Edition, 1951]

———. "Matter of Inspiration," *Saturday Review of Literature,* XXXIV (Oct. 13, 1951), 27–28, 64. [essay]

———. "Mental Annuity," *Vogue,* Sept. 15, 1955, pp. 108–9. [essay]

———. "Modern Lighting," *Saturday Review of Literature,* V (Oct. 27, 1928), 294. [essay]

———. "The Modern Novel and the Theme of Love," *New Republic,* CXXVIII (May 11, 1953), 18–19. [essay-review]

———. "The Next Book," *Now and Then,* Autumn 1948, pp. 11–12. [anticipating *The Heat of the Day*]

———. Introduction to *North and South* by Mrs. Gaskell. London: John Lehmann, 1951. [a brief introduction to the 1855 novel]

———. *"Persuasion," London Magazine,* IV (1957), 47–51. [essay]

———. "The Power in the Cave," *Listener,* XXXVII (March 20, 1947), 431–32. [essay on imagination]

———. Preface to *Pride and Prejudice.* London: Williams and Norgate, 1948.

———. "Rx for a Story Worth the Telling," *New York Times Book Review,* August 31, 1958, pp. 1, 13. [essay]

———. "The Search for a Story to Tell," reprinted in *Highlights of Modern Literature: A Permanent Collection of Memorable Essays from the New York Times Book Review,* ed. Francis Brown. New York: New American Library, 1954. [a 1952 essay]

———. *Seven Winters.* Dublin: Cuala Press, 1942. [This edition of the short autobiography was limited to 450 copies. The book was also published in London at the same time by Longmans, Green.]

———. *The Shelbourne: A Center in Dublin Life for more than a Century.* London: George G. Harrap and Co., 1951. [An American edition of this history, called *The Shelbourne Hotel,* was published at the same time in New York by Alfred A. Knopf.]

———. "So Much Depends," *Woman's Day,* September 1951, pp. 72, 149–50, 152–58. [short story]

———. "Sponge of the Present," *Saturday Review of Literature,* XXXVI (June 20, 1953), 11, 43–44. [essay]

———. *Stories by Elizabeth Bowen.* New York: Alfred A. Knopf, 1959. [Miss Bowen's selection, with a preface]

———. *A Time in Rome.* New York: Alfred A. Knopf, 1960. [an account of seven months in Rome]

———. *To the North.* London: Victor Gollancz, 1932. [novel republished in Cape Collected Edition, 1952]

———. *Anthony Trollope: A New Judgment.* Oxford University Press, 1946. [a 1945 radio play, also reprinted in *Collected Impressions*]

———. "Truth and Fiction," *Listener,* LVI (October 25, November 1, November 8, 1956), 651–52, 704–6, 751–52. [three-part essay on the novel]

———. "The Virgins and the Empress," *Harper's Magazine,* CCXIX (Nov. 1959), 50–55. [essay incorporating material from *A Time in Rome*]

———. "What We Need in Writing," *Spectator,* CLVII (Nov. 20, 1936), 901–2. [essay]

———. *Why Do I Write? An Exchange of Views between Elizabeth Bowen, Graham Greene, and V. S. Pritchett.* London: Percival Marshall, 1948. [a series of open letters on the role of the novelist]

———. *A World of Love.* London: Jonathan Cape, 1955. [novel]

———. "Writer's Peculiar World," reprinted in *Highlights of Modern Literature.* [See "The Search . . . to Tell" above.]

Breit, Harvey. "A Talk with Miss Bowen," *New York Times Book Review,* Mar. 26, 1950, p. 27. [interview]

Brooke, Jocelyn. *Elizabeth Bowen.* London: Longmans, Green and Co. for the British Council and the National Book League, 1952. [This short monograph mixes criticism with "appreciation" to the detriment of both.]

C. E. [Christian Edwards?]. Review of *Castle Anna, Spectator,* CLXXX (Mar. 5, 1948), 285.

Cecil, Lord David. "Chronicler of the Heart," *Vogue,* Nov. 1, 1953, pp. 118–19. [an impressionistic profile of Elizabeth Bowen by a friend, containing biographical information not available elsewhere]

Daiches, David. "The Novels of Elizabeth Bowen," *English Journal,* XXXVIII (June 1949), 305–13. [a general critical essay]

De Vries, Peter. "Touch and Go (with a Low Bow to Elizabeth Bowen)," *New Yorker,* Jan. 26, 1952, p. 30. [parody of an Elizabeth Bowen short story]

Frierson, William C. *The English Novel in Transition: 1885–1940.* Norman: University of Oklahoma Press, 1942. [brief account of the earlier novels]

Gold, Herbert. "Random Dreams, True and False," *Hudson Review,* VIII (Spring 1955), 150–55. [includes a review of *A World of Love*]

Greene, Graham. "The Dark Backward: a Footnote," *London Mercury,* XXXII (Oct. 1935), 562–65. [essay on the presentation of time in the novel, with special reference to *The House in Paris*—one of earliest essays other than reviews to consider Miss Bowen's work]

———. "Two Novels," *Spectator,* CLXI (Oct. 7, 1938), 578. [In this review of *The Death of the Heart,* Greene argues that Miss Bowen's achievement can be compared to that of Henry James in *The Awkward Age.*]

Hardwick, Elizabeth. "Elizabeth Bowen's Fiction," *Partisan Review,* XVI (November 1949), 1114–21. [an argument that Elizabeth Bowen's work has been greatly overvalued]

Harkness, Bruce. "The Fiction of Elizabeth Bowen," *English Journal,* XLIV (December 1955), 499–506. [like the Daiches essay, an attempt to discuss too much writing in too few pages]

Hartley, L. P. Review of *Encounters, Spectator,* CXXXI (July 21, 1923), 91–92.

———. Review of *A World of Love, Spectator,* CXCIV (Mar. 11, 1955), 293–94. [In this second review, Hartley comments on the thirty-two years separating his reviews of her first book and her most recent one.]

Hutchens, John K. "On an Author," *New York Herald Tribune Book Review,* March 26, 1950. [interview]

Kiely, Benedict. "Elizabeth Bowen," *Irish Monthly,* LXXVIII (1950).

Lehmann, John. *I Am My Brother.* New York: Reynal, 1960. [This second volume of Lehmann's autobiography includes reminiscences of Elizabeth Bowen during the second world war.]

———, ed. *The Craft of Letters in England.* London: The Cresset Press, 1956. [Miss Bowen's work is discussed by Francis Wyndham on pp. 46–51, 55–56; by Philip Toynbee on p. 62.]

Ludwig, J. B. "The New World of Elizabeth Bowen," *New Republic,* CXXXII (January 31, 1955), 18–19. [review of *A World of Love*]

Mason, H. A. "Measure for Measure: or Anglo-American Exchanges,"

Scrutiny, XVI (March 1949), 3. [dismisses the work of Elizabeth Bowen as not worth consideration]

Morley, Christopher. "Their Untouchable Selves," *Saturday Review of Literature,* IV (April 7, 1928), 740. [This review of *The Hotel* is one of the first American responses to Miss Bowen's work.]

Mortimer, Raymond. Review of *The Death of the Heart, New Statesman and Nation,* XVI (Oct. 8, 1938), 534. [one of the most interesting discussions of this novel]

Mullen, Thomas P. "Progress Toward Disaster: A Study of the Novels of Elizabeth Bowen." Unpubl. B.A. honors thesis, Amherst College, 1950.

Newby, P. H. *The Novel: 1945–1950.* London: Longmans, Green and Co. for the British Council, 1951. [discusses Elizabeth Bowen as a traditional novelist, pp. 19–20]

O'Faolain, Sean. *The Short Story.* London: Collins, 1948. [contains a lengthy analysis of "Her Table Spread"]

———. *The Vanishing Hero: Studies in Novelists of the Twenties.* London: Eyre and Spottiswoode, 1956. [Miss Bowen's novels are discussed in a chapter entitled "Elizabeth Bowen, or Romance does not Pay," pp. 167–90.]

Owen, Sally. "Sonnet," *Now and Then* (publ. by Jonathan Cape), Autumn 1951, p. 16. [about *The Death of the Heart*]

Pendry, E. D. *The New Feminism of English Fiction: A Study in Contemporary Women-Novelists.* Tokyo: Kenkyusha Ltd., 1956. [Chapter Six, pp. 120–52, is devoted to a discussion of Elizabeth Bowen as "the most feminine of contemporary novelists"]

Prescott, Orville. *In My Opinion.* New York and Indianapolis: Bobbs-Merrill, 1952. [Prescott finds Miss Bowen and Ivy Compton-Burnett typical of a modern decadence, too subtle and abstract to be important, pp. 101–5.]

Pritchett, V. S. "The Future of English Fiction," *Partisan Review,* XV (October 1948), 1063–70. [argues that the "dispossessed poets" Elizabeth Bowen and Henry Green are obliquely historians of "the crisis in civilization"]

———. "Prospects for the English Novel," *New York Times Book Review,* April 17, 1949, pp. 1, 21, 22.

Read, Herbert. *English Prose Style.* Boston: Beacon Press, 1955. [In this 1952 revision of the 1928 book, Read has included the opening paragraphs of *The Heat of the Day* as an example of "the impressionistic style."]

Reed, Henry. *The Novel Since 1939.* London: Longmans, Green and Co. for the British Council, 1948. [includes a discussion of *Look at All Those Roses* and *The Demon Lover*]

Rowse, A. L. "The Use of History" in *The English Spirit: Essays in History and Literature.* London: Macmillan, 1946. [*Bowen's Court* is discussed on pp. 256–59.]

Sackville-West, Edward. *Inclinations.* London: Secker and Warburg, 1949. [Elizabeth Bowen and Ivy Compton-Burnett are discussed in a chapter called "Ladies whose bright Pens . . . ," pp. 78–103.]

Sarton, May. *I Knew a Phoenix.* New York: Rinehart, 1959. [describes a visit to Elizabeth Bowen's home in Regent's Park, pp. 215–18]

Schneider, Dorothy Leona. "The Novels of Elizabeth Bowen." Unpubl. M.A. thesis, Washington University, 1952.

Schorer, Mark. "With Intellectual Iron," *New Republic,* CXXVII (Nov. 3, 1952), 18–19. [review of the reissue of *The Last September*]

Seward, Barbara. "Elizabeth Bowen's World of Impoverished Love," *College English,* XVIII (October 1956), 30–37. [discusses Elizabeth Bowen as a writer who "explores a persistent theme—the tragic dangers of romantic excess in the twentieth century"]

Snow, Lotus. "The Uncertain 'I': A Study of Elizabeth Bowen's Fiction," *Western Humanities Review,* IV (Autumn 1950), 299–310. [discusses the fiction as presenting the passionate person's search for identity in a hostile society]

Strachey, John. "The Golden Age of English Detection," *Saturday Review of Literature,* XIX (Jan. 7, 1939), 12–14. [praises the novels, especially *The Death of the Heart,* from a Marxist point of view]

Strong, L. A. G. *Personal Remarks.* New York: Liveright, 1953. [emphasizes the Irishness of Elizabeth Bowen, pp. 132–45]

Time Magazine. Review of *The Death of the Heart,* XXXIII (Jan. 30, 1939), 65–66. [calls Elizabeth Bowen "more promising" than Elizabeth Madox Roberts, Willa Cather, Virginia Woolf]

Tindall, William Y. *Forces in Modern British Literature: 1885–1946.* New York: Alfred A. Knopf, 1947. [finds Elizabeth Bowen "no less excellent" than Katherine Mansfield as a short-story writer, calls *The Death of the Heart* "one of the best and bitterest novels of recent years"]

Vallette, J. "Elizabeth Bowen," *Mercure de France,* CCCVII (September 1949), 166–69. [one of few critical essays not English or American]

Williams, Raymond. "Realism and the Contemporary Novel," *Partisan Review,* XXVI (Spring 1959), 200–213.

Woolf, Virginia. *A Writer's Diary.* London: Hogarth Press, 1953. [includes several references to Elizabeth Bowen, although her name is not indexed]

Worsley, T. C. Review of *Castle Anna, New Statesman and Nation,* XXXV (March 6, 1948), 193.

Wyndham, Francis. Review of *A World of Love, London Magazine,* II (June 1955), 86–89.

Young, Vernon. "Hell on Earth: Six Versions," *Hudson Review,* II (Summer 1949), 311–18. [includes a review of *The Heat of the Day*]

Index